Michael Schoenfeldt's fascinating study explores the close relationship between selves and bodies, psychological inwardness and corporeal processes, as they are represented in early modern literature. After Galen, the predominant medical paradigm of the period envisaged a self governed by humors, literally embodying inner emotion by locating and explaining human passion within a taxonomy of internal organs and fluids. It thus bestowed a profoundly material basis upon behavioral phenomena, giving the poets of the period a vital and compelling vocabulary for describing the ways in which selves inhabit and experience bodies. In contrast to much recent work on the body which has emphasized its exuberant leakiness as a principle of social liberation amid oppressive regimes, Schoenfeldt establishes the emancipatory value that the Renaissance frequently located not in moments of festive release, but in the exercise of regulation, temperance, and self-control.

MICHAEL C. SCHOENFELDT is Professor of English at the University of Michigan. He is the author of *Prayer and Power: George Herbert and Renaissance Courtship* (1991) and of numerous published essays on Spenser, Shakespeare, Jonson, Donne, Herrick, Milton, and Amelia Lanyer.

Cambridge Studies in Renaissance Literature and Culture 34

Bodies and Selves in Early Modern England

Cambridge Studies in Renaissance Literature and Culture

General editor
STEPHEN ORGEL
Jackson Eli Reynolds Professor of Humanities, Stanford University

Editorial board
Anne Barton, *University of Cambridge*
Jonathan Dollimore, *University of York*
Marjorie Garber, *Harvard University*
Jonathan Goldberg, *Johns Hopkins University*
Nancy Vickers, *Bryn Mawr College*

Since the 1970s there has been a broad and vital reinterpretation of the nature of literary texts, a move away from formalism to a sense of literature as an aspect of social, economic, political and cultural history. While the earliest New Historicist work was criticized for a narrow and anecdotal view of history, it also served as an important stimulus for post-structuralist, feminist, Marxist, and psychoanalytical work, which in turn has increasingly informed and redirected it. Recent writing on the nature of representation, the historical construction of gender and of the concept of identity itself, on theatre as a political and economic phenomenon and on the ideologies of art generally, reveals the breadth of the field. Cambridge Studies in Renaissance Literature and Culture is designed to offer historically oriented studies of Renaissance literature and theatre which make use of the insights afforded by theoretical perspectives. The view of history envisioned is above all a view of our own history, a reading of the Renaissance for and from our own time.

Recent titles include

29. Dorothy Stephens, *The limits of eroticism in post-Petrarchan narrative: conditional pleasure from Spenser to Marvell*

30. Celia R. Daileader, *Eroticism on the Renaissance stage: transcendence, desire, and the limits of the visible*

31. Theodore B. Leinwand, *Theatre, finance and society in early modern England*

32. Heather Dubrow, *Shakespeare and domestic loss: forms of deprivation, mourning, and recuperation*

33. David M. Posner, *The performance of nobility in early modern European literature*

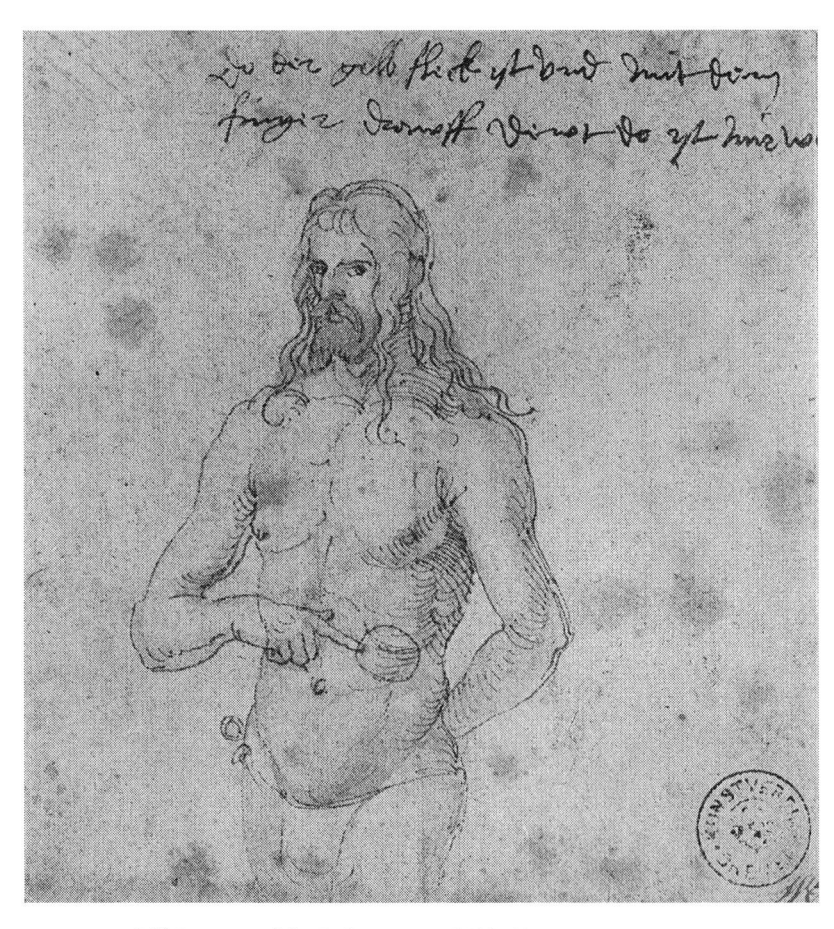

Self-Portrait of the Sick Dürer, c. 1512–13

Bodies and Selves in Early Modern England

Physiology and Inwardness in Spenser, Shakespeare, Herbert, and Milton

Michael C. Schoenfeldt

CAMBRIDGE
UNIVERSITY PRESS

CAMBRIDGE UNIVERSITY PRESS
Cambridge, New York, Melbourne, Madrid, Cape Town, Singapore, São Paulo

Cambridge University Press
The Edinburgh Building, Cambridge CB2 8RU, UK

Published in the United States of America by Cambridge University Press, New York

www.cambridge.org
Information on this title: www.cambridge.org/9780521630733

© Michael C. Schoenfeldt 1999

This publication is in copyright. Subject to statutory exception
and to the provisions of relevant collective licensing agreements,
no reproduction of any part may take place without the written
permission of Cambridge University Press.

First published 1999

A catalogue record for this publication is available from the British Library

Library of Congress Cataloguing in Publication data

Schoenfeldt, Michael Carl.
Bodies and selves in early modern England: physiology and inwardness in Spenser,
Shakespeare, Herbert, and Milton / Michael C. Schoenfeldt.
    p. cm. – (Cambridge studies in Renaissance literature and culture: 34)
Includes index.
ISBN 0 521 63073 8 (hardback) – ISBN 0 521 66902 2 (paperback)
1. English literature – Early modern, 1500–1700 – History and criticism.
2. Body, Human, in literature. 3. Shakespeare, William, 1564–1616 – Knowledge –
Physiology. 4. Spenser, Edmund, 1552?–1599 – Knowledge – Physiology.
5. Herbert, George, 1593–1633 – Knowledge – Physiology. 6. Milton, John, 1608–1674 –
Knowledge – Physiology. 7. English literature – Psychological aspects. 8. Mind and
body in literature. 9. Psychology in literature.
10. Renaissance – England. 11. Self in literature I. Title. II. Series.
PR428.B63S36   1999
820 – dc21   99-11231 CIP

ISBN 978-0-521-63073-3 hardback
ISBN 978-0-521-66902-3 paperback

Transferred to digital printing 2007

Contents

List of Illustrations		*page* x
Preface		xi
1	Bodies of rule: embodiment and interiority in early modern England	1
2	Fortifying inwardness: Spenser's castle of moral health	40
3	The matter of inwardness: Shakespeare's Sonnets	74
4	Devotion and digestion: George Herbert's consuming subject	96
5	Temperance and temptation: the alimental vision in *Paradise Lost*	131
Afterword		169
Notes		173
Index		198

Illustrations

Self-Portrait of the Sick Dürer, c. 1512–13, reproduced by
permission of the Kunsthalle, Bremen. *Frontispiece*
1 Thomas Walkington, *The Optick Glasse of Humors*
(London, 1607), fol. 39v, reproduced by permission of
The Folger Shakespeare Library. *page* 4
2 Robert Fludd, *Utrusque cosmi . . . historia* (Oppenheim,
1619), II, 1, 105, reproduced by permission of The Folger
Shakespeare Library. 5
3 Nicholas Culpepper, *The Anatomy of the Body of Man*
(London, 1677), illustration between pages 14 and 15,
reproduced by permission of The Huntington Library,
San Marino, California. 27

Preface

This project began in a year at Clare Hall, Cambridge, and was enriched by a variety of conversations that took place that year, particularly with Michael McVaugh, Gillian Beer, Paul Marquis, Terri Apter, Catherine Bates, Victor Caston, Dympna Callaghan, Richard Todd, Lori Anne Ferrell, and Jeremy Maule. It is my deep personal regret that Jeremy did not live to see the book published, so that he could tell me all that was wrong and right with it. He did help the manuscript as much as he could along the way.

I have been blessed with many patient and probing audiences as I worked out the ideas that congealed into this project. I would like to thank in particular audiences at the University of Reading, Oxford University, Cambridge University, Keele University, the University of Chicago, Sarah Lawrence University, the University of London, the British Milton Seminar, and the University of Michigan. The wonderfully informal Works-in-Progress group in the Department of English at the University of Michigan has been a feast for mind and body; thanks to Tobin and Jill Siebers for supplying the venue and the desserts. I continue to learn much from my splendid colleagues in early modern studies at the University of Michigan: Steven Mullaney, John Knott, Linda Gregerson, Ejner Jensen, Carla Mazzio, Ralph Williams, P. A. Skantze, David Porter, and Bill Ingram. Valerie Traub deserves special mention here, for generously demanding of this project the kind of theoretical rigor that her own work always exhibits. Many individuals have read and responded to portions of the manuscript, including David Loewenstein, Richard Strier, William Shullenberger, Debora Shuger, Leonard Barkan, George Bornstein, Claude Summers, Sidney Gottlieb, Jonathan Post, David Hillman, Ted-Larry Pebworth, Russell Fraser, Donald Friedman, Michael MacDonald, Richard Burt, Robert Appelbaum, and Neils Herold. Elise Frasier proved an able editor and critic, and Angela Balla was a blessedly fastidious proofreader. Patrick Cheney ruined a summer vacation by reading the entire manuscript, for which I, and any readers the book happens to muster, must be grateful. I have learned much about the connections among literature, history, and medicine in conversations with Dr. Howard Markel. I have benefited from the unerring and enabling support of departmental chairs while I worked on this project; Robert Weisbuch was Chair when I began, and Martha Vicinus when I finished. I owe a debt of gratitude to the Michigan Institute for Humanities, where the initial thinking that led to this project began; and to the Office of the Vice President for Research at the University of Michigan, for the two grants that gave me the time off to begin and conclude the project. Josie Dixon, my editor at Cambridge, showed great faith in the project, even in its early stages, and continually offered insight as the manuscript progressed. As an early reader of selected chapters for the Press, Katharine Maus graciously saw virtues in the project I had been unable to grasp, and insightfully pointed me in the directions that occupied my next two years. As its last, best reader, Stephen Orgel saved the manuscript from several infelicities, and urged me to follow through on several missed opportunities.

Friends who have cheered and sustained me while I worked on this book include John Wagner, John Whittier-Ferguson, Kerry Larson, John Kucich, Jonathan Freedman, and Leslie Atzmon. I regret that my mother did not live to see this book, since she taught me much about the way selves can inhabit afflicted bodies with patience and grace. My father and stepmother, Charles and Charlene Schoenfeldt, bolstered me with love and encouragement as I worked on this book. My brother Patrick reminds me continually of the abiding affection that flesh is also heir to. I dedicate the book with pleasure to Ben and Aaron Schoenfeldt, whose own precious, messy bodies and sweet original selves have taught me so much while they redeemed the pain of living, laboring, and learning.

For permission to reprint, I owe thanks to Routledge, which published a shorter version of Chapter 1 in *The Body in Parts: Fantasies of Corporeality in Early Modern Europe*, ed. David Hillman and Carla Mazzio (1997); to the University Press of Kentucky, which published a shorter version of Chapter 2 in *Worldmaking Spenser: Explorations in the Early Modern Age*, ed. Patrick Cheney and Lauren Silberman (1999); to Garland, which published a shorter version of Chapter 3 in *Shakespeare's Sonnets: Critical Essays*, ed. James Schiffer (1998); and to *The George Herbert Journal*, which published a shorter version of Chapter 4 in *George Herbert in the Nineties: Reflections and Reassessments*, ed. Jonathan F. S. Post and Sidney Gottlieb (1995).

All references to the Bible are to the 1611 Authorized Version. All references to Shakespeare's plays are to *The Riverside Shakespeare*, ed. G. Blakemore Evans *et al.* (Houghton Mifflin, 1974). Spelling and punctuation have been kept as close as possible to the originals, but I have modernized *u, v, w, i, j*.

To Ben and Aaron

1 Bodies of rule: embodiment and interiority in early modern England

> Sir Toby: Does not our lives consist of the four elements?
> Sir Andrew: Faith, so they say, but I think it rather consists of eating and drinking.
> Sir Toby: Th' art a scholar; let us therefore eat and drink.
>
> *Twelfth Night*, 2.3.10–12

Around 1512, Albrecht Dürer attempted to describe to a physician friend a pain he felt in his side. The result is the searching self-portrait that graces the frontispiece of this book. The finger points to the region of the spleen, the organ responsible for the production of melancholy, the humoral fluid whose effects so fascinated and apparently troubled Dürer (witness his famous engraving of *Melancholia*). At the top of the page is written in German: "There where the yellow spot is and the finger points, there it hurts me."[1] Like Dürer, the writers we will look at attempt to express inwardness materially. They will point to various regions of their bodies to articulate what we would call a psychological state. Yet they will not display the promiscuous inwardness of the anatomized corpse, splaying itself for all to see, a phenomenon which has been explored with such insight by Jonathan Sawday.[2] Rather they will aspire to the mysterious inwardness toward which living, intact flesh can only point. In this book I show that bodily condition, subjective state, and psychological character are in this earlier regime fully imbricated.

Like the famous self-portrait that Dürer made in 1500, the *Self-Portrait of the Sick Dürer* has Christic echoes. As Joseph Leo Koerner remarks, "Pointing to his side and gazing out of the picture, Dürer assumes the traditional pose of Christ as Man of Sorrows, displaying his wounds to the viewer" (p. 179). The slightly exaggerated crease, just inside the circle that pinpoints the agony, is shadowed like the wound in Christ's side. As in so many of the works that we will examine in this book, the sensations of pain and pleasure will demand a deep attention to the body, and a resultant scrutiny of the self. This attention will itself be the root of a kind of psychological inwardness that we value deeply, and that we often associate with the most valued works of the Renaissance. Classical ethics and

Judeo-Christian spirituality together emphasize this deeply physical sense of self, even while these disparate realms of value are frequently in conflict themselves over the particular meanings the body yields.

This book, then, will explore a form of materialist psychology, but not the kind dramatized by Ben Jonson. Jonson, remarks Katharine Maus,

> conceives a materialist psychology to entail a complete availability of self to observers.... The apparent "flatness" of the Jonsonian humours character... may be due to this impossibility of his possessing hidden depths, some implied level of experience from which the audience is excluded. A character like Asotus cannot have "that within which passeth show."[3]

I want to show how humoral psychology makes available not only the deliberately superficial characterizations that mark Jonsonian comedy but also the convoluted depths of Shakespeare's Sonnets. In the Dürer *Self-Portrait*, which marshals all the resources of his art for largely diagnostic purposes to show what is within, we glimpse both the effort to express the material self as a site of inwardness, and the elusiveness of that self, the way it seems always to be receding both from the matter in which it takes form, and the medium in which it is expressed. Despite Hamlet's eloquent and psychologically necessary articulation of his own inscrutability at the corrupt court of King Claudius, the real mystery is not to announce that one has "that within which passeth show," but rather to try to manifest what is within through whatever resources one's culture makes available. Each of the writers we will look at explores the mysteries of psychological inwardness that are folded into the stories of the body told by contemporaneous medicine.

The central element in these stories is humoral theory. First espoused by the Hippocratic writers, and later developed and systematized by Galen, this particular set of doctrines and beliefs held that physical health and mental disposition were determined by the balance within the body of the four humoral fluids produced by the various stages of digestion – blood, phlegm, yellow bile, and black bile.[4] These fluids are then dispersed throughout the body by spirits, mediators between soul and body. Andrew Wear estimates that "between 1500 and 1600 there were published around 590 different editions of works of Galen."[5] Under this regime, illness is not the product of an infection from without but rather is the result of an internal imbalance of humoral fluid. Although this account of behavior appears at once deeply materialist and incorrigibly determinist, in actual practice it was possible to manipulate the humoral fluids and their concomitant behaviors through diet and evacuation. Indeed, much of the literature we will be looking at explores just the possibility of managing these fluids in order to live longer, to have healthy male children, to assuage certain characterological flaws, and to exploit similar flaws in others. The choleric man, for example, is angry because he has too much choler. He needs to purge this excess, and/or assimilate substances that are cold and wet to counterbalance the hot and dry qualities of excess choler. The goal of medical intervention was thus to restore each individual's proper balance, either through ingestion of substances possessing opposite traits, or purgation of excess, or both. Although this regime imagined that bodies were perpetually in danger of poisoning themselves through their own nutritive material, it also made available a vast array of therapies for purging this harmful excess, and urged frequent and thorough deployment of them.

It is easy for us, benefiting daily from our own very different medical and psychological regimens, to underestimate both the seductive coherence of Galenic humoral theory and its experiential suppleness. This theory possesses a remarkable capacity to relate the body to its environment, and to explain the literal influences that flow into it from a universe composed of analogous elements. In Figure 1, from Thomas Walkington's *Optick Glasse of Humors*, we can see how the various humors were correlated with the elements, with a time of life, with a season, with one of the four winds, with a planet, and with the zodiac.[6] The four elements to which Sir Toby Belch would reduce human life in the epigraph to this chapter are themselves part of the network of humoral flow. The activities of "eating and drinking" that Sir Andrew Aguecheek proposes to supplant this elemental philosophy are in fact the media by which these elements enter human bodies and so influence human conduct. Even Paracelsus, who mounts the major attack against Galenism in the period, characterizing it as the product of a stale scholasticism which his "new" learning will replace, retains a significant amount of Galenic theory in his elaborate theories of correspondence and influence. The illustration from Robert Fludd's *Utrusque cosmi ... historia* (Oppenheim, 1619; see Fig. 2) demonstrates how the Paracelsian physiological self is poised at the intersection of a variety of climatological forces. Because the body is a microcosm of the universe, its visceral inwardness supplies the center that is interpenetrated by the universal forces of choler, blood, phlegm, and feces (rather than Galen's melancholy). Humoral theory is not the dry recounting of Aristotle or Galen that it is often construed to be – particularly by Paracelsians, or partisans of a self-proclaimed scientific revolution – but rather a remarkable blend of textual authority and a near-poetic vocabulary of felt corporeal experience.

Indeed, when one gets over the initial unfamiliarity of a particular description of a bodily process, one is struck by the fact that this is indeed how bodies feel as if they are behaving. So different from our own counterintuitive but more effective therapies, these accounts describe not so much the actual workings of the body as the experience of the body. In his

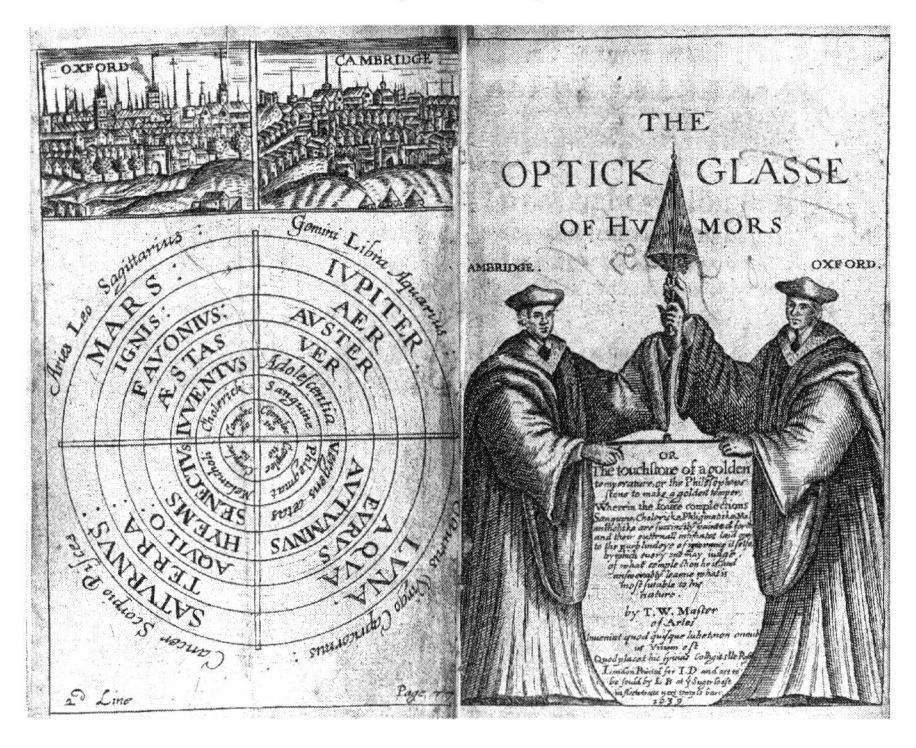

Figure 1 From Thomas Walkington, *The Optick Glasse of Humors* (London, 1607)

brilliant depiction of the ancient regime of the self, Peter Brown stresses the enormous difference between early and contemporary accounts of the body:

The learned treatises of the age collaborated with ancient commonsense notions to endow the men and women of late antiquity with bodies totally unlike those of modern persons. Here were little fiery universes, through whose heart, brain, and veins there pulsed the same heat and vital spirit as glowed in the stars. To make love was to bring one's blood to the boil, as the fiery vital spirit swept through the veins, turning the blood into the whitened foam of semen. It was a process in which the body as a whole – the brain cavity, the marrow of the backbone, the kidneys, and the lower bowel region – was brought into play, "as in a mighty choir." The genital regions were mere points of passage. They were the outlets of a human Espresso machine. It was the body as a whole, and not merely the genitals, that made orgasm possible. "In a single impact of both parts," wrote the somber but well-read Christian, Tertullian, "the whole human frame is shaken and foams with semen, as the damp humor of the body is joined to the hot substance of the spirit."[7]

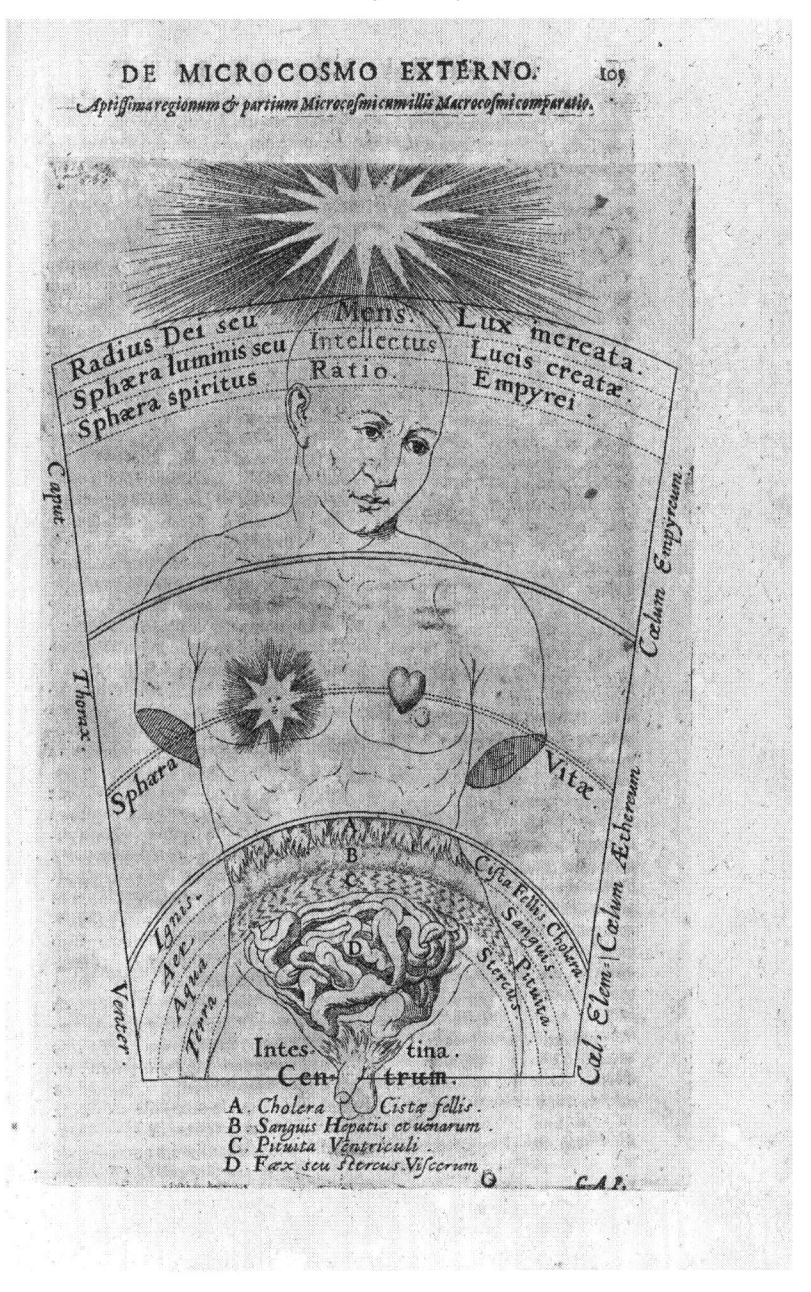

Figure 2 From Robert Fludd, *Utrusque cosmi . . . historia* (Oppenheim, 1619)

Brown has good reasons for heightening the sense of difference between present and past. It is an effective strategy for shaking readers out of the complacence that vague notions of the classics sometimes precipitate. But I question whether these ancient and outmoded doctrines produced "bodies totally unlike those of modern persons." I have found in my research for this book a focus on the body to bring these writers from the past as near to me as the skin and organs we share, even though discursive explanations for corporeal phenomena frequently vary as widely as Brown suggests.

Bodies have changed little through history, even though the theories of their operations vary enormously across time and culture. We all are born, we eat, we defecate, we desire, and we die. The explanations made available by this earlier regime, moreover, are frequently less estranging than our own clinical vocabularies. When reading these earlier descriptions, even those used by Brown to exemplify a gulf of difference between past and present, I have been struck by the fact that this language yields an account of what it feels like to experience certain corporeal phenomena. Indeed, the lexicon of Galenic medicine has survived the demise of its intellectual framework in part because of its cogent experiential basis and its profoundly sentient terminology. We still get choleric, feel phlegmatic or sanguine or melancholy. Anger still feels hot to us, and requires that we "cool down." Although it may have offered little actual help (and a significant amount of harm) to those who sought its physiological and psychological remedies, Galenic medicine provided a range of writers with a rich and malleable discourse able to articulate and explain the vagaries of human emotion in corporeal terms.

It could, for example, explain those fascinating conjunctions of physiology and psychology that are blushing and blanching. In Lodowick Bryskett's *Discourse of Civill Life* (1606), we learn that

the minde finding that what is to be reprehended in us, commeth from abroade, it seeketh to hide the fault committed, and to avoide the reproach thereof, by setting that colour on our face as a maske to defend us withall. . . . But feare which proceedeth from imagination of some evill to come, and is at hand, maketh the mind which conceiveth it to startle, and looking about for meanes of defence, it calleth al the bloud into the innermost parts, specially to the heart, as the chiefe fort or castle; whereby the exterior parts being abandoned and deprived of heate, and of that colour which it had from the bloud and the spirits, there remaineth nothing but palenesse. And hereof it commeth to passe that we see such men as are surprised with feare, to be not only pale, but to tremble also, as if their members would shake off from their bodies: even as the leaves fall from the tree as soone as the cold wether causeth the sappe to be called from the branches to the roote, for the preservation of the vertue vegetative.[8]

Galenic medicine here yields a colorful, experiential, even lyrical vocabulary of the physiology of inner emotion.

Even though the ideological underpinnings of Galenic physiology seem to inhabit a universe completely alien to the explanations available in modern medicine, the various therapies frequently resemble the available treatments in what is now tellingly termed "alternative medicine." We now understand the random and relentless ways that diseases descend upon their victims, but we still long to have health and longevity be the product of a regimen of dietary choices and physical exercises. In its emphasis on temperance as a central strategy for the maintenance of physiological and psychological health, locating both at the mid-point of unhealthy extremes, Galenic physiology provides a compelling model of just how good health could emerge from good living. As temperance became a central ethical virtue for the Renaissance, health assumed the role of a moral imperative, just as it still is in many ways for us. Illness in turn was perceived as a symptom of immorality. One of the more troubling aspects of Galenic medicine is that while it makes the patient the agent rather than the victim of his or her health, it also provides a framework for blaming the patient for the illness that arbitrarily afflicts him or her.

Reading the descriptions of corporeal processes available in works of Renaissance medicine, one is frequently struck by an uncanny experience of familiarity and strangeness. This is in part because the vocabulary is one we still use today, but the meanings of the terms have shifted. "Complexion," for example, meant not skin tone but, in the definition of Sir Thomas Elyot, author of one of the most popular health manuals in the period, *The Castel of Helthe*,

> a combynation of two dyvers qualities of the four elementes in one body, as hotte and drye of the fyre: hotte and moyste of the Ayre, colde and moyst of the Water, colde and dry of the Erth. But although all these complexions be assembled in every body of man and woman, yet the body taketh his denomination of those qualyties, whiche abounde in hym, more thanne in the other.[9]

Because skin tone was one indicator of such internal qualities, the modern meaning of the word began to emerge from this mode of explanation. As these various traits were assumed to reflect a climatological influence, "complexion" assumed the racial meanings that underpin its modern applications. Familiar terms such as "temper," "humor," "passion," "heat," "blood," "spirit," and "temperature" all derive from this earlier lexicon of the self, but mean something very different in early modern usage. "The balance of humors," remarks Nancy Siraisi, "was held to be responsible for psychological as well as physical disposition, a belief enshrined in the survival of the English adjectives sanguine, phlegmatic, choleric, and melancholy to describe traits of character."[10] This medical ideology made available a particular corporeal lexicon of inner emotion. As Katharine Maus points out:

> In vernacular sixteenth- and early seventeenth-century speech and writing, the whole interior of the body – heart, liver, womb, bowels, kidneys, gall, blood, lymph – quite often involves itself in the production of the mental interior, of the individual's privates. Humours psychology is perhaps the most systematic working out of this premise.[11]

We still locate our psychological inwardness in corporeal terms, giving those we love pictures of our body's hydraulic pump on Valentine's Day, although we realize the deeply metaphorical nature of this act, particularly in an age where heart transplants are increasingly common.[12] But in the writers we will be looking at, such embodiments of emotion will not be enactments of dead metaphors but rather explorations of the corporeal nature of self. As David Hillman has recently argued, selfhood and materiality

> were ineluctably linked in the pre-Cartesian belief systems of the period, which preceded, for the most part, any attempt to separate the vocabulary of medical and humoral physiology from that of individual psychology. When, therefore, characters on the early modern stage speak of "my heart's core, ay . . . my heart of heart" (*Hamlet* 3.2.73), or of "the heat of our livers" (*2 Henry IV* 1.2.175) – or, indeed, of being "inward search'd" (*Merchant of Venice* 3.2.86) or afflicted with "inward pinches" (*Tempest* 5.1.77) – we would do well to regard these as far from merely metaphorical referents, and to try to discover how they figure into an overall understanding of bodily – and therefore psychological – interiority in a given play.[13]

By urging a particularly organic account of inwardness and individuality, Galenic medical theory gave poets a language of inner emotion whose vehicles were also tenors, whose language of desire was composed of the very stuff of being. The texts we will be examining emerge from a historical moment when the "scientific" language of analysis had not yet been separated from the sensory language of experience. Whereas our post-Cartesian ontology imagines psychological inwardness and physiological materialism as necessarily separate realms of existence, and thus renders corporeal language for emotion highly metaphorical, the Galenic regime of the humoral self that supplies these writers with much of their vocabulary of inwardness demanded the invasion of social and psychological realms by biological and environmental processes.[14]

The philosophical question which such a notion of self entails, for us and for the Renaissance, is just how the physical body and non-physical spirit interact. The Renaissance inherits and elaborates an enormous dissonance and inconsistency in the available doctrines of the relationship between bodies and souls, and between reason and the passions. Plato in the *Timaeus* was among the first to locate what we would call emotions in bodily organs. He lists what he terms "pathemata" by name, ascribing the rational part of the soul to the head, the soul's faculty of courage and anger to the part of the body near the heart "between the diaphragm and the neck," and desire to the lower part of the body.[15] In a work that became notorious for articulating an atheistic materialism, the *Quod Animi Mores*, Galen marshals the authority of both Plato and Aristotle to argue that the behavior of the soul depends on the temperature of the body:

Those who do not agree that the soul derives benefit and harm from the mixture of the body have no explanation whatsoever to give of differences in children, or of the benefits derived from regimen, or of those differences in character which make people spirited or otherwise, or intelligent or otherwise.[16]

In the immensely popular *The Examination of Men's Wits* (1594), Juan Huarte boldly endorses Galen's materialist psychology while giving it a particular climatological, nationalist, and implicitly racist spin:

Galen writ a booke, wherein he prooveth, That the maners of the soule, follow the temperature of the body [*Quod animi mores*], in which it keepes residence, and that by reason of the heat, the coldnesse, the moisture, and the drouth, of the territorie where men inhabit, of the meates which they feed on, of the waters which they drinke, and of the aire which they breath: some are blockish, and some wise: some of woorth, and some base: some cruel, and some merciful.... And to proove this, he cites many places of Hippocrates, Plato, and Aristotle, who affirme, that the difference of nations, as well in composition of the body, as in the conditions of the soule, springeth from the varietie of this temperature: and experience it selfe evidently sheweth this, how far are different Greeks from Tartarians: Frenchmen from Spaniards: Indians from Dutch: and Æthiopians from English.... Finally, all that which Galen writeth in this his booke, is the groundplot of this my Treatise.[17]

In *The Optick Glasse of Humors*, Walkington more typically qualifies Galen even while conceding Galen's central point. Walkington argues that the soul follows "the crafts and temperature of the body," but assures the reader that "Wee must not imagine the mind to be passible, being altogether immaterial, that it selfe is affected with any of these, corporall thinges, but onely in respect of the instruments which are hand-maids of the soule."[18] Recourse to an altogether immaterial core self allows Walkington to shun some of the more disturbing aspects of the psychology implied by Galenic physiology. For if morals really are a function of physiology, then a particularly severe form of predestination is manifested in the body. Similarly, Edward Reynolds argues in *A Treatise of the Passions and Faculties of the Soule of Man* (1640), that while

the Reasonable part of Man ... depends in all its ordinarie and naturall operations, upon the happie or disordered temperature of those vitall Qualities, out of whose apt and regular commixion the good estate of the Body is framed and composed.... But yet this dependance on the Body is not so necessarie and immutable, but that it may admit of variation, and Soule be in some cases vindicated from the impression of the Body ... as Hard Bones being steeped in vinegar and ashes... doe lose their Nature, and grow so soft, that they may be cut with a thred; So the toughest, and most unbended natures by early and prudent discipline may be much Rectified.[19]

The stunning image of hard bones being softened in vinegar represents the theoretical power of discipline in this regime to rectify the distortions of physiology. Locating and explaining human passion amid a taxonomy of internal organs, and manipulating their fluid economies for the desired physiological, psychological, and ethical outcome, Galenic physiology issues in a discourse in which, to use a phrase that Slavoj Zizek borrows from Hegel, "the spirit is a bone."[20] In this discourse, that is, the purportedly immaterial subject is constituted as a profoundly material substance.

It is a difficult framework for those of us who are the inheritors of the Cartesian philosophical tradition to grasp. "Despite some trends in recent philosophy and medicine," remarks Anthony Fletcher, "we are mostly still good Cartesians at heart. That is we experience ourselves as a self which has or is within a body."[21] As Descartes himself remarks in a letter to Princess Elizabeth of Bohemia: "It does not seem to me that the human mind is capable of conceiving at the same time the distinction and the union between body and soul, because for this it is necessary to conceive them as a single thing and at the same time to conceive them as two things; and this is absurd."[22] Descartes here brilliantly articulates a kind of uncertainty principle for a true philosophy of the subject. Yet it is just this complex mode of connection between body and mind towards which contemporary medicine, with all its mechanistic presuppositions, is being driven to endorse by its own researches into the body. As Antonio Damasio, a neurologist, remarks in *Descartes' Error*:

This is Descartes' error: the abyssal separation between body and mind, between the sizable, dimensioned, mechanically operated, infinitely divisible body stuff, on the one hand, and unsizable, undimensioned, un-pushpullable, nondivisible mind stuff; the suggestion that reasoning, and moral judgment, and the suffering that comes from physical pain or emotional upheaval might exist separately from the body. Specifically: the separation of the most refined operations of mind from the structure and operation of a biological organism . . .

The idea of a disembodied mind also seems to have shaped the peculiar way in which Western medicine approaches the study and treatment of diseases. The Cartesian split pervades both research and practice. As a result, the psychological consequences of the diseases of the body proper, the so-called real diseases, are usually disregarded and only considered on second thought. Even more neglected are the reverse, the body-proper effects of psychological conflict. How intriguing to think that Descartes did contribute to modifying the course of medicine, did help it veer from the organismic, mind-in-the-body approach, which prevailed from Hippocrates to the Renaissance. How annoyed Aristotle would have been with Descartes, had he known.[23]

It is easy to be too hard on Descartes, since he is in many ways just the inheritor of a dualism central to western thought since Plato (although Plato's own account of morality is deeply materialist[24]). Descartes is, moreover, famous for having located the soul in a material organ, the pineal gland, in part because it was a single organ, and in part because it could be hard to locate in an anatomized corpse, suggesting that something in the body had departed at the moment of death.[25] But his emphasis on the central question of how rationality can be a property of material substance, and his definition of existence in terms of rational thought, as separate from the mechanisms of the body – the force of the famous "Je pense, donc je suis" – produced a pronounced dissociation of essential self from body, a dissociation from which we are still trying to recover. Although the therapeutic gains have been enormous, one cannot but feel that something was lost as well as gained when the body became primarily a machine. In John Purcell's *A Treatise on Vapours or, Hysterick Fits* (1702), we can hear the "new science" proudly mocking earlier doctors who did not know "the true mechanism of Man's Body.... Nothing is now acceptable but what is explain'd Mechanically by Figure and Motion."[26] It is typical of the ironies that repeatedly dog such hubristic statements, including those of our own moment, that much of the task of cutting-edge neurology is dedicated to undoing the intellectual complacence that frequently underpins professedly revolutionary claims.

The purpose of this book is to recover as much as possible this earlier understanding of self, not as an inert and alien body of knowledge, but rather as a vibrantly inconsistent but brilliantly supple discourse of selfhood and agency. I intend to show how in early modern England, the consuming subject was pressured by Galenic physiology, classical ethics, and Protestant theology to conceive all acts of ingestion and excretion as very literal acts of self-fashioning. At each meal, the individual was enmeshed in the process identified by Charles Taylor as "remak[ing] himself by methodical and disciplined action."[27] The argument of the book is in dialogue, and sometimes in explicit disagreement, with a presupposition that structures much current work on the Renaissance. Where New Historicism has tended to emphasize the individual as a victim of the power that circulates through culture, I stress the empowerment that Galenic physiology and ethics bestowed upon the individual. This is a book, then, about control, but not the authoritarian state that so frequently characterizes New Historicist descriptions of Renaissance England; I emphasize rather the self-control that authorizes individuality. It is about how to fortify a self, not police a state. Its focus is a regime of self-discipline which an earlier culture imagined as a necessary step towards any prospect of liberation. I hope to show how in this earlier regime, control could be enabling as well as inhibiting. As Henry Peacham remarks in *The Complete Gentleman*, "And albeit true it is that Galen saith, we are commonly beholden for the disposition of our minds to the temperature of our bodies, yet much lieth in our power to keep that fount from empoisoning by taking heed to ourselves."[28] It is the disordered, undisciplined self, subject to a variety of internal and external forces, that is the site of subjugation, and the subject of horror. I want to analyze a particularly physiological mode of self-fashioning, one that turns inward as much as outward, and pays particular attention to those moments of eating and evacuation that demarcate the cusp between inner and outer. Emphasis on the physiological underpinnings of the early modern self, I argue, allows us to see that this self is far more than just an effect of discourses, or the product of socio-cultural discourses, institutions, and practices. Looking closely at these past discourses allows us to see what these individuals made of the materials of their culture, and their bodies, as well as what their culture and bodies made of them. Indeed, much of the physiological work of the period arises as an explicit response to the famous injunction of the Delphic oracle, "Know thyself." In a commentary note "To the Readers" prefacing Phineas Fletcher's *Purple Island* (itself an extended imitation of the trip through the alimentary tract that constitutes Spenser's Castle of Alma), the Conformist divine Daniel Featley remarks, "he that would learn *Theologie*, must first studie *Autologie*. The way to God is by our selves: It is a blinde and dirty way; it hath many windings, and is easie to be lost: This Poem will make thee understand that way."[29] Traversing this "blinde and dirty way," through the interior spaces of the consuming subject, is a voyage that a surprising number of early modern writers felt to be an essential part of the project of self-knowledge.

Behind the presuppositions of New Historicism, as well as the terms in which I dispute them, is the work of Michel Foucault. In the earlier work of Foucault – *The Archaeology of Knowledge*, *Discipline and Punish*, *The Order of Things* – it seemed as if subjectivity was inexorably produced and secured through society's power over the individual.[30] Likewise, even through the introductory volume of *The History of Sexuality*, Foucault was locating the rupture that produced modern configurations of the sexual self in the seventeenth century. In the last two published volumes of *The History of Sexuality*, and in the various published and unpublished lectures he gave late in his life, Foucault signaled a major departure from this work, as he turned to classical Greece and Rome to discover a "care of the self" which anticipates modern subjectivity.[31] In his pursuit of the problematization of sexuality back to Stoic and early Christian discourse, Foucault discovered a message of individual liberation amid a regime of self-control. In *The Use of Pleasure*, Foucault argues that the classical ideal of moderation (the same virtue to which Spenser and Milton will give such ethical force) epitomizes the individual's liberation: "Sophrosyne [moderation] was a state that could be approached through the exercise of self-mastery and through restraint in the practice of pleasures; it was characterized as a freedom" (p. 78). For Foucault, then, control becomes a discourse of liberation, not of suppression. The unexpected and unfinished leap (Foucault was, of course, no classicist) from the breezy historical generalizations of the Introduction to the comparatively plodding work on Stoic and early Christian modes of self-control has been relatively ignored by literary critics and historians. The point of this last phase of Foucault's remarkable career, however, is the way that individual subjectivity, and individual liberty, is secured through the individual's exercise of self-discipline.

It is this emphasis on the productive function of discipline that differentiates my work from recent work on the body in the Renaissance that has drawn its conceptual models from Mikhail Bakhtin's important work on Renaissance festivity.[32] Bakhtin's fascinating book on Rabelais, a stunningly original attempt to remind us of the social functions of a nearly forgotten repertoire of practices deliberately segregated from everyday life, has itself become a paradigm of early modern consumption that needs to be dislodged. Bakhtin's powerful formulations about eating and festive release have been in some ways too influential, generating an opposition between the classically immured body and the precivilized, unregulated body that is belied by the very regime that produced the discourses of health and sickness.[33] As the Dutch physician Levinus Lemnius observes, God "created so many wayes and passages to purge forth the humours, and to wash away the excrements, lest a man might be oppressed by the abundance of them." Indeed, the body is in this regime a dynamic and porous edifice continually producing "superfluous excrements" which must be removed:

So the head purgeth it self by the Nostrills, Ears, the Palate, and unburdens it self by [s]neesing and spitting: The Breast and Lungs by the vocal artery send forth flegme by coughing: the Stomach and Ventricle cleanseth its sink by vomit and belching; The Intestines purge themselves by the belly, and with breaking wind backward, the guts are cleansed from their excrements: The Reins and Bladder send away the Urine by urinary passages, but the superficies of the body discusseth all fumes and sweat through the skin that is full of holes and pores.[34]

The stomach is at the center of an organic system demanding perpetual, anxious osmosis with the outside world. Obstruction rather than flow is cause and evidence of illness. As Lady Grace Mildmay, one of the many female health practitioners in the period, remarked in her medical papers, "If there be obstructions in the stomach and bowels and rhume in the head, then must the body be kept soluble."[35]

Indeed, the body's emunctory capacities are so important to the health of the organism that curing hemorrhoids can result in sickness and even death. As Sir Thomas Elyot remarks,

> Hemorroides be vaynes in the foundement, of whome do happen sundry passions, sometyme swellyng, without bledynge, sometyme superfluous bloud by the puissance of nature, is by them expelled, and than be they very convenient, for by them a man shall escape many greate sycknesses, which be ingendred of corrupted bloude, or of melancoly. Semblably, if they be hastylye stopped from the course, whiche they have bene used to therby do increase the said syknesses, whiche by them were expelled.[36]

This critical link between health and flow urges revision of the account of the ideal classical body we have inherited from Bakhtin's compelling work on Rabelais. Under the Galenic regime of the humors, which imagines all illness as an imbalance among the four nutritive fluids produced by digestion, soundness of mind and body is achieved not by immuring bodily fluids but rather by carefully manipulating them. As Thomas Venner remarks in *Via Recta ad Vitam Longam*, "they that have their belly naturally loose and open . . . are not easily affected with sicknesse: whereas of the contrary, they that have the same bound up, . . . have for the most part, often conflicts with sicknesse." This is because "the keeping of those ordinary and daily excrements, is very offensive to the body by reason of the noysome fumes that ascend from them, which of all other parts do chiefly annoy the head, causing dimnesse of the sight, dulnesse, heavinesse, head-ach, inflammation of the head; and not these only of the head; but the mind it selfe is oftentimes hereby disturbed, and malancholikly [*sic*] affected."[37] This physiology demands not the seamless corporeal enclosure that Bakhtin identifies with the classical body but rather the routine excretory processes that he displaces onto lower-class festivity.

Moreover, as Michel Jeanneret points out, regimens of humoral regulation are widespread in the literature of the sixteenth century, and "even crop up where they are least expected: in the middle of Rabelaisian frolics."[38] The story of Gargantua is in fact one of a deleterious carnivalesque excess giving way to salubrious dietary self-regulation; Gargantua, Jeanneret observes, "comes a long way from the feasts of his childhood to the scientifically measured out meals of his adolescence" (p. 87). By focusing only on the former, readers of Rabelais, and of Renaissance literature, have told a powerful but partial story. Relatedly, the very etymology of *carnival*, the concept from which so much work on early modern bodies departs, derives from the farewell to the flesh (the literal meaning of *carne-vale*) that is celebrated by a brief but intense indulgence in carnal desire. To view carnival in isolation from this calendrical process of self and communal regulation is seriously to misread its social function. In this book I want to show that selves emerge not just in heightened moments of carnivalesque inversion and excess, but in the mundane activities of eating and defecating.

The relative analytical weight given to the carnivalesque body is a signal difference between my argument and that which emerges in the book that pioneered work on the humoral body in recent criticism, Gail Kern Paster's *The Body Embarrassed*.[39] Paster's work has had an appropriately wide influence because it reminded literary critics of the frequency and cogency of humoral terminology. But where Paster links "the humoral body's corporeal flux" to "Bakhtin's description of the grotesque body" (p. 14), I want to show how humoral theory encouraged not carnivalesque liquefaction but rather the careful maintenance of constitutional solubility. Paster tends to pathologize the leaky body, to see it as the site of something socially embarrassing, where I argue that Galenic medicine renders the obstructed body the source of mortal pathogens. Throughout the book I look at the ways that what Paster aptly terms a "caloric economy" could be manipulated by the subjects of it, rather than recording, as does Paster, the manipulations of gender and class that it so frequently sanctioned. Paster offers a fascinating theoretical mapping of Lacanian psychoanalytic theory onto both Bakhtinian carnival and Norbert Elias's powerful account of civilization as a series of advancing thresholds of shame.[40] By emphasizing the individual subject's willing and unembarrassed adoption of therapies of self-regulation, I want to show how self-discipline not only entailed the forced assimilation of corporeal urges to societal pressure but also produced the parameters of individual subjectivity.

I intend throughout the book to generate a dialogue between past and present models of the self. I explore the striking differences, and powerful but latent connections, between psychoanalytic and earlier models of self. For example, Freud's theory of repression argues that painful memories get shoved down into the unconscious, where they become the source of neurotic symptoms and physical expressions like hysteria. Psychoanalytic practice is based on the idea that purging these memories is the key to renewed mental health; as the patient releases denied feelings – especially negative ones, such as hatred for a parent – the neurotic symptoms dissipate and the patient is able to move on. It is, I would assert, fascinating just how different, even contrary, this notion of the beneficial release of emotions is from a Neostoic privileging of self-control, whereby physical and psychological health is imagined to derive from the capacity to control rather than to vent emotion. Even more fascinating, though, is just how much this structure depends on a therapeutic model derived from Galenic medicine, making the purgation of something inward and potentially noxious the dominant curative mode. Where Galenic medicine imagines humoral excess as the source of illness, psychoanalysis locates dangerous excess on the plane of the verbal, the imaginary, and the mnemonic. Drives rather than humors constitute the hydraulic forces coursing through the individual. Where the one locates illness in repressed memory, the other in excess corporeal matter. The goal of both regimes, though, is to scour the subject of deleterious inwardness.

A central difference is the status of what we have come to call repression. The early modern regime seems to entail a fear of emotion that resembles our own fear of repression. As we will see, the status of emotion is one of the most contested areas of early modern psychology, a dispute with roots going back to Augustine's reading of Cicero. But emotion, or what is called in the early modern lexicon "passion" or "affection," was frequently linked with disease, even by those who were engaged in the project of validating its proper deployment. In *The Passions of the Minde*, a work dedicated to exploiting the rhetorical function of passions, Thomas Wright notes that "there is no Passion very vehement, but that it alters extreamly som of the foure humors of the body." Such alterations were invariably harmful: "Passions," concludes Wright, "cause many maladies, & welnigh all are increased by them." "Seeing that the affections and perturbations of the mind are of such force for the overthrowing of the health and welfare of the body," notes Thomas Venner, "I advise all such as are respective of their health, to bridle all irrational motions of the mind, by the reason and understanding and labour by all means to observe a mediocrity, in their passion, wherein consisteth the tranquillity both of mind and body." An anonymous physician, advising a gentleman on matters of health, warns that untoward emotion can threaten the health of even the most health-conscious individual: "For though we live in a sweet and pure aire, observe a strict diet, use sleepe and exercise according to the rules of Physicke, and keepe fit times and measure in expelling superfluities out of our bodies; yet if we have not quiet, calme and placable mindes, we shall subject our selves to those diseases that the minde, yeelding to these passions, commonly inflicteth upon the body: these are many in number, grievous to suffer, and dangerous to life."[41]

We do injustice to this constitutive discipline of emotion when we pathologize it as repression. Discussing the Roman moralists, and those Renaissance writers who follow their severe pronouncements on emotion, Katharine Maus advises:

It is false to call their hostility to emotional indulgence merely repressive, because the whole concept of harmful repression involves the assumption, denied by Roman psychological theory, that an impulse unnaturally suppressed will pop out uncontrollably in some unexpected and usually grotesque fashion. Since they do not accept the Platonic-Augustinian-Freudian notion of an economy of drives, the Roman moralists see no reason for this to be true.[42]

Where we imagine desire as the locus of self, the Roman moralists "imagine desire as an alien intruder upon the tranquil, rational soul."[43] When Stoics are criticized in the early modern period, it is more typically for their pride than for their suppression of emotion. In the *Institutes,* for example, Calvin denounces the philosophers who "have burst foorth into so great licentiousnesse, that they have boasted that it is indeed Gods gift that we live, but our owne that we live well and holily."[44] The marginal note to this passage reads "Seneca" – the author who formulated most fully the Stoic principles of absolute independence as a source of freedom. The autonomy and self-sufficiency of the Stoic threaten the Christian's absolute dependence on divine grace for the true happiness of salvation.

In the early modern regime, it is unfettered emotion that is most to be feared, while in the modern psychoanalytic regime it is the unhealthy effect of those fetters. In *Civilization and Its Discontents* Freud suggests that civilization requires repression – a generalization with which each of the authors featured in this book would agree – and yet Freud also offers the brilliant but paradoxical formulation that the very repression necessary to civilization produces behavioral pathologies that are dangerous both to civilization and to individuals. I am not denying that repression can be a powerful analytical tool for understanding texts from the past. But I am maintaining that not all exercises in self-control are occasions of pathological repression. Where in *Civilization and Its Discontents*, the psyche looks like a sadomasochistic dungeon, with the superego imposing cruel but necessary torments on the hapless ego and the troublesome id, in Book 2 of *The Faerie Queene* (the subject of Chapter 2) the self is a hospitable but fortified castle of temperate pleasure.

In a powerful but much disputed essay, "Psychoanalysis and Renaissance Culture," Stephen Greenblatt argues that in both psychoanalysis and Renaissance thought "the self is at its most visible, most expressive . . . at moments in which the moral will has ceded place to the desires that constitute the deepest stratum of psychic experience."[45] I would maintain on the contrary that this is where they most fully diverge. The Renaissance seems to have imagined selves as differentiated not by their desires, which all more or less share, but by their capacity to control these desires. Psychoanalysis and early modern psychology are linked in that both require fastidious attention to the inner promptings of various appetites and urges. But where psychoanalysis tends to locate identity in terms of which objects are desired among the various available possibilities, how intensely they are desired, and how these desires have been fashioned by the experiences of early infancy, the Renaissance locates identity in the more or less successful regulation of a series of desires shared by all. Greenblatt rightly questions "the universalist claims of psychoanalysis," which remain for the most part "unruffled by the indifference of the past to its categories" (p. 215). One of the purposes of this book is to allow the past to ruffle these claims. To do so is not to credit this earlier culture from which we derive with "an entirely different system of consciousness" (p. 217), but it is to respect and to learn from those differences that do emerge.

The early modern fetish of control, moreover, does not demand the unequivocal banishment of emotion. Indeed, the ethical status of emotion supplies an occasion when the blend of classical and Christian cultures that defines the Renaissance, for us and for the period, is revealed in all its explosive instability. The fact that in England the Renaissance was also experienced as a religious reformation only heightens the agitation between the comparative ethical value of classical Stoic apathy and Christian affect, between the rigorous self-control that temperance demands and the absolute dependence on God that Protestantism counsels, between finding happiness in a paradise within and locating the source of happiness in a divinity outside oneself. For writers such as Justus Lipsius, these tensions could be dismissed by emphasis on the common vocabulary and ethical goals of discipline and moderation shared by classical and Christian writers. Not only did they share a similar set of vices; as Anthony Levi remarks, "It was the ambiguity of the term 'reason' as much as any other single factor which enabled Justus Lipsius to seem to unite stoic ethical doctrine with orthodox Christianity ... the terminology is Senecan, the interpretation Christian."[46] But as early as Augustine, Christian sentience had been in excruciating contrast with Stoic imperturbability. In *The City of God*, Augustine suggests that the status of emotion is what differentiates the Roman from the Christian regime: "In our discipline it is not asked whether the pious spirit will be angry, but why it is angry; nor whether it is sad, but for what cause it is sad; nor whether it fears, but why it fears."[47]

The Renaissance inherited a confused intellectual legacy, what William Bouwsma has aptly termed "The Two Faces of Humanism: Stoicism and Augustinianism." And Renaissance writers were notoriously inconsistent in their application of these contrary principles.[48] Neostoicism, moreover, developed in England in very different ways from what it had come to mean on the Continent. As J. H. Salmon notes,

Tacitean Neostoicism became a vehicle for discontent in Jacobean court circles. The particularly English confluence of the streams of Senecan and Tacitean ideas, which occurred at about the time of the Essex coup, differed somewhat from Lipsius's intermixing of the two. With Lipsius the way lay open for rational statecraft and the prudential participation of the subject as the servant of the absolutist state. It was not so with those English malcontents who devised their own blend of Senecan and Tacitean influence under the pressure of plots, rivalries and disappointments in late Elizabethan and early Jacobean times. For them Tacitus politicized Senecan philosophy and gave it a cynical bent, while Seneca strengthened the lessons, already suggested in Tacitus's history of Roman tyranny and civil war, that private prudence and withdrawal were the best policies.[49]

In England, that is, Neostoicism became a vehicle of political discontent, rather than the absolutist code it had become on the Continent. This difference was only heightened by the fact that in the seventeenth century, the English royal court came to define itself in terms of the kinds of sensual indulgence that Neostoicism castigated. In *Paradise Lost*, the Puritan revolutionary Milton will battle valiantly to reclaim an ethic of pleasure from this court, while in *Paradise Regained* he will use a Neostoic deployment of temperance to reject the entire inheritance of Greece and Rome, including Neostoic self-sufficiency. In both works, food will play a central role, as a site of sensuality, obedience, and transgression. Behavior towards food will determine the ethical success of the subject.

Tellingly, the works under consideration here emerge in the historical moment when the English meanings of "diet" are beginning to migrate from their original Greek meaning of "a daily mode of life," or "a regular way of living," to the more specific, food-related, contemporary connotations. Attention to dietary patterns will reveal much about the specific regimens of self that Galenic medicine makes available. My work will sometimes draw on the accounts of the social meanings of dietary structures of purity and impurity, of the raw and the cooked, available in the work of Claude Levi-Strauss and Mary Douglas.[50] But my emphasis will be less on the dietary patterns of a culture, and more on the decisions that individuals make on a daily basis as they attempt to put these structures into practice. Under the Galenic dispensation in particular, dietary regimes organize not just societies but also selves. This is especially true when the issue is not a series of blanket dietary taboos, such as those announced in Leviticus, but rather questions of excess and of purity, which are different for each individual, and at different times. In *Powers of Horror*, Julia Kristeva argues that Christianity entails a redefinition of the cultural role of food in terms of the ephemeral economies of inner purity:

It is through abolishment of dietary taboos, partaking of food with pagans, verbal and gestural contact with lepers, as well as through its power over impure spirits that the message of Christ is characterized. . . . What is happening is that a new arrangement of difference is being set up, an arrangement whose economy will regulate a wholly different system of meaning, hence a wholly different speaking subject. An essential trait of those evangelical attitudes or narratives is that abjection is no longer exterior. It is permanent and comes from within.[51]

Christianity then entails an increase in dietary freedom, and dietary anxiety, an anxiety that is further accented by Protestantism. When, as Paul announced, to the pure all things are pure, how is one to determine the critical moment when sustenance slides into gluttony, when the consuming subject is itself tainted by impurity, except by scrupulous self-examination that reproduces in detail the trajectory, circumstances, and parameters of appetite? The authors I will be looking at are not "hunger artists" of the type that Maud Ellmann has described but writers who discover interiority in the therapeutic process of regulating their consumption and excretion.[52]

Galenic medicine and Christian ethics conspire to highlight the particular physiological and psychological makeup of the individual. They demand of the ethical subject, that is, participation in a discourse of deeply embodied inwardness. Anne Ferry's important study of the verbal resources of inwardness to Renaissance poets, *The "Inward" Language*, is limited by its dismissive account of the physiological discourse of the inner self in the Renaissance; she calls it "a collection of inconsistencies in which observations, concepts, superstitions garnered from many periods were bundled together indiscriminately."[53] I would argue on the contrary that the eclecticism and inconsistency that Ferry bemoans are not marks of its inadequacy but rather signs of its tractability. It is, moreover, a discourse that allows at once for generalization – the four personality types that emerge from the predominance of each of the four humors – and for individuation – since each person is comprised of a unique mix of humors. This discourse has been the subject of painstaking scholarship by what might be termed an older historicism.[54] I want to show how humoral psychology is a more versatile discourse of motive and emotion than these previous studies, concerned largely to diagnose characters by humoral type or to reveal the "Renaissance idea of man," would suggest. It is at least as precise and nuanced as the procedures we use to organize and analyze selves. In returning to this vocabulary, then, I am not seeking to replace one kind of procrustean taxonomy of behavioral types with another. There is no single "idea of man (or woman)," but a variety of different and competing models deployed (sometimes by the same author, in the same paragraph) to different ends.

Galenic medical theory gave poets the tools necessary to diagnose human motive, and the therapies required to alter it. The Galenic regime demands that one pay careful attention to the self, in order to know its whims, its desires, and its weaknesses, in order to determine which foods are most appropriate to one's humoral constitution. Diet here is just another version of medicine. As Juan Luis Vives remarks: "Those two arts of Dietetics and Medicine are so much alike, are bound up so closely with one another, that sometimes medicine is thought to be dietetics and vice versa."[55] To choose one's diet is in this regime an act of self-fashioning in the most literal sense, and requires intense self-scrutiny. In *The Castel of Helthe*, Thomas Elyot describes how the attempt to eat healthily produces a kind of necessary introspection in the consumer: "The quantitie of meate muste be proporcioned after the substaunce and qualitie therof, and accordinge to the complexion of hym that eateth." One must attend not only to one's complexion, or particular humoral temperament, but also to one's occupation and environment:

Wherefore of men, which use moch labor or exercise, also of them, which have very cholerike stomackes here in Englande, grosse meates may be eaten in a great quantitie; and in a cholerike stomake biefe is better dygested than a chykens legge, forasmoche as in a hotte stomacke fyne meates be shortly aduste and corrupted. Contrarywise in a colde or fleumatyke stomake grosse meate abydeth longe undigested, and maketh putrified matter: lyght meates therfore be to suche a stomacke more apt and convenyent. The temperate bodye is beste nourysshed with a lyttell quantitie of grosse meates: but of temperate meates in substaunce and qualytie, they maye safely eate a good quantitie.[56]

Consumption is part of a highly complex network of influences on character and health. The porousness of the stomach is symptomatic of the overall porousness of the individual.

For Robert Burton, author of the immensely popular *Anatomy of Melancholy*, the particulars of each consumer's situation must be weighed so carefully that the dietary recommendations to which he devotes so many pages must finally be subordinated to the superior authority of idiosyncrasy: "our owne experience is the best Physitian; that diet which is most propitious to one, is often pernitious to another; such is the variety of palats, humors, and temperatures, let every man observe, and be a law unto himselfe." The introspection that consumption demands precipitates an arena of radical individuation. Even Paracelsus, whose medical writings in many areas repudiate the Galenic system on which Burton's claims are based, imagines the stomach as an inherently distinctive organ: "If the physician is to understand the correct meaning of health, he must know that there are more than a hundred, indeed more than a thousand, kinds of stomach; consequently, if you gather a thousand persons, each of them will have a different kind of digestion, each unlike the others."[57] Necessarily situating dietary authority within, the early modern consumer becomes "a law unto himself," cultivating a self whose unique experience and temperament mandate axioms superior to the prescriptions of external authority.

Although frequently used to denote superficial characterological types, then, the humoral vocabulary was capable of expressing the uniqueness of each individual, and of giving each individual the tools for introspection, as well as a reason for doing so. Juan Huarte, whose *Examination of Men's Wits* counseled parents in the proper procedures for producing healthy male children, expresses wonder at the fact that such a variety of individuals can emerge from the mixture of only four fluids, and suggests that medical treatment should respect this variety:

of so slender a number of parts [4], nature maketh so many proportions, that if a 100000 men be begotten, ech of them comes to the world with a health so peculier and proper to himselfe . . . everie man who falleth sicke, ought to be cured conformable to his particular proportion.[58]

Sir Francis Bacon opens his Essay "Of Regiment of Health" with the suggestion that individual experience ultimately outweighs all medical rules – "There is a wisdom in this beyond the rules of physic: a man's own observation what he finds good of, and what he finds hurt of, is the best physic to preserve health." Bacon, moreover, concludes that the best doctor is not necessarily the one with the deepest knowledge of the rules of medicine but the one who is "best acquainted with your body."[59]

So Galenic medicine led individuals to a kind of radical introspection, an introspection whose focus was physiological as well as psychological. The Galenic body achieves health not by shutting itself off from the world around it but by carefully monitoring and manipulating the inevitable and literal influences of the outside world, primarily through therapies of ingestion and excretion. "Physicke," notes Robert Burton in *The Anatomy of Melancholy*, "is naught else but *addition and substraction*."[60] This principle at once empowers the individual consumer and puts immense ethical and medical pressure on the type and quantity of food consumed. Like so many of the humors books, *The Anatomy of Melancholy* contains elaborate descriptions of the effect of a variety of foods on the humoral disorder of melancholy. Not only are medicine and diet closely aligned in this discourse, but they are seen to blend with ethics and religion. Burton, for example, describes over-eating in a vocabulary that fuses psychology, medicine, and ethics:

As a lamp is choked with a multitude of oil, or a little fire with overmuch wood quite extinguished, so is the natural heat with immoderate eating strangled in the body . . . an insatiable paunch is a pernicious sink, and the fountain of all diseases, both of body and mind. (p. 226)

Burton, moreover, proceeds to articulate in detail the processes by which body and soul work upon each other:

as the body works upon the mind by his bad humours, troubling the spirits, sending gross fumes into the brain, and so *per consequens* disturbing the soul, and all the faculties of it . . . so, on the other side, the mind most effectually works upon the body producing by his passions and perturbations miraculous alterations, as melancholy, despair, cruel diseases, and sometimes death itself; insomuch that it is most true which Plato saith in his Chamides [*sic*], ... all the mischiefs of the body proceed from the soul. (p. 250)

The mental and emotional health of the individual is made largely dependent upon the health of the body, a health which is itself dependent on the quantity and propriety of the food the individual consumes.

In the *Directions for Health*, William Vaughan posits that

if it be true, that the soule is in the bloud, and dispersed thorow every part of the same, (as God is wholly in the world, and wholly in every part of the same) then surely must it follow, that the variety of the bloud doth change and diversifie the understanding, and also that the actes of the understanding soule, doth change the humours of the body: that out of these diversities of tainted humours, there are ingendred strange and wandring phantasies.

Physicians, continues Vaughan, "likewise affirme it for irrefragable doctrine, that such as the bloud is, such are the spirits (for they issue from the bloud its selfe) and such as the spirits are, such is the temper or distemper of the braine and heart; and such as the braine is, well or ill disposed, so also are the vertues of imagination, understanding, and memory, well or ill disposed" (p. 137). In *Mystical Bedlam*, Michael MacDonald remarks of the therapies that such ideas encouraged: "Because they believed so strongly that there was a sympathy between body and soul, Tudor and Stuart doctors employed physical remedies to heal mental diseases ... almost every one of Napier's mentally disturbed patients was purged with emetics and laxatives and bled with leeches or by cupping." Lady Grace Mildmay recommends the following definition of and treatment for madness: "The humour being gotten into the fantasy increaseth it and the fantasy working upon the humour increaseth it also, for befriending each other. Therefore at first expel the humour by violent evacuations."[61]

In *The Touchstone of Complexions*, Lemnius explores the strong link between mind and body, between physiology and mood, by attending to the critical role of the spleen: if the spleen

throughly perfourme the offyce, for which it was ordeyned and doe exactly drinck up the drossy seculency of Bloude, it maketh a man there uppon wonderful meary and jocunde. For when the Bloud is sincerely purefied, and from all grossenesse and seculency purged, the Spyrites consequently are made pure, bright, and cleare shining: Whose purity and clearnes causeth the mynd to rejoyce, and among meery companions to laughe and delight in prety devyses, mery concepts, and wanton Phansyes ...

Contrariwyse if it bee surcharged and overwhelmed with too much confluxe of filthy Humour, and be debarred or disappoynted of the ordinary helpe and ayde of the Lyver, eyther through imbecillity or obstruction, then bryngeth it many discommodities and annoyaunces, no lesse hurtfull and prejudiciall to the mynde then to the body, as Heavinesse, sorrowe, sadnesse, feare and dread of missehap to come, carefulnesse, thought, desperation and distrust.[62]

Bodies are in continual need of internal purification, a process that occurs primarily in the stomach and the spleen, the organs to which the sick Dürer points. As Oswei Temkin remarks of the Hippocratic and Galenic medicine that underwrites Burton, and so much of early modern medical principle, "The coupling of right diet and virtue was an essential part of Galenic philosophy. Proper regimen balanced the temperament of the body and its parts, and with them the psychic functions. Correct and incorrect diet could determine health and disease, and because it was under human control, the choice of diet gave a moral dimension to health and sickness."[63]

Diet and digestion were seen to affect not just mental capacity but even the ineffable realms of the soul. "Now for the soules faculties," asks William Vaughan, "how is it possible, but that the smoaky vapours, which breathe from a fat and full paunch, should not interpose a dampish mist of dulnes betwixt the body and the bodies light?"[64] The title of a work by John Downame demonstrates the close relationship that existed between spiritual and physical health: *Spiritual physicke to cure the diseases of the soule, arising from the superfluitie of choller, prescribed out of Gods word* (London, 1600). The Elizabethan *Homilie Against Gluttony and Drunkennesse*, moreover, makes good digestion dependent upon divine grace: "except GOD give strengthe to nature to digest, so that we may take profite by [our meats], either shall we filthily vomite them up again, or els shal they lie stinking in our bodies, as in a lothsome sinke or chanell, and so diversely infect the whole body."[65] Not only is every act of eating a performance of our fragile dependence upon the recalcitrant graces of a predatory world; the processes of corporeal assimilation demand the continual intervention of divine grace to accomplish the miracle of digestion.

Like so many of his contemporaries, Robert Burton divides the body into a political triumvirate: the brain, the heart, and the belly:

As the first of the Head in which the Animal Organes are contained, and Braine it selfe, which by his Nerves give sense and motion to the rest, and is (as it were) a privy Councellour, and Chancellour to the Heart. The second Region is the Chest, or middle Belly, in which the heart as king keepes his court, and by his Arteries communicates life to the whole body. The third Region is the lower Belly, in which the liver resides as a *Legat a latere*, which the rest of those naturall Organes, serving for concoction, nourishment, expelling of excrements.

The heart, he says, is "the seat and fountaine of life, of heat, of spirits, of pulse and respiration, the Sunne of our Body, the King and sole commander of it: The seat and Organe of all passions and affections," while the brain is "the most noble Organ under Heaven, the dwelling house and seat of the Soule, the habitation of wisdom, memory, judgement, reason, and in which man is most like unto God." Yet it is to the belly that Burton's attention will turn most frequently over the course of his massive book, the region that he compares to "some sacred Temple or Majesticall Pallace" in which one may "behold not the matter onely, but the singular Art, Workmanship, and counsell of this our great Creator."[66] As we will see in Chapter 4, George Herbert's *Temple* of devotion will be deeply involved in matters of the belly. The stomach, the organ that accomplishes digestion, provides Burton, and so many of the writers we will look at, with a particularly intense focus of inwardness because it is the part of our body that makes its needs felt most frequently and insistently. It demands to be filled at least a couple of times a day, and to be emptied at least once. When these demands are not met, the entire organism suffers. The exigencies of the stomach require the individual to confront on a daily basis the thin yet necessarily permeable line separating self and other. The stomach, remarks Bacon in *Historia Vitae et Mortis*, is "the master of the house as they say, upon whose strength all the other digestions depend."[67] Much of the medical literature of the period is devoted to explanations of digestion, that magical yet mundane moment when dead animal and vegetable matter is ingested to sustain life, when something alien is brought into the self and something alien is excreted by the self, when the object of appetite is rendered the source of repugnance. Far more involuted, conceptually and physiologically, than the voracious orifice of indiscriminate consumption immortalized by Comus, the belly god of Jonson's *Pleasure Reconciled to Virtue* and of Milton's *A Masque*, the stomach occupies a central site of ethical discrimination and devotional interiority in early modern culture.

An elaborate technology of digestion was invoked to explain the process by which the stomach accomplishes the critical activity of separating nutritive material from the pernicious dross that inevitably suffuses it, and preparing the nutritive material for assimilation. Even the notorious diagnostic examination of urine and feces by physicians was simply a technique for investigating just how effectively the patient was accomplishing the critical activities of assimilation and excretion. The process of digestion was imagined to occur in three stages. The first, occurring in the stomach proper, is termed concoction, and converts food into chyle, a fluid that the body can begin to absorb. The next stage occurs in the liver, and converts the chyle into blood, which can be distributed to the different members of the body through the network of veins. The third stage takes place in the various parts of the body that attract what nourishment they need from the blood. Digestion thus is not something that happens exclusively in the stomach, but occurs throughout the organism. The human body is from this perspective a giant stomach, a torus through which food passes. Digestion, moreover, is a very literal assimilation of something that is not part of one to the essence of one's being; as Thomas Elyot describes it in his *Castel of Helthe* (1541), "concoction is an alteration in the stomacke of meates and drynkes, accordynge to their qualities, wherby they are made lyke to the substance of the body."[68] Digestion is a continual process of liquefaction and rarefaction, with each stage producing a purer form of nutrition by expelling what is not useful and converting what is. Semen in the male, and milk in the female, are the most rarefied forms of blood. Each stage of digestion, moreover, produces its own excrement: in the stomach, the excrement is feces; in the liver, urine; and in the various parts of the body, sweat, hair, nails, and mucus.

Together with its corollary organs of digestion – the liver and the spleen – the stomach was imagined to complete physiologically a process that begins in the ethical judgment: the discrimination of dross from nutrition, of good from bad. The stomach is at the center of a system demanding perpetual, anxious osmosis with the outside world. Nicholas Culpepper's translation of John Veslingus's *Anatomy of the Body of Man*, from which Figure 3 is taken, outlines the stomach's ventricular capacities as well as its complex but sometimes cozy relationship to the surrounding organs:

The inferior Orifice which is on the right side, the Ancients called *Pylorus*, or *Janitor*; for by this the meat digested passeth to the next Guts as by a gate; the heat of the Bowels round about the Stomach, quallify its cold and dry Temperature: the Stomach is in form like the Bag of a pair of Bag-pipes; it is placed by the Wisdome of God in the left *Hypochondrium* under the *Diaphragma*; The right part is committed to the Liver, the left to the Spleen; below, it is cherished by the *Omentum*, and underneath it lies upon the Sweet bread, as it were upon a Pillow.

Indiscriminately mixing anthropomorphic, thermal, musical, domestic, and architectural imagery, Culpepper at once conveys the labyrinthine architecture of the abdomen and infers the intricate processes that the stomach performs in every act of digestion.

Thomas Vicary's *A Profitable Treatise of the Anatomie of Mans Body* offers a similar vision of the stomach's relation to other organs, transforming the stomach's architectonic centrality into a narrative of its physiological priority:

It hath the lyver on the right side, chafing & heating him with his lobes or figures: & the Splen on the left syde, with his fatnes, and veynes sending to him melancolie, to exercise his appetites: and above him is the Harte, quickening him with his Arteries: Also the brayne, send to him a braunch of Nerves to geve him feeling.[69]

The stomach, according to Vicary, is the recipient of the assiduous attentions of a constellation of internal organs. The liver, Vicary continues,

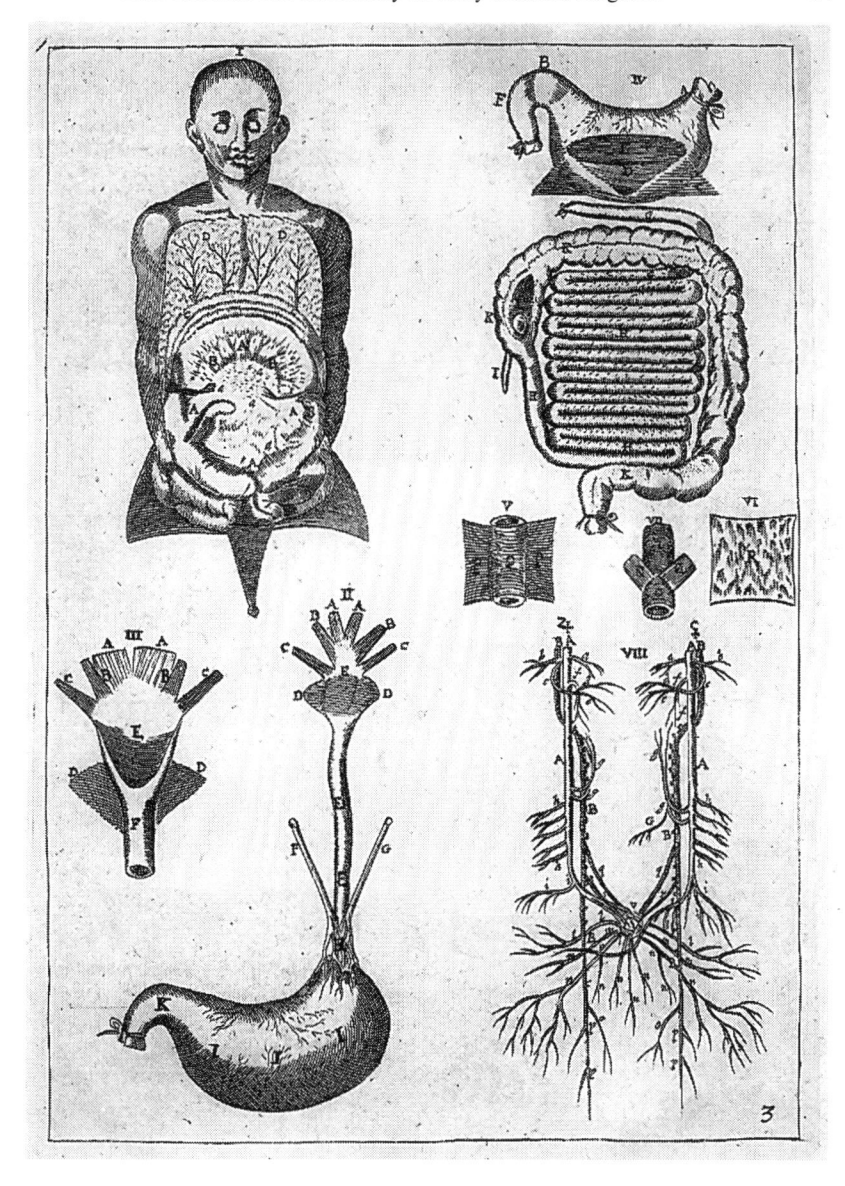

Figure 3 From Nicholas Culpepper, *The Anatomy of the Body of Man* (London, 1677)

assumes its particular shape and texture because "it should be plycable to the stomacke, like as a hande dothe to an apple, to comforte her digestion; for his heate is to the stomacke as the heate of the fyre is to the Potte or Cauldron that hangeth over it" (p. 69). In both Culpepper's and Vicary's digestive structures, a feeling of snug domesticity alternates with a vocabulary of technical precision.

Vicary's comparison of the stomach to a cauldron heated by the liver's fire involves one of the most frequently used images for the stomach – the comparison of its mechanisms to culinary techniques practiced outside the organism. A very literal kind of cooking occurs within the stomach – "concoction," the technical term for digestion, derives from the Latin *concoctus*, "to boil together" – readying food for delivery to various parts of the body as a cook prepares meals. "Our stomake is our bodies kitchin," remarks William Vaughan in his popular *Directions for Health*. Joshua Sylvester's translation of *Du Bartas His Divine Weekes and Workes* (1605) calls the stomach "That ready cook concocting every Mess," and explores in some detail the culinary processes involved:

> in short time it cunningly converts
> Into pure Liquor fit to feed the parts;
> And then the same doth faithfully deliver
> Into the *Port-vein* passing to the Liver,
> Who turns it soon to blood; and thence again
> Through branching pipes of the great *Hollow-vein*,
> Through all the members doth it duly scatter:
> Much like a Fountain, whose divided Water
> Itself dispersing into hundred Brooks,
> Bathes some fair Garden with her winding crooks . . .
> Even so the Blood (bred of good nourishment)
> By divers Pipes to all the body sent,
> Turns here to Bones, there changes into Nerves;
> Here is made Marrow, there for Muscles serves,
> Here skin becoms, there crooking veins, here flesh,
> To make our Limbs more forcefull and more fresh.

Du Bartas imagines the body as a variegated garden nourished by a fountain whose liquid is transformed into the parts it nourishes. Accomplishing the salutary liquefaction of food mass, the stomach is the vital center of a vast system of food preparation and distribution, concocting food solids into nutritive fluid that can then be dispersed through the blood to the different parts of the body as needed.[70]

The stomach, then, is not a passive receptacle but the great feeder of parts. This physiological fact explains in part why, in the most famous literary account of the stomach in English Renaissance literature, Menenius Agrippa's fable of the belly in Shakespeare's *Coriolanus*, Agrippa is able to quiet the rebellion of a hungry and angry mob by means of the rather unexpected comparison of aristocrats to the belly. One would not normally think of defending a voracious aristocracy in a subsistence society by likening it to the organ of digestion. In hierarchical readings of bodily organs, moreover, the belly is normally linked to the lower classes, while the upper classes are aligned with the heart or brain. In the marginalia of Fletcher's *Purple Island*, for example, the commentator asserts that

> The whole body may be parted into three regions: the lowest, or belly; the middle, or breast; the highest, or head. In the lowest the liver is soveraigne, whose regiment is the widest, but meanest. In the middle the heart reignes, most necessarie. The brain obtains the highest place, and is as the least in compass, so the greatest in dignitie.[71]

Against this typical interpretation of the political order of the body, Agrippa strategically replaces a hierarchy based on the distinction between low and high with a hierarchy based on the distinction between center and periphery, and so underscores the vast importance given to the digestion and distribution of food in the maintenance of the individual body. When the belly is accused of idleness, that "only like a gulf it did remain / I' th' midst a' th' body, idle and unactive, / Still cupboarding the viand, never bearing / Like labor with the rest," the belly responds by conceding

> That I receive the general food at first
> Which you do live upon; and fit it is,
> Because I am the store-house and the shop
> Of the whole body . . .
> I send [food] through the rivers of your blood,
> Even to the court, the heart, to th' seat o' th' brain,
> And, through the cranks and offices of man,
> The strongest nerves and small inferior veins
> From me receive that natural competency
> Whereby they live . . .
>   all
> From me do back receive the flour of all,
> And leave me but the bran.

Fantasizing that a society's resources naturally trickle down from its most to its least privileged members, Agrippa uses the physiological centrality of the stomach to mystify a doctrine of social inequality and to obscure the actual labor that is part of the production and distribution of provisions.[72]

Indeed, in a defense of high taxation in 1483, Bishop Russell likens the royal court not to the head or the heart but "to the chief of the 'principal' members, the stomach," and develops the image in ways that directly invoke the political meanings that Agrippa squeezes from physiology:

That bodye is hole and stronge whois stomake and bowels is ministered by the utward membres that suffiseth to be wele digested; for if the fete and hondes, whych seme to doo most paynefulle labour for mannys lyving, wolde complayne ageynste the wombe [abdomen] as ageynste an idelle and slowthfulle parte of the body, and denye the provysyon of syche necessarye foode as the stomake calleth for, hyt might sone happe, that faylynge the belye for lake, the guttes and intestines compressed and shut by drynesse, alle the other membres shold nedes peryshe togedyr. And therfor hyt ys undoubted in nature that thys middelle membres of the body . . . be not unoccupied, but hafe ryght a besy office; for when they be fed they fede agayne, yeldynge un to every parte of the bodye that withoute the whyche no man leve. . . . What ys the bely or where ys the wombe of thys grete publick body of Englonde but that there where the kyng ys hym self, hys court and hys counselle? For there must be digested all maner metes, not onely servyng to commyn foode but alleso . . . some tyme to medicines, such as be appropred to remedye the excesses and surfettes committed at large.[73]

In a signal act of bad policy derived from good physiology, Russell endows the most voracious consumers in his culture with a critical role in the sustenance of that culture.

In *A Treatise of the Passions and Faculties of the Soule of Man*, Edward Reynolds likewise endorses the wisdom of "the Fable of the Faction betweene the Belly and Members" when applied by Agrippa to "a Rebellion amongst the people of Rome" because it showed "how unnaturall a thing it is, and how pernicious to the parts themselves, to nourish their owne private Discontents, when the Weale publique is together therewithall endangered."[74] Even Coriolanus's temperamental stubbornness is given a physiological explanation by Menenius, the author of the belly fable:

> He was not taken well; he had not dined:
> The veins unfilled, our blood is cold, and then
> We pout upon the morning, are unapt
> To give or to forgive; but when we have stuffed
> These pipes and these conveyances of our blood
> With wine and feeding, we have suppler souls
> Than in our priest-like fasts: therefore I'll watch him
> Till he be dieted to my request.   (5.1.50–57)

Apparently, the way to a superior's heart is very literally through his stomach.

The critical role the stomach plays in the emotional and physiological life of the organism makes it a central medium for therapies that alter body and mind. The stomach, notes Thomas Vicary, "is a necessarie member to al the body; for if it fayles in his working, al the members of the body shal corrupte." Humor, notes Peter Lowe in *The Whole Course of chirurgerie*, is "a thinne substance, into the which our nourishment is first converted, or it is an naturall *Jus* that the bodie is intertained, norished, or conserved with."[75] Our bodies flourish to the degree that they remain *au jus*, and the stomach is the key site of this salubrious liquefaction of nutritive material. In *The Touchstone of Complexions*, Levinus Lemnius explicitly links digestive concerns to a humoral physiology and psychology, which connects mental and physical illness to the excess or dearth of one of the four fluids produced by digestion known as humors:

> These [humors] accordinge to the nature of nourishment received, are increased or diminished.... And albeit these humoures beying of greate force divers wayes, and sondrily affecting the body, yea ye mynde also with fulsome and unpleasant exhalations and sentes is oftentimes greatlye annoyed and encumbred, even as ill and naughty wyne bryngeth to the brayne affects both hurtfull and daungerous...
>
> For if the body shoulde not be susteined with nourishment, or if the humoures (which moisten every perticular member) should lacke the preservatives and fomentations wherewith they be mayntayned, the whole frame of mans body must of necessity decay, and be utterly dissolved.[76]

No firm line could be drawn separating food from medicine. "Physicians hold," notes William Vaughan, "that men be diversly affected, according to the dyet which they use."[77] The point made repeatedly in the vast literature on medical self-help is that all foods do something in one, and to one, physically and mentally. As Huarte asserts in *The Examination of Men's Wits*: "albeit a good stomacke do parboile and alter the meat, and spoile the same of his former quality, yet it doth never utterly deprive itself of them: for if we eat lettice (whose qualitie is cold and moiste) the bloud engendred therof, shalbe cold and moist ... for it is impossible, (as Galen avoucheth) that the humors should not retaine the substances and the qualities, which the meat had, before such time as it was eaten."[78] Like the humors they nourish, foods are predominantly either hot or cold, moist or dry, and bestow that disposition on the consumer.

The stomach, moreover, supervises the necessary discrimination of edible from inedible matter, a discrimination that is ethical as well as physiological. The process of disposing of what Spenser calls the "fowle and wast" material is as important to the health of the organism as is the process of nutritive assimilation. "The Guttes," notes Thomas Vicary, "were ordeined in the fyrst creation to convey the drosse of the meate and drinke, & to clense the body of their superfluities." Good digestion demands not just the assimilation of nutritive material but also the expulsion of superfluity. As Sir Thomas Elyot asserts, "these excrementes be none other, but matter superfluouse and unsavery, which by natural powers may not be converted in to fleshe, but remayning in the body corrupt the members, and therfore desireth to have them expelled."[79] Indeed, most illness in the period is imagined to derive from the body's inability to rid itself of excess humors. As a result, nearly all medical interventions in the period short of surgery are intended to mimic and enhance the body's emunctory capacities, through purgation, phlebotomy, or clyster.

Perhaps this is why the spiritual autobiographies of the period pay such close attention to digestion. As their common etymology would suggest, the regulation of diet and the keeping of diaries are engaged in corollary forms of diurnal inwardness.[80] At the beginning of the *Reliquiae Baxterianae*, Richard Baxter explains why he observes the conditions of his body in a work intended to measure the progress of his soul: "because the Case of my *Body* had a great Operation upon my Soul, . . . I shall here together give you a brief Account of the most of my Afflictions of that kind." A typical passage records that: "My chief Troubles were incredible Inflations of Stomach, Bowels, Back, Sides, Head, Thighs, as if I had been daily fill'd with Wind."[81] Baxter, moreover, blames these inward afflictions on his youthful diet – "I am now fully satisfied that all proceeded from Latent Stones in my Reins, occasioned by unsuitable Diet in my Youth" – and imagines their cure in the careful regulation and manipulation of substances that enter and exit his adult body – "My chiefest remedies" for illness are:

> 1. Temperance as to quantity and quality of Food: for every bit of spoonful too much, and all that is not exceeding easie of digestion, and all that is flatulent, do turn all to Wind, and disorder my Head.
> 2. Exercise till I sweat . . .
> 3. A Constant Extrinsic Heat, by a great Fire, which may keep me still near to a Sweat, if not in it: (for I am seldom well at ease but in a Sweat).
> 4. Beer as hot as my Throat will endure, drunk all at once, to make me Sweat.[82]

For Baxter, health is contingent upon the continual application of therapies of purgation – therapies which themselves offer a physiological version of the spiritual phenomenon of repentance. Tempering what enters the body, and sweating out one's inevitable excess, become essential components of the spiritual life of the subject. In *Via Recta ad Vitam Longam*, Thomas Venner remarks in a section entitled "why doth the health of body much consist in the due and daily avoiding of [excrements]":

> For in every concoction some excrements are ingendred, which residing in the body condense and oppilate, and so become the roots of divers diseases. Now the thicker sort of excrements which arise from the first and second concoction of the stomack and liver, are avoided by sensible evacuation, as by Stoole and urine; but the thinner that come of the third concoction in the limbs are wasted by transpiration, and purged forth by exercise, which causeth sweat in those which wish to live in health.[83]

The sweat that Baxter cultivates is just another form of beneficial excretion. By continually sweating, that is, Baxter manifests physiologically the necessity of continually purging sin. Just as the self is always producing sins that need confession, so is it always manifesting noxious humors that demand evacuation.

An even more remarkable nexus of spirituality and corporeality is recorded in the diary of Ralph Josselin, another seventeenth-century clergyman. Josselin remembers an occasion where "I was ill in my stomacke, and yett very loth to enter into a course of phisicke[.] this weeke I had a great looseness and griping of my body, avoyding thereby much choller, which I looke upon as a good providence of god towards me." God apparently works in mysterious ways, approaching his creatures even through their digestive tract. As John Harington remarks in his scurrilous *Metamorphosis of Ajax*, "a good stoole might move as great devotion in some man, as a bad sermon."[84]

The stomach and its corollary organs of digestion will assume a surprisingly central role in the epic and lyric works that this study foregrounds. The next chapter, "Fortifying Inwardness: Spenser's Castle of Moral Health," will explore in detail the book of Edmund Spenser's *Faerie Queene* devoted to temperance, the classical virtue by which appetite is made subject to discipline. The notorious episode of the Castle of Alma in Book 2 will be at the center of this chapter, as it is at the conceptual center of Spenser's legend. Giving the well-worn metaphor of the self as a castle a particular emphasis, and elaborating the cozy domesticity that suffused the portraits of the stomach in Vicary and Culpepper, Spenser will lead Arthur and Guyon on a tour of the alimentary tract, entering through the mouth and proceeding down the gullet in order to explore the stomach, the most literal site of human inwardness. In his larger project of bestowing upon the intrinsically inglorious ethic of temperance the grandeur of heroic action, Spenser endows this life-sustaining system of nutritive addition and excretory subtraction with the bustling stability of a baroque structure. Like Arthur and Guyon, we are meant to view the continual processing of food, and the perpetual discrimination of noxious from nutritive matter, as a "goodly order" which solicits our admiration for the "great workmans skill" behind it.

Where Spenser is so overt in his engagement with corporeal processes that he has been criticized for grotesqueness, Shakespeare in the Sonnets is so subtle that the vocabulary of physiological process largely escapes mention. In Chapter 3, "The Matter of Inwardness: Shakespeare's Sonnets," I will show how the Sonnets use the Galenic vocabulary of corporeal emotion to underscore their portrait of desire as a disease that threatens physical and mental health, and to underpin their ideal of the well-balanced self. Throughout the Sonnets, Shakespeare develops links between the corollary appetites for food and love not so much to provide strategies for rendering both hygienic as to explore the relevance of the necessary periodicity of hunger to the ebb and flow of erotic desire. I argue that Sonnet 94, "They that have power to hurt," vexes us in large part because we unintentionally vex it with an anachronistic model of self and desire. Probably the most discussed of the Sonnets in the twentieth century, this poem needs to be read against the medical and moral culture from which it derives in order to see the premium that Shakespeare's own articulations of desire place on the self-control the poem praises. Throughout the chapter I look at how Shakespeare asks the genre of the sonnet – a genre traditionally dedicated to articulating passion – to investigate instead the dangers that passions pose to health of mind and body, and to describe a corollary longing for stasis and self-control. The sonnet – a taut, restrained form demanding immense discipline – becomes the perfect vehicle for articulating severely constrained desire.

Where Shakespeare's Sonnets describe a cultural conflict between the Stoic eradication of disturbing emotion and the outpouring of powerful emotion, Herbert attempts to synthesize the aggressive moderation of Stoic ethics with the emotional extremity of Christian devotion. Chapter 4, "Devotion and Digestion: George Herbert's Consuming Subject," looks at a writer whose spirituality is frequently articulated in terms of an unexpected but stunning corporeality, and who deals with digestion and indigestion as states of devotional inwardness. Herbert makes taste the primary experience of community with God. Yet it is a pleasure that is valued only to the degree that it is subject to fastidious regulation. Food's progress from the external liturgies of sacred and secular consumption to the internal labyrinths of digestion allows Herbert to trace the inner contours of the Christian devotional subject. In this chapter, I demonstrate how the *Treatise of Temperance and Sobrietie* that Herbert translated – a work arguing that all illness derives from the ingestion of something either excessive or bad – shares with the poetic *Temple* of devotion he composed a concern with the ways in which the inner self is constructed by regulating carefully the substances that enter and exit the physical body. In "The Church-porch," Herbert advises: "Lose not thy self, nor give thy humours way: / God gave them to thee under lock and key" (lines 143–44). Here and throughout *The Temple*, Herbert uses the Galenic theory of the humors to portray the self as a principle of containment amid a series of pernicious fluids ready to overrun the self. In his profound engagement with issues of diet and devotion, Herbert transforms the ambivalences that suffuse eating and excreting into the punishments and rewards of the Christian dispensation.

In the final chapter, "Temperance and Temptation: The Alimental Vision in *Paradise Lost*," I explore the works of John Milton, a writer whose lifelong engagement with issues of self-regulation will lead him to re-enact throughout his career scenes of gastronomic temptation. It will also lead him to value the virtue of temperance that shields one from the effects of temptation. Milton's account of this virtue will be shaped in large part by Spenser, whom he termed "our sage and serious Poet ... whom I dare be known to think a better teacher then Scotus or Aquinas."[85] I explore Milton's lifelong engagement, from the Latin *Elegies* and *Comus* through *Areopagitica* and *Paradise Regained*, with the moral and physiological components of eating and drinking. Rejecting for theological reasons both the Eucharistic feast and the holy fast – two central occasions for exploring the religious meaning of food – Milton nevertheless endows eating with immense moral and spiritual value. Every meal is a moral test, a temptation to transgress what the Lady in *Comus* terms "the holy dictate of spare temperance." This preoccupation with consumption reaches its apex in *Paradise Lost*, where Milton attempts to justify the ways of God to men and women by reminding us that we, not God, introduce into the world the illnesses from which we suffer through our past and present behavior before food. The mechanics of digestion, moreover, exemplify for Milton the principles of spiritual transformation that animate his hierarchical yet meritocratic universe. From the brutal exigencies of the cannibalism of Sin and her children to the baroque elegance of table manners in heaven, eating encompasses for Milton the highest and lowest possibilities of moral existence. Milton vigorously rewrites Spenser's sinful Bower of Bliss as Eden; in Milton's telling, sensual Paradise is destroyed not by a knight representing temperance but by an act of intemperate eating. Milton's emphasis on the positive role of regulated pleasure redeems an ethic of gustatory delectation from royalist bondage, and reclaims for Puritanism a morally authentic code of moderate behavior. Milton thus establishes a *via media* of the self in explicit opposition to those Anglican apologists who would make it the exclusive property of adherence to a theology of the middle way. An exertion of discipline over desire, of reasoned choice over sensual appetite, Miltonic temperance ameliorates the incurable diseases that ensue from that first act of intemperate eating, and that are nourished by the gluttony that re-enacts that inaugural moment.

Although my discussion of the early modern self ranges among a variety of non-canonical materials and writers, it concentrates on four canonical male authors, authors whose centrality to our culture explains in part why we continue to articulate our inwardness in a language inherited from them. The one area in which Galenic physiology has received a lot of recent attention is the one which I attend to least here – the area of gender.[86] As Thomas Laqueur and others have shown, Galenic medicine was frequently in collusion with patriarchal ideology to give a physiological "explanation" to the asserted inferiority of women.[87] Women were imagined to be inverted men, lacking the natural heat required to push out the analogous organs of generation. They were also frequently assumed to be physiologically less capable of the regimens of self-discipline than were men. In *The Secret Miracles of Nature*, Lemnius gives an elaborate humoral explanation for what he believes to be women's innate inability to exercise self-control:

> women are subject to all passions and perturbations... a woman enraged, is besides her selfe, and hath not power over her self, so that she cannot rule her passions, or bridle her disturbed affections, or stand against them with force of reason and judgement...
> For a woman's mind is not so strong as a mans.... If any man desires a natural reason for it, I answer him thus, that a womans flesh is loose, soft and tender, so that the choler being kindled presently spreads all the body over, and causeth a sudden boyling of the blood about the heart.... If any man would more neerely have the cause of this explain'd and desires a more exact reason; I can find no nearer cause that can be imagined, than the venim and collections of humours that she every month heaps together, and purgeth forth by the course of the moon; For when she chanceth to be angry, as she will presently be, all that sink of humours being stirred fumeth, and runs through the body, so that the Heart and Brain are affected with the smoky vapours of it, and the Spirits both vitall and animal, that serve those parts are inflamed... reason being but weak in them, and their judgment feeble, and minds not well order'd, they are sharply enraged, and cannot rule their passions.[88]

The comparative lack of muscle mass in females, combined with the phenomenon of menstruation, is used by Lemnius to "explain" why women have less self-control than men. When the discourse could so fully pathologize the very being of women, it is perhaps unsurprising that women did not find in its lexicon a hospitable tool for articulating their interiority.

Yet Galenic medicine was more a matter of degree than absolute difference, and the very fact that its terminology was relational rather than absolute could be turned to undo the masculinist framework it was so frequently used to buttress. In *A woman's woorth, defended against all the men in the world*, Anthony Gibson argues that women have "greater wisdom in their speech" because they are not so physiologically predisposed to choler as men.[89] In the chapter on Shakespeare's Sonnets, I discuss several examples in which the excess natural heat that was seen to separate men from women could be similarly construed as a site of female superiority. An overriding emphasis on gender has sometimes skewed the interpretation of Galenism, making fluidity the exclusive province of female corporeality.[90] Female bodies may have been imagined as fluid, but so were male bodies; both sexes aspired through a variety of unpleasant therapies to attain the solubility necessary to stay alive. Despite Lemnius's description of the psychopathology of menstruation, females were sometimes thought to possess a physiological advantage because their monthly menstrual flow functioned as a purge, accomplishing naturally what men would have to achieve through the comparatively invasive technique of blood-letting. All bodies, male and female, need to be ventilated and purged regularly; indeed, men and women are advised to sleep "rather open mouth'd then shut, which is a great help against internall obstructions, which more ensweeteneth the breath, recreateth the spirits, comforteth the braine, and more the cooleth the vehement heat of the heart."[91]

The physiological and psychological inwardness on which I focus, moreover, is less frequently gendered. As Jonathan Sawday notes of the anatomy books, which were more often intent on the revelation of inner and outer sexual difference than the Galenic health manuals: "For men and women, *the sexually undifferentiated body-interior* is a region of eerie unfamiliarity."[92] When Robert Burton offers a brief tour of the parts of the body, he turns away, not out of embarrassment but out of indifference, from the genitals, the organs in whose presence and desires we would locate the essence of identity: "Members of generation are common to both sexes, or peculiar to one; which because they are impertinent to my purpose, I doe voluntarily omit."[93] Perhaps we over-read the importance of the genitals to this earlier regime because in our own regime they occupy a centrality that they shared with a nexus of other organs – the stomach, the heart, and the brain – in the Renaissance. Where we are prone to situate identity on the axis of sexual desire, the Renaissance tended to locate identity amid the control of a variety of appetites, including the sexual. At Tilbury Queen Elizabeth had famously announced that "I may have the body of a weak and feeble woman, but I have the heart and stomach of a king," strategically suggesting that the traits traditionally identified with male rulers were available to her bodily interior, even if her physical exterior failed to exhibit them.[94]

Although there are many recipe books by women that employ a mixture of Galenic medicine and folk wisdom, the women writers of the period turn more frequently to religious discourse than to physiological self-regulation to articulate their inwardness. This may in part derive from the cultural fact that women were often allowed the spiritual literacy deemed necessary to save their souls, but were barred from education in the medical discourse that produced this highly theorized form of physiological interiority; as Margaret Cavendish complained in 1655, "I never read of anatomie nor never saw any man opened, much less dissected, which for my better understanding I would have done."[95] Although women were certainly patients and practitioners of the healing arts of manipulating humoral flow, I could not find an example of a woman writer practicing the philosophically rigorous and literarily intense engagement with physiological inwardness that marks the four canonical male writers under examination.

Caroline Walker Bynum has situated in medieval studies a series of brilliant and influential studies of the ways that women's bodies became the site of a particularly material kind of religiosity.[96] I have learned much from this rich body of work and analysis. Yet her work has sometimes produced a sense that materials such as food had little meaningful traffic with the male subject. By stressing spectacular moments of diet, starvation, and wounding, moreover, she has inadvertently made such moments analytically normative, and so has distracted attention from the carefully regulated pleasure and nourishment that constitutes quotidian consumption. In a different vein, I have also learned much from Jonathan Sawday's erudite and precise study of Renaissance anatomy, *The Body Emblazoned*. But where Sawday emphasizes the spectacle of flayed bodies, I explore the mundane inwardness of living, inhabited bodies. And where Sawday seeks out a teleology of the scientific revolution, I am interested in the surprising survival of old ways of construing amid the discovery of ideas that discount them.[97] I intend the present book to be not so much a repudiation of as a complement (in both senses) to Katharine Maus's brilliant study of theatrical inwardness, *Inwardness and Theater*.[98] Where Maus, though, situates inwardness on the stage, I look at the genres of epic and lyric. The inward explorations of lyric, and the overt exertions of epic, are bound to produce different configurations of embodiment than the exuberant theatricality of drama. And where Maus focuses on ways that religious, political, and legal discourses contributed to the vocabulary of inwardness, I emphasize the physiological.

What I concentrate on, then, is a particularly literal mode of self-fashioning, one that turns inward as much as outward, and that pays particular attention to moments of eating and excreting as urgent but quotidian occasions for demarcating the porous cusp between self and other, and between matter and spirit. I am not arguing that Galenic physiology provides the only or even the predominant vocabulary of inwardness in the period. Religious devotion and erotic courtship exert a powerful claim there. But I am trying to call attention to a cogent and flexible discourse that possessed the remarkable ability to render inwardness tangible. It is, moreover, a discourse that is often in collusion with or just behind the period's other discourses of inwardness, needing only the amplification of knowledge to awaken its resonances. Table manners, medical advice, and religious injunction function as a series of sometimes contradictory ethical narratives by which early modern selves and societies attempt to reclaim the fiction of bodily control against the inevitable seepages and compulsory atrophies of mortal existence. I hope to demonstrate that recent criticism has too frequently framed its analyses of bodies and subjects in terms of an opposition between release and control. Both Rabelaisian festivity and fastidious discipline are attempts to stave off the mortality that one inevitably confronts in the act of eating – the one by drowning the tediousness of daily life in festive release, the other by deliberately disguising the squalid violence of eating in the proliferation of arbitrarily rarefied practices. I want to look closely at the resources available to the period for imagining inner space, and for describing and delimiting desire. The self becomes for so many of these writers a little kingdom, filled with insurrectionary forces, and in continual need of monitoring from within and without. The very resemblance of this internal kingdom to the larger world of political power can make self-discipline an extension of governmental control. But it can also bestow upon the individual an authority whose government contests rather than buttresses that of the terrestrial monarch it resembles. As Milton in particular shows, the kingdom of the self, arising from a carefully cultivated paradise within, can become the site of political resistance. By asking models of political authority to delineate the inner contours of the individual, the discourse of self-regulation, arising from models of the self so different from our own, may nevertheless begin to make a space for something recognizably modern.

2 Fortifying inwardness: Spenser's castle of moral health

> Intestines stretch out all the way to the curvatures of the brain. The two don't look much different, and they aren't and they are.
>
> Norman Maclean[1]

In Lodowick Bryskett's *A Discourse of Civill Life*, a work that offers a combination of courtesy book and moral philosophy characteristic of Renaissance eclecticism, an interlocutor named "Maister Spenser" is allowed to pose one of the central questions of Renaissance ethical psychology: "how cometh it to passe . . . that the soule being immortall and impassible, yet by experience we see dayly, that she is troubled with Lethargies, Phrensies, Melancholie, drunkennesse, and such other passions, by which we see her overcome." The narrator responds to this question of how body affects spirit by drawing a distinction between "the Intellective soule, which is immortal, and the passible understanding," which

> being an inward sense, and therefore tyed to the bodie, feeleth the passions of the same.... And in like manner are the words of Aristotle to be understood, where he saith, that such whose flesh is soft are apt to learne, and they that are melancholy to be wise. For that the Sensitive vertue taketh more easily the formes or kindes of things in such subjects according to their nature, and representeth them to the understanding, from whence knowledge and understanding proceedeth.... And this happeneth not onely in these passions, but also in all other alterations, as of gladnesse, of sorow, of hope and of feare.[2]

Bryskett and Spenser were longstanding friends, and both had served Lord Grey in Ireland. The *Discourse* itself is meant to represent a discussion in Ireland among Bryskett, Spenser, Dr. John Long, Sir Robert Dillon, and others. Although the *Discourse* is in large part a translation of Giambattista Giraldi's "Tre Dialoghi della vita civile," the second part of *De gli hecatommithi* (1565), it is telling that Spenser, who is otherwise rather reticent in the conversation because he has "already undertaken a work tending to the same effect, which is in *heroical verse*, under the title of a *Faerie Queene*" (*Discourse*, p. 22), intervenes at this moment, since one of the central concerns of that poem, and particularly of Book 2, is the relationship between physiology and morality, between matters of the body and conditions of the spirit. By depicting in detail the quietly heroic effort demanded by the virtue of temperance, Spenser investigates the close relationship between bodies and souls.

Throughout the book, that is, temperance allows Spenser to explore the ethics of human physiology. As Spenser announces at the beginning of canto 9,

> Of all Gods workes, which do this world adorne
> There is no one more faire and excellent,
> Then is mans body both for powre and forme,
> Whiles it is kept in sober government;
> But none then it, more fowle and indecent,
> Distempred through misrule and passions bace:
> It growes a Monster, and incontinent
> Doth loose his dignitie and native grace. (2.9.1)[3]

What emerges here is an intimate link between ethics and aesthetics, between the individual's capacity to order a physiological self and the inner and outer beauty of that self. The body, Spenser suggests, preternaturally "growes a Monster," and must be "kept in sober government" in order to achieve the "powre and forme" of which it is capable. This dynamic sense of ethical physiology allows Spenser to articulate at once a humanist definition of ideal humanity but also a Calvinist conviction of human deprivation. Spenser intends the book not just to inculcate admiration for God's workmanship in the human body but also to demonstrate the Sisyphean effort required to sustain a well-tempered body.

The virtue of temperance also requires that Spenser explore the relationship between classical ethics and Christian belief, since temperance, unlike holiness or chastity (the two other virtues explored in the 1590 *Faerie Queene*), is a virtue available both to Jerusalem and to Rome. But the treaty between the two cities remains a vexed one at best. The portrait of the virtue of temperance offers a moment when the compound of classical and Christian cultures that characterizes the Renaissance, for us and for the period, exhibits a volatile splendor. As we move from Book 1's Legend of Holiness to Book 2's Legend of Temperance, we see emerging a tension between the absolute dependence on God that Protestantism counsels and the rigorous self-control that temperance demands. As the trip through the Castle of Alma will demonstrate in detail, the castle was built by God, whose workmanship one is to admire, but it is maintained by heroic human labor of regulation. This tension between divine and human action is manifested most explicitly in the fact that Redcrosse, the hero of Book 1, and Guyon, the hero of Book 2, almost do battle at the beginning of Book 2, egged on by Archimago. In this near battle, Spenser dramatizes one of the central issues of Renaissance Christian humanist culture – the disparity between the Augustinian emphasis on the object of emotion and the Stoic stress on the intensity of emotion.[4] For the Stoic, all emotion is to be routed out, so that the rational self may rule unfettered by the claims of emotion. The goal is not extremity but moderation. For the Christian, on the other hand, emotion is either good or bad according to the object to which it is directed. As the Puritan divine William Ames remarks in *The Marrow of Theology* (1639) amid a praise of the virtue of temperance: "It is obvious that the mean has no place in some virtues. The love of God is to be praised not when it is not too much but when it is most ardent. Here the measure is without measure."[5] An extreme love of God would be a properly directed, even rational passion. Spenser makes a similar point when he has Guyon, the exemplar of temperance, tell Arthur that if he knew the beauty of his Faerie Queene's mind, it would "infinite desire into your spirite poure" (2.9.3). Even the epitome of temperance imagines an appropriate outlet for the "infinite desire" to which temperance is theoretically opposed.

A related tension emerges amid the lexicon of virtue made available by classical ethics; as critics have frequently observed, Spenser seems to elide the difference between continence, feeling temptations but resisting them, and temperance, being so well-balanced that one no longer feels the temptations at all.[6] Perhaps this is why the virtue is represented by two figures in the first place – where Guyon feels the desires he must contain, the Palmer coolly tempers, and even at critical moments directs, Guyon. The opening lines of Ben Jonson's "Epode" describe well these two possibilities of moral existence:

> Not to know vice at all, and keep true state,
>   Is virtue, and not Fate:
> Next, to that virtue, is to know vice well,
>   And her black spite expel.[7]

Where the Palmer seems "Not to know vice at all," Guyon knows it well and battles to expel its "black spite." In *The Book of the Courtier*, the interlocutors discuss the relative virtues of temperance and continence in terms that have great significance for Book 2 of *The Faerie Queene*. When Lord Octavian taxes continency for being tainted with the passions it contains, Lord Julian objects:

If I have well understood, you have saide that Continencie is an unperfect vertue, because it hath in it part of affection [passion]: and me seemeth that the vertue (where there is in our mind a variance between reason and greedie desire) which fighteth and giveth the victory to reason [i.e., Continence], ought to be reckoned more perfect than that which overcommeth, having neither greedie desire nor any affection to withstand it.

Octavian responds by conceding the point, and develops an image for the internal victories of continence and temperance that is akin to Spenser's primary metaphor for the action of virtue in the world – warfare.

> You have judged aright. And therefore I say unto you, that continencie may be compared to a Captain that fighteth manly, and though his enemies bee strong and well apointed, yet giveth he them the overthrow, but for all that not without much ado and danger. But temperance free from all disquieting, is like the Captaine that without resistance overcometh and raigneth. And having in the mind where she is, not onely aswaged, but cleane quenched the fire of greedy desire, even as a good prince in civil warre dispatcheth the seditious inward enimies, and giveth the scepter and whole rule to reason.[8]

Where temperance is literally a static virtue, a physiological and psychological *state* achieved through proper humoral balance, continence is a perpetually active virtue, a dynamic and ethical program demanding unending vigilance to exercise damage control over the eternally burning "fire of greedy desire." Throughout Book 2 Spenser will oscillate between these two ethical possibilities, honoring both the peaceful harmonies of temperance and the heroic struggles of continence.

These conceptual and narrative dissonances derive in part from the very audacity of Spenser's declared project – making a virtue whose essence is moderation suit a pattern of heroism based on strife and excess. Spenser's moral fiction is roiled by the paradox that the primary model he possesses for dramatizing the virtue of temperance is the decidedly intemperate act of fighting. In portraying temperance, then, he is forced to depict an inherently relational virtue by means of a binary model of physical contest. That is why temperance at the end of the book begins to look like what it would come to mean in twentieth-century America – a drastic abstinence that would eradicate any possibility of temptation, rather than a moderate partaking of an incremental pleasure.[9] In practice always a kind of moral tightrope walking, temperance inhabits a far murkier ethical territory than the decidedly dichotomized moral terrain of Book 1. This murky territory becomes a veritable bog when Phaedria, an exemplar of intemperance, is allowed to quote compellingly from the Sermon on the Mount (2.6.15) in her temptation to a life of careless ease. Here the peaceful faith in a caring God exemplified by Jesus's words –"Consider the lillies of the field, how they grow: they toile not, neither doe they spinne" (Matt. 6.28 [AV]) – becomes in Phaedria's mouth an exhortation to surrender to pleasure: "The lilly," which "neither spinnes nor cardes, ne cares nor frets," "Bid[s] thee to them thy fruitless labours yield, / And soone leave off this toylesome wearie stoure" (2.6.16). Likewise, to seek for danger when pleasure is available is "wilfully [to] make thyself a wretched thrall" (2.6.17); here Phaedria reverses the language of servitude that is normally deployed to describe the proper place of pleasure in the virtuous life. As is often remarked, moreover, Phaedria sounds remarkably like Medina, an early exemplar of productive mediocrity, when she makes peace between Guyon and Cymochles, proposing that they turn their energies to "Another warre ... lovely peace, and gentle amitie" (2.6.34-35). Here we see that temperance is not only a relational virtue, but also a situational one. To be temperate with the intemperate is to belie rather than fulfill the demands of temperance.

Although frequently defined as a middle ground between disagreeable opposites, temperance is continually driven to extremity by the situations in which it is enacted. The enforcement of temperance begins to demand forms of extreme violence that replicate the forces it intends to harness. The more ethical pressure Spenser puts on temperance over the course of the book, the more its maintenance requires intemperate action. This process reaches its apotheosis in the troubling destruction of the Bower of Bliss, where we are made to experience Spenser's immense ambivalence about whether extremity in defense of the virtue of temperance is a vice. Spenserian temperance occupies an elusive and anxious mean between the distasteful figure of "selfe-consuming Care" (2.7.25) that guards the cave of Mammon and the seductive carelessness that Acrasia exemplifies, but partakes of both extremes. Throughout the book we are made to experience the immense difficulty of responding to temptation in a way that is at once moderate and heroic, gloriously decisive yet philosophically tempered. By emphasizing rather than dampening these dissonances present in the philosophical and physiological traditions he inherits, Spenser produces a magnificent portrait of the quotidian struggle necessary to create and sustain an inner self.

Indeed, the first adventure proper of Guyon – the meeting with Amavia – provides not only the book's narrative occasion (revenging their deaths) but also the book's conceptual structure. Amavia's husband Mordant had succumbed to Acrasia's charms, and when he tries to leave she poisons him. Amavia subsequently kills herself. Spenser tells us that Mordant "was flesh (all flesh doth frailty breed)" (2.1.52). The book at large is a series of responses to the congenital frailty of flesh, a frailty which is at once physiological and moral. Even Ruddymane, the unfortunate offspring of Mordant and Amavia, is involved in the hygienic regimens of temperance. An infant discovered grotesquely playing in the pool of blood issuing from his mother's body, Ruddymane provides an emblem of the congenital nature of sin – what Spenser calls "bloudguiltinesse" (2.2.4). The blood is not to be washed from his hands (thus his name, "ruddy": red; "manus": hand) in part because it may be "infected" with "secret filth" that derives from the "great contagion" produced by Acrasia's charms (2.2.4). "We come into this world," remarks Donne in a sermon, "as the Egyptians went out of it, swallowed and smothered in a red sea, *Pueri sanguinum, & infirmi*, weake, and bloudy infants at our birth."[10] The image of Ruddymane's stained hands works in a similar way: Spenser takes an image advertising the taint of original sin, and applies it with particular force to the regimens of temperance intended to ameliorate such taints.

The water in which Guyon and the Palmer attempt to wash off such blood, moreover, issues from a well that is itself involved in a narrative of integrity and inviolability. It is the result of the constant virtue of a nymph who, when chased by an overheated Dan Faunus, asks Diana to "let her die a mayd." Diana responds by "Transform[ing] her to a stone from stedfast virgins state" (2.2.8). Her symbolic inviolability becomes the clinching reason that the blood cannot be washed off in this well of her tears. Her waters are "chast and pure, as purest snow, / Ne lets her waves with any filth be dyde, / But ever like her selfe unstained hath beene tryde" (2.2.9). Her constant virtue provides a pointed contrast to the emotional extremity of Amavia and Mordant.

Yet the stone that epitomizes and assures this virtue is not an unequivocal good. Stone is a common image both of Stoic constancy and of Stoic insensibility. In the next chapter, we will see how Shakespeare's use of the image of stone in Sonnet 94 deliberately stirs positive and negative connotations simultaneously. Spenser is in fact far more interested in the active, dynamic nature of the virtue of temperance than he is in its ability to generate static tableaus of emblematic meaning. That is why Book 2 also follows the adventures of another nymph, one whose similar virtues are far more active and dynamic – Belphoebe. Belphoebe is, we learn, composed of a "goodly mixture of complexions due" (2.3.22). She possesses, that is, a humoral disposition which provides the physiological correlative to her moral virtue. Spenser compares her body, moreover, to a temple: "Like two faire marble pillours [her legs] were seene, / Which doe the temple of the Gods support" (2.3.28). As in George Herbert's *Temple*, the well-disciplined self supplies an apt arena for devotional exercise. Spenser emphasizes the way that Belphoebe shares a marmoreal constancy with the nymph, but reminds us that unlike the nymph she is active, mobile. Belphoebe, moreover, is no fleeing virgin but an armed maiden ready to battle whatever threatens. She carries a spear and bow-and-arrow "wherewith she queld / The salvage beastes in her victorious play" (2.3.29). The beasts, of course, are both external threats and conventional representatives of the internal passions that she so expertly controls in her deliberate and active virginity. In response to Braggadocchio's suggestion that she belongs at court, where her beauty could be admired, Belphoebe responds that the way to real honor is labor: "Before [honor's] high gate high God did Sweat ordaine, / And wakefull watches ever to abide" (2.3.40–41). Attacking ease – "Where ease abounds, yt's eath to doe amis" – and praising the man "who his limbs with labours, and his mind / Behaves with cares ... Who seekes [honor] with painfull toile" (2.3.40), Belphoebe offers a dynamic contrast to the constant but inert virtue of the nymph who becomes a stone.

Belphoebe, that is, represents the continual effort that for Spenser is required to live a temperate life. The architectural model of the self implicit in the comparison of her legs to the columns of a temple exemplifies the process of constructing the self through a discourse of self-control that is the mission of Book 2, and that will reach its apotheosis in the Castle of Alma. Belphoebe's surprising emphasis on sweat – "Before [honor's] high gate high God did Sweat ordaine" (2.3.40) – not only represents the immense effort that induces such virtue but also the excrement that for Spenser is always at the core of moral effort. Remembering that in the physiological framework the blood oozing from Amavia, the tears welling from the nymph, and the sweat produced by Belphoebe's moral exertions, are just bodily excrements will help us prepare for the prominent role that waste disposal plays in the Castle of Alma. By emphasizing the labor behind Belphoebe's virginity, Spenser marries a Protestant work ethic to the classical ethic of temperance. Through an emphasis on the labor involved in the moral effort to battle innate frailty, Spenser's Calvinistic pessimism joins hands with his humanistic constructionism. The virtue of temperance allows Spenser to elide some of the essential dissonances between these two systems, since it is a virtue that assumes great ethical importance in both systems.

Yet Acrasia too has her occasions for labor, an effort which produces the "few drops" of sweat, "more cleare then Nectar," that trill down Acrasia's snowy breast "through languour of her late sweet toyle" (2.12.78). Acrasia's sweat not only reprises and eroticizes Belphoebe's moral effort, but also reminds us of the lassitudinous labors that await those who succumb to temptation.[11] Virtue is work in part because vice works so hard in its pursuit of pleasure.

Part of the problem of understanding the temperance that Book 2 prescribes derives from the fact that Spenser and the classical philosophy from which he draws ask the same ethical vocabulary to apply to both food and sex. Temperance, remarks Bryskett in *A Discourse of Civill Life*, "is exercised specially about the senses of tasting and feeling, but chiefly about the wanton lusts of the flesh."[12] This elision was not much of a problem for the Greeks, for whom sex and food were in so many ways analogous appetites, to be indulged in moderation. But the moral ambivalence about even licit forms of sexuality that Christianity inherits and intensifies from classical Rome produces dissonance when the same virtue is asked to apply to both appetites. Belphoebe and the nymph both practice not sexual temperance but sexual abstinence. They repudiate sex absolutely rather than indulge in it moderately. An analogous abstinence in regard to food is impossible to practice, at least without divine intervention. Guyon faints after three days without food in Mammon's cave, but no one faints in Spenser's world for lack of sex. Indeed, refusing sexuality has an unequivocally positive effect on the knights who do so successfully. The discourse of moderation, then, becomes somewhat dysfunctional when applied to sexuality: where Spenser can clearly imagine consuming "a little food," he obviously has trouble imagining "a little sex." The two become fused in Guyon's violent refusals of drink in the Bower of Bliss. When the Genius of the Bower offers Guyon a "Mazer bowle of wine," Guyon "overthrew his bowle disdainfully" (2.12.49), and when a "comely dame" named Excess offers Guyon a cup of "sappy liquor," Guyon grabs the cup

> out of her tender hond,
> The cup to ground did violently cast,
> That all in peeces it was broken fond,
> And with the liquor stained all the lond.   (2.12.56–57)

Here, we can see the twentieth-century meaning of temperance as abstinence from alcohol beginning to emerge. For Spenser, drink serves at once as synecdoche for the pleasures of the flesh and as an occasion of dangerous relaxation. "All drunkenness," maintains Lemnius, "is pernicious, because the nerves being soked continually with much Wine, are softened, and the whole frame of the body dissolved."[13] Drink precipitates the liquefaction of the constructed self. It is not until Book 3's portrait of chastity, or sexual desire legitimated in the bond of marriage, that Spenser will imagine a realm of legitimate sexuality. Indeed, at the beginning of Book 3 Britomart, the exemplar of chastity, unhorses Guyon, the champion of temperance, not only suggesting the perpetual tension between the dampening of desire and the directing of desire (a tension that stretches back to Augustine's quarrel with Cicero) but also implying that the carefully directed emotion of chastity is superior to the completely dampened desire of temperance. But in Book 2, sexual desire threatens the desiring subject, whereas food sustains it.

The Palmer interprets the tableau of the dead Amavia as "the image of mortalitie, / And feeble nature cloth'd with fleshly tyre, / When raging passion with fierce tyrannie / Robs reason of her due regalitie, / And makes it servant to her basest part" (2.1.57). Spenser epitomizes the triumph of passion over reason in this suicidal scenario. Passion usurps the role of reason, producing internal insurrection and tyranny. But this contestatory model of internal government is immediately correlated with a very different model based on the idea of the mean:

> The strong through pleasure soonest falles, the weake through smart.

> But temperance (said he) with golden squire
> Betwixt them both can measure out a meane,
> Neither to melt in pleasures whot desire,
> Nor fry in hartlesse griefe and dolefull teene.
> Thrise happie man, who fares them both atweene. (2.1.58)

By theorizing temperance as a cool mean between two over-heated extremes, Spenser prepares a conceptual path to the House of Medina, Guyon's next adventure.[14] The middle of three sisters, Medina embodies the mean not as a site of stasis but rather as the product of a continual struggle. Her two sisters, Elissa (too little) and Perissa (too much), battle constantly, and join together only to trouble her: "Still did they strive, and dayly disagree; / The eldest did against the youngest goe, / And both against the middest meant to worken woe" (2.2.13). Where Elissa the eldest is continually discontented, Perissa observes "no measure in her mood, no rule of right, / But poured out in pleasure and delight" (2.2.36). In this brief episode – a rehearsal for the visit to the Castle of Alma – Spenser portrays the immense if invisible effort required to occupy the mean. "If temperance is heroic," remarks Kathleen Williams, "and in a way of course it is – it is so in virtue of its ability to take up day after day a task which (it seems at this point in the poem) can never be lightened. Medina's balance is precarious and difficult to maintain, and one has to keep working at it."[15] In the Castle of Medina, Spenser shows how the mean is achieved out of a kind of architectural tension, accomplishing great labor by achieving the temporary stasis of carefully balanced contrary forces.

It is significant that Perissa's repudiation of rule is enacted not just in her behavior but also in her romance with Sansloy, whose name means "without law." Throughout the book, temperance comes to mean the work of self-control, the daily, even hourly, effort to govern a series of forces from within and without that threaten the integrity of the subject. Under this regime, selves are established and maintained through rule. To reject rule is to reject the possibility of becoming a self, and to become like Grill, the creature who will prefer to remain a hog. Discussing Phedon, who has killed his wife out of mistaken jealousy, the Palmer laments: "most wretched man, / That to affections does the bridle lend . . . / Strong warres they make, and cruell battry bend / Gainst fort of Reason, it to overthrow" (2.4.34). The self is on the one hand a spirited horse requiring firm control and on the other a kind of military outpost, always threatened by temptation from without and insurrection from within. One's task in the moral world of Book 2 is not to eradicate the affections, but rather to keep the reins held tightly on them, and so to participate in the simultaneously dynamic and architectonic construction of a self.

By "affections" here, Spenser specifically means feelings, passions, desires, those forces coursing through one's being that are potentially opposed to reason. The affections, moreover, are directly tied to the humors, which they can both cause and issue from. In the masque *Hymenaei*, in which Jonson imagines the four humors and four affections together threatening the marriage ceremony, Hymen announces: "The four untempered humors are broke out, / And with their wild affections go about / To ravish all religion." Then Reason speaks, and "At this the humor and affections sheathed their swords and retired amazed to the sides of the stage" (lines 140-41). In his note on the passage, Jonson explains: "as in natural bodies, so likewise in minds, there is not disease or distemperature but is caused either by some abounding humor or perverse affection."[16] The humors and affections are the same phenomenon in different physiological media.

"Inordinate affections," argues Thomas Wright in *The Passions of the Minde*, "many ways disquiet the minde, and trouble the peaceable state of this Common-weale of our soule." Wright proceeds to catalog the ways that self-rule at once mimics and epitomizes the rule of kingdoms:

By two wayes the subjects of every Common-weale, usually disturbe the State, and breede civill broyles therein: The first is, when they rise up and rebel against their King: the second is, when they brawle one with another, and so cause riots and tumults: the former is called Rebellion, the latter sedition. After the same manner, Passions either rebell against Reason their Lord and King, or oppose themselves one against another.... This internall Combat and spirituall Contradiction every spirituall man daily perceiveth, for inordinate Passions, will he, nill he, cease not almost hourely to rise up against Reason, and so molest him, troubling the rest and quietnesse of his Soule.... For these rebellious Passions are like crafty pioners, who, while souldiers live carelesly within their Castle, or at least not much suspect, they undermine it, and breake in so upon them, that they can hardly escape: in like manner these affections undermine the understandings of men.[17]

The affections, then, exist inside the self, but are imagined as something outside the self. Physiological double agents, these internal forces threaten the fragile constructions of the self, both by direct assault and by a kind of sabotage. Moral existence entails a continual cold war. The self must be in a perpetual state of alertness, always seeking for signs that these crafty pioneers are undercutting its fragile foundations. It is a warfare, furthermore, that is constructive rather than destructive of the self, both because of the radical inwardness such introspection demands and because the battle prevents the self from being overrun by a series of undifferentiated passions. In this regime, all experience the assault that

>   strong affections do apply
> Against the fort of reason evermore
> To bring the soule into captivitie:
> Their force is fiercer through infirmitie
> Of the fraile flesh, relenting to their rage,
> And exercise most bitter tyranny
> Upon the parts, brought into their bondage.   (2.11.1)

What individuates humans is not their desires but their success at battling this internal usurpation by desire. The congenital infirmity of frail flesh only gives insurrectionary desire a foothold in the very being attempting to conquer such desires. In Spenser's universe, to succumb to the affections is finally to become a beast. Self-control is the vehicle for self-rule, and finally for freedom.

We need to remember that Alma's castle is "Attempred goodly well for health and *for delight*" (2.11.2); it is a place of pleasure as well as discipline, and demonstrates remarkable hospitality for a place under constant siege, once its doors are finally opened. It is not temperance but intemperance that is finally opposed to pleasure; as Montaigne argues, "Intemperance is the plague of sensual pleasure; and temperance is not its scourge, it is its seasoning . . . temperance is the moderator, not the adversary, of pleasures."[18] Temperance, then, entails not a turn from the body and its pleasures but a redirection of fastidious attention to them. It is telling that the comparatively inert temptations in Mammon's cave have less effect on Guyon than the fact that he goes three days without food, and subsequently faints from weakness. Spenser here intends to remind us not just of the inherent frailty of even virtuous flesh – its critical need for sustenance – but also of the organism's dependence on just the digestive and defecatory processes that are detailed in the Castle of Alma. In order to live, bodies must be porous, must have openings to let in nutritive material and expel waste, yet these openings become the source of enormous anxiety. The moral job of the upright self is to police these necessary thresholds between the outside world and the inner self.

The Castle of Alma, in many ways the allegorical core of the book, entails a trip into the mouth and through the digestive tract of the body in order to stress the ethical and physiological importance of digestion, not to deny the importance of corporeal pleasure. The self is a castle, but one that must trade continually with the outside world while dealing with treachery within. It can do so only by placing at each gate a sentinel capable of repelling the enemy. In *The Passions of the Minde*, Thomas Wright locates a danger to the self in the senses, and particularly the eyes: "All senses no doubt are the first gates wherby passe and repasse all messages sent to passions: but yet the scriptures in particular wonderfully exhort, command,

and admonish us to attend unto the custodies and vigilance over our eyes."[19] One of the many reasons that Spenser's fantastic voyage through the body ends up in the head is that what goes on there with sensory data is exactly like what goes on in the stomach with gustatory matter. In both cases, the self must police its necessarily porous borders with a potentially harmful world, winnowing the matter that is allowed in, and expelling any material that could harm the self.

Pyrochles and Cymochles, those figures of elemental opposition to temperance, exemplify the consequences of inadequately completing this process. Each represents the kind of single-minded attachment to a humor soon to be mocked in Jonsonian comedy of the humors. Pyrochles, who shouts "I burn, I burn," and complains "O how I burne with implacable fire, / Yet nought can quench mine inly flaming side" (2.6.44), is choleric.[20] Cymochles, who succumbs to Phaedria's soporific song and allows "In slouthfull sleepe his molten hart to steme" (2.6.27), is phlegmatic, tending in his lack of effort at self-regulation to liquefy the matter that ought to maintain an architecturally sturdy moral self.[21] Pyrochles is walking proof of a lesson often forgotten in contemporary work on the humors: that heat, although frequently invoked to explain male superiority – men are hot and dry, while women are cool and wet, lacking the natural heat to push their sexual organs outward – could also be the cause of a desire that threatened the kinds of self-control on which any conception of manhood rested.[22] Pyrochles here provides a cogent contrast to the maid who becomes cold stone in order to flee a satyr "Inflamed ... to follow beauties chace" (2.2.7).

Even Maleger, who leads the assault on the Castle of Alma, can be understood to represent a predominant humor: his "leane and meagre" physiognomy and his "cold and drery" complexion denote melancholy (2.11.22). His arrows, moreover, deliver wounds that cannot be healed because they fester "inly" (2.11.21). It is likewise significant that both Maleger and his troops exemplify a strangely disembodied state: we learn that Maleger was "of such subtile substance and unsound, / That like a ghost he seem'd, whose grave-clothes were unbound," while his troops are hard to kill "For though they bodies seeme, yet substance from them fades" (2.11.20; 2.9.15). Maleger, moreover, must be separated like Antaeus from the earth from which he draws strength before he can be defeated. Arthur's victory over Maleger certainly is representative of a kind of victory over the flesh, as it has been frequently allegorized, but it is also a victory on behalf of the flesh against the forces that assault it.[23]

When we enter the Castle of Alma, then, we move from a world of elementary opposition to a system of alimentary processing. Very popular (and frequently imitated) in its own day, the Castle of Alma has seemed to most subsequent readers a counter-productive grotesquerie. Critical opinion of this episode has altered little since John Hughes wrote in 1715 that the allegory of the House of Temperance is "debas'd by a Mixture of too many low Images, as *Diet, Concoction, Digestion*, and the like; which are presented as persons."[24] Underpinning Hughes's criticism is a deeply anachronistic notion not only of literary decorum, but also, and more tellingly, of the relationship of body to self. Hughes presumes a realm of low and therefore irrelevant corporeal processes from which Spenser misguidedly draws the material for his allegory of the temperate self.[25] In *The Anatomy of Melancholy*, by contrast, Robert Burton asks a question which demonstrates great sympathy for the possible motives for including an account of the body's sundry details in a depiction of the construction of an ethical self:

And what can be more ignominious and filthie ... then for a man not to knowe the structure and composition of his owne body, especially since the knowledge of it, tends so much to the preservation of his health, & information of his manners.[26]

For Burton, unlike Hughes, true filthiness inheres not in attending to the sordid details of corporeal processes but in ignoring them. Spenser suggests that each of us possesses a "Selfe, whome though we do not see / Yet each doth in him selfe it well perceive to bee" (2.12.47). Part of the point of Book 2 is to help make this self more visible, and so to aid in the larger project of self-knowledge. Underpinning both Burton's and Spenser's somatic explorations of the interior self is the assumption that knowledge of physiology is knowledge of psychology, that knowing the body is not just gaining information about the corporeal machine the self inhabits but actually learning something about the self. Both assume, moreover, that the discrimination of noxious from nutritious matter in digestion is a physiological version of the discrimination of good and evil. If the alimentary path traversed by Spenser's knights seems to us a particularly grotesque and inappropriate route to knowledge of self, as I think it still does, perhaps the fault lies not so much in Spenser's aesthetic as in our own historically contingent and severely attenuated conceptions of what areas of knowledge pertain to the comprehension of self. Our inability to apprehend and appreciate the controlled corporeality that is at the core of Spenserian temperance measures our distance from Spenser, and from the early modern regime of the self he helped to shape.

It is in the development of this paradigm of self, so different in many ways from current models, that my differences with two of the most persuasive recent accounts of Book 2 – Stephen Greenblatt's in *Renaissance Self-Fashioning*, and David Miller's in *The Poem's Two Bodies* – emerge.[27] Where Miller emphasizes the absence of the genitals in the Castle of Alma's tour through the body, Greenblatt argues that the resistance to temptation that culminates in the destruction of the Bower of Bliss is symptomatic of a damaging pathological repression of the erotic at the core of Western culture. Both, that is, deploy a kind of Freudian framework to locate the self on the axis of genital eroticism, and find Spenser's subordination of such eroticism to the larger project of control to constitute a kind of sickness. Where Greenblatt sees such repression in collusion with the colonial suppression Spenser defended, Miller links it to a larger squeamishness about sex. Where Miller focuses on what is absent in the Castle of Alma, Greenblatt leaves out the Castle of Alma altogether. What emerges when one steps back from their powerful but deeply partial arguments is a sense of the enormous difference between the regime of the temperate self and our own presuppositions about the pathologies of discipline.

I, in turn, want to emphasize the constitutive nature of this self-control within the paradigm that Spenser inherits and develops. Self-control is for Spenser a means of legitimating, not negating, desire. It is the total release of one's passions, represented by characters such as Pyrochles, which is most feared. Indeed, Book 2's account of self-discipline entails not a discourse complicit with colonial repression, but something very different: a discipline intended to inculcate the internal stability that makes possible a liberation from the passions that seethe within and without the human subject. It is not temperance but rather intemperance that is portrayed in terms of political violence and unjust subjugation: "When raging passion with fierce tyrannie / Robs reason of her due regalitie, / And makes it servant to her basest part" (2.1.57). What is needed is an account of the Book which comprehends both the destructive exertions of the Bower and the complex production of the Castle of Alma, and investigates, moreover, the relationship between the two episodes.

One thing that unites the two episodes is the importance of the militarized self. Where the Castle of Alma is surrounded by enemies and under constant siege, Guyon is in the Bower surrounded by sensual temptations whose pull he feels strongly. Both episodes, then, imagine figures in isolation who are assaulted, and who must exercise vigilance in order for virtue to achieve victory. Both, moreover, depend upon the military metaphor not just for defense, but also for offense. Attack becomes the primary mode of responding to the internal subterfuge and external challenge that temptation presents. Together, the two episodes represent for Spenser the destructive and constructive aspects of the virtue of self-control. Where Guyon can literally take or leave the material temptations that Mammon displays, the Bower of Bliss entails an entirely different situation: the revenge of Mordant that inaugurated the Book, the wish to liberate all those whom Acrasia has made captive, and the deeply compelling nature of the temptations, all cry out for a vigorous response. In the Bower, extremity in the defense of the virtue of temperance proves no vice; it demands instead a powerful if troubling exertion of unequivocal force. Spenser in the Bower of Bliss chooses to record the costs as well as the benefits of the self-control he endorses, lavishing his poetic gifts on a range of sensuous details that are destroyed. Ben Jonson writes in his marginal notes on the lush passages, "An excellen D[escription] of a most pleasant [place]."[28] In contrast to the fulsome description of the Bower's delights, the destruction happens quickly – in one stanza, 2.12.83 – testimony both to the insubstantiality and ephemerality of the pleasures of the Bower, and to Spenser's refusal to participate in a narrative that sadistically relishes the details of their destruction.

Spenser, though, never suggests that force is irrelevant to the maintenance of self in a world filled with external temptation and a moral physiology rife with insurrectionary forces. The gates of the Castle of Alma are "fast barred ... / And every loup fast lockt, as fearing foes despight," even to the two virtuous knights who request entry (2.9.10). An ethic of hospitality here collides with an image of the self in a continual state of war. Spenser is fascinated by the immense military effort required to achieve the apparent stasis of a deeply moral life, and to resist the Pyrochles-like fire of "horrors, and unrests, / In our inflamed breasts." The self achieves at best a fragile and flammable stability continually threatened by passions and affections.

We can sense some of the necessity of this effort by exploring the detailed contrast Spenser develops between the thresholds of the Castle of Alma and of the Bower of Bliss. Like the Castle of Alma, the Bower of Bliss also has gates, but its gates are not installed to ensure the integrity of the Garden; rather, they are "wrought of substaunce light, / Rather for pleasure, then for battery or fight" (2.12.43). These are thresholds established not for the purposes of physiological and moral discrimination but rather for the erotic pleasure of transgressing them. In Alma's "Barbican," or mouth, sits a "Porter ... Day and night duely keeping watch and ward" (2.9.25). It also has thirty-two "warders, ... all armed bright / In glistring steele, and strongly fortifide: / Tall yeomen seemed they, and of great might, / And were enraunged ready, still for fight" (2.9.26). At the threshold of the Bower of Bliss, by contrast, is the bad "genius," who "of this Gardin had the governall, / And Pleasures porter was devizd to bee." Where each of Alma's warders is armed to the teeth, the porter at the Bower of Bliss is found "Holding a staffe in hand for mere formalitee," not because he might actually use it to bar entrance (2.12.48). Fascinatingly, Renaissance moral physiology here leads Spenser to reverse an ethic that praises hospitality and welcome to strangers. Guyon and Arthur are ultimately greeted with hospitality at the Castle of Alma, but only after "ween[ing] fowle reproch / Was to them doen, their entrance to forstall" (2.9.11), and only after they have skirmished with

Maleger's troops. Acrasia, by contrast, exemplifies an ethic of hospitality; feasting with open table all those who happen by. "It was her guise, all Straungers goodly so to greet," notes Spenser, with corrosive irony (2.12.56).

It is telling of the effort involved that Arthur and Guyon seek the Castle's shelter because they are exhausted, and need to recover. Guyon is in a swoon from his three days without food or rest in the Cave of Mammon, while Arthur is tired from defending Guyon against Pyrochles, Cymochles, Archimago, and Atin. When Arthur and Guyon are finally allowed in, Alma "gentle court and gracious delight ... to them made, with mildnesse virginall, / Shewing herself both wise and liberall" (2.9.20). Arthur and Guyon ask Alma for a tour of the Castle, and first are led to view the Castle wall, which is "not built of bricke, ne yet of stone and lime / But of thing like to that Ægyptian slime, / Whereof king Nine whilome built Babell towre" (2.9.21). Spenser here describes the skin as slime not just to emphasize the fragility and mortality of the structure ("Soone it must turne to earth"), but also to underscore a tension between the unqualified awe the form inspires ("So goodly workemanship") and the sinful matter from which the form is made. Here Spenser's humanist constructionism chafes against his Protestant disgust (2.9.21).

This chafing is abated somewhat in what has been for readers since the seventeenth century the most enigmatic stanza in the poem:

> The frame thereof seemd partly circulare,
> And part triangulare, O worke divine;
> Those two the first and last proportions are,
> The one imperfect, mortall, foeminine;
> Th'other immortall, perfect, masculine,
> And twixt them both a quadrate was the base,
> Proportioned equally by seven and nine;
> Nine was the circle set in heavens place,
> All which compacted made a goodly diapase. (2.9.22)

Kenelm Digby, Spenser's seventeenth-century commentator, remarks that in this mysterious stanza Spenser

seems onely to glance at the profoundest notions that any Science can deliver us, and then on a sudden (as it were) recalling himself out of an Enthusiasme, he returns to the gentle Relation of the Allegoricall History he had begun, leaving his Readers to wander up and down in much obscurities.[29]

Digby astutely notices that this stanza involves something very different from the surrounding material. In lieu of the playful joy of identifying teeth as warders and vertebrae as steps on a ladder, this stanza seems at once to solicit and to defy interpretation in the bewildering numerical shorthand it employs.

It is a solicitation Digby cannot refuse. "Tis evident," he continues, "that the Authors intention in this Canto is to describe the bodie of a man inform'd with a rationall soul." "But in this Stanza," argues Digby, Spenser "comprehends the generall description of them [body and soul] both, as (being joyned together to frame a compleat Man) they make one perfect compound" (*Variorum*, 2.473). Digby, then, sees the canto, and the stanza in particular, as inhabiting the same philosophical territory as the question that Bryskett has Master Spenser propose in his *A Discourse of Civill Life* about the relationship between the soul and the body. According to Digby, Spenser intends to compare the mind to the part of the frame that is circular, and the body to that part that is "Triangular." Digby then compares the three corners of a triangle to "the 3 great compounded Elements in mans bodie, to wit, Salt, Sulphur and Mercurie which mingled together make the naturall heat and radical moysture, the 2 qualities whereby man liveth" (*Variorum*, 2.474). Digby here refers to the Paracelsian elementals, rather than to the Aristotelian/Galenic elements of earth, air, fire, and water. But when he glosses the "Quadrate [that] was the base" of the system, he is firmly back in Galenic medicine, suggesting that the quadrate refers to

the foure principall humors in mans Bodie, viz. *Choler*, *Blood*, *Phleme*, and *Melancholy*: which if they be distempered and unfitly mingled, dissolution of the whole doth immediately ensue: like to a building which falls to ruine, if the foundation and Base of it be unsound or disordered. (*Variorum*, 2.475–76)

Digby's architectural metaphor here is apt; as we have seen, Spenser's depiction of temperance continually compares the achievement of a physiological balance of the humoral fluids to the construction of a building. Selves are in Spenser's world established on the precarious cusp of matter and spirit.

The stanza uses a bewildering blend of Galenic physiology and mystical geometry to explain this enigmatic conjunction of matter and spirit. The part that is "triangular," Spenser indicates, is "imperfect, mortall, foeminine," while the part that is "circulaire" is "immortall, perfect, masculine" (2.9.22). Digby glosses the lines by recourse to the Galenic model of heterosexual attraction and procreation:

as the feminine Sex is imperfect and receives perfection from the masculine: so doth the Body from the Soul, which to it is in lieu of a male. And as in corporall generations the female affords but grosse and passive matter, to which the Male gives active heat and prolificall vertue: so in spirituall generations (which are the operations of the minde) the body administers onely the Organs, which if they were not imployed by the Soul, would of themselves serve for nothing. And as there is mutuall appetence between the Male and the Female, betweene matter and forme; So there is betweene the bodie and the soul of Man, but what ligament they have, our Author defineth not (and it may be Reason is not able to attaine to it). (*Variorum*, 2.475)

Digby, then, likens the attraction between matter and soul to that between man and woman, and describes their conjunction as a kind of hermaphroditical joining of different realms of existence like that which concludes Book 3 of the 1590 *Faerie Queene*. The sexual difference between men and women, then, comes to stand for the metaphysical difference between matter and spirit. And on a hierarchy whereby spirit is higher than matter, males are likened to spirit. This is mapped onto an Aristotelian account of generation, whereby woman supplies the matter and man the form. But the situation is even more complex than Digby's gender-based scheme allows. The tour itself is conducted by a woman who in most accounts represents the soul, which in this scheme is supposed to be masculine. And she leads the knights on a tour through a body that is probably masculine, although Digby's scheme makes matter feminine. Most readers, that is, have interpreted the "wandering vine" and "wanton yvie" over the portcullis as a male-specific moustache (2.9.24).[30] The sexual ideology at work here is certainly masculinist, but it aspires to locate the highest existence not in a rigidly narrow masculinity, but in a conjunction of traits confusedly endowed with masculine and feminine meaning.

On the next leg of what A. C. Hamilton wittily refers to as "their Cook's tour" of the Castle of Alma, Arthur and Guyon pass through the well-guarded mouth:

> And round about the porch on every side
> Twise sexteen warders sat, all armed bright
> In glistring steele, and strongly fortifide:
> Tall yeoman seemed they, and of great might,
> And were enraunged ready, still for fight.   (2.9.26)

This barricaded mouth is so different from the Gulf of Greediness, that orifice of indiscriminate consumption that borders the Bower, a "griesly mouth . . . Sucking the seas into his entralles deepe" (2.12.6). Arthur and Guyon are then led down the gullet in order to explore the stomach, the place where the substance of a dead other is made into something familiar and alive, where nutritive material begins the remarkable transformation into the quadrate of humoral fluids which will sustain mortal flesh.[31] Giving the well-worn metaphor of the self as a castle a particular emphasis, Spenser likens the passage to the stomach to a

> stately Hall,
> Wherein were many tables faire dispred,
> And ready dight with drapets festivall,
> Against the viaundes should be ministred.   (2.9.27)

Just as the gates of the castle are guarded by many figures, so is the kitchen inhabited by many creatures of authoritative discrimination. The hall is presided over by a steward, a "comely personage" named "Diet," a figure "rype of age, / And in demeanure sober, and in counsell sage." His marshal is "A jolly yeoman" named "Appetite," who "did bestow / Both guestes and meate, when ever in they came, / And knew them how to order without blame." The social hierarchy these characters inhabit represents the complex order that Spenser imagines as necessary for physiological maintenance. They also demonstrate a kind of obedience to the soul by the body in the gestures of deference they show to Alma: "They both attone / Did dewty to their Lady, as became" (2.9.28).

These figures of dietary and social order usher Alma, Guyon, and Arthur into "the kitchin rowme," the stomach proper, which is

> a vaut ybuilt for great dispence,
> With many raunges reard along the wall;
> And one great chimney, whose long tonnell thence
> The smoke forth threw. And in the midst of all
> There placed was a caudron wide and tall,
> Upon a mighty furnace, burning whot
> More whot, then Aetn', or flaming Mongiball:
> For day and night it brent, ne ceased not,
> So long as any thing it in the caudron got. (2.9.29)

This eternal flame is the source of the life of the body. It is what makes possible the survival of the organism. Yet even this necessary flame is not an unequivocal good, but must be tempered by the lungs, "An huge great paire of bellowes, which did styre / Continually, and cooling breath inspyre" (2.9.30). A dynamic balance between the heat necessary for cooking and the cooling breath of respiration – a balance central to definitions of temperance as a form of moderation between extremes – is thus attained in the organic disposition of the well-ordered body.

The stomach, moreover, is not a passive receptacle but an area of immense bustle:

> About the Caudron many Cookes accoyld,
> With hookes and ladles, as need did require;
> The whiles the viandes in the vessell boyld
> They did about their businesse sweat, and sorely toyld.
>
> The maister Cooke was cald Concoction,
> A carefull man, and full of comely guise:
> The kitchin Clerke, that hight Digestion,
> Did order all th' Achates in seemely wise,
> And set them forth, as well he could devise.
> The rest had severall offices assind,
> Some to remove the scum, as it did rise;
> Others to beare the same away did mind;
> And others it to use according to his kind. (2.9.30–31)

The turbulent complexity of the digestive process is indicated by the number of figures and jobs Spenser finds it necessary to include. Each well-governed stomach is for Spenser like the royal kitchen, filled with a baffling array of tasks and workers. Apparently for Spenser, too many cooks do not spoil this roiled broth, but are required to accomplish the nearly magical transformation of dead matter into the nutritive fluid which sustains life.

This passage on the stomach echoes the operation at the center of the Cave of Mammon – the mining and purifying of metal:

> One with great bellowes gathered filling aire,
> And with forst wind the fewell did inflame;
> Another did the dying bronds repaire
> With yron toungs, and sprinckled oft the same
> With liquid waves, fiers Vulcans rage to tame,
> Who maistring them, renewd his former heat;
> Some scumd the drosse, that from the metall came;
> Some stird the molten owre with ladles great;
> And every one did swincke, and every one did sweat.   (2.7.36)

Spenser here identifies a striking if unoriginal resemblance between the cooking that constitutes digestion and the purifying of metal from ore. Indeed as we will see in Chapter 5, Milton in *Paradise Lost* uses the alchemical transformation of metal to explain the corporeal transubstantiation that is digestion. But Spenser intends to emphasize the contrast: where the one produces inert riches, the other sustains life. Where the one is an unnatural temptation away from the flesh, making Guyon forget to eat and sleep, the other is the central activity of healthy flesh.

Spenser's portrait of the stomach as a kind of kitchen draws on a vast literature which uses culinary metaphors to explain digestive processes. "Our stomake is our bodies kitchin," remarks William Vaughan in his popular *Directions for Health*.[32] "Concoction," one of the characters inhabiting Spenser's great vault, is the technical term for digestion, and derives from the Latin *concoctus*, "boiled together." A very literal kind of cooking occurs within the stomach of the individual consumer, carefully preparing the food for delivery to various parts of the body as a cook prepares meals. The stomach receives such extensive attention in Spenser's account of the well-tempered individual because it is a concentrated site of physiological and psychological inwardness. If the stomach does not work well, the entire being suffers and/or dies. Indeed, the name of the figure who presides over this castle, "Alma," may be short-hand for "anima," "soul," as many commentators urge, but it also means "nourishing," and this without having to buy any vowels or consonants. For the pre-Cartesian regime of the self Spenser inhabits, soul does not reside in a realm separate from the body but is in large part constituted by it.[33] The stomach, moreover, is the primary organ through which one can actually alter the temperature of the body – a concept which is at once physiological and psychological. Digestion is then not simply a function of some lower bodily stratum, to borrow a phrase from Bakhtin, but a central process of psychological and physiological self-fashioning.

In *A View of the Present State of Ireland*, Spenser endorses Galen's principle that the psychological proclivities of the soul are in large part derived from the humoral temperature of the body. Irish wet nurses can have a pernicious influence on the English infants to whom they give suck, Spenser warns, because the infants "draw into themselves together with their suck, even the nature and disposition of their nurses, for the mind followeth much the temperature of the body."[34] A similar concern emerges in Bryskett's *A Discourse of Civill Life*:

> To the end therefore that the child receive not any vicious habit by the qualities of his first food and nourishment; wise men have advised, that the nurse to be chosen for a child, should not be base or of vile condition, that the child might be the apter to be brought up to vertue: that she be not of strange nation, lest she should give it strange or unseemely manners, unfit or disagreeable to the customes and conditions of the house or citie wherein it is borne, and wherein it is to live: and lastly, that she be of good and commendable behaviour, to the end that with the milk it may suck good conditions, and an honest disposition to vertuous life.[35]

Juxtaposed with Spenser's frequent recourse to the recurrent dualisms of neoplatonic spirituality, then, is an aggressively materialist notion of self, a notion that puts particular ethical and psychological pressure on all acts of consumption. In the most literal way, you are what and how you eat. Under this regime, temperance assumes a double urgency: it is a virtue that not only exhibits proper ethical conduct, but also actively alters the moral condition of the self that practices it. That is why the central arena in the Book of Temperance is the body.

A key task in the preparation of food is the separation of edible from inedible matter: "Some to remove the scum as it did rise; / Others to beare the same away did mind" (2.9.31). Likewise, a critical issue in the assimilation of nutritive material is the successful and thorough elimination of what cannot be digested. In *The Secret Miracles of Nature*, Lemnius explicitly links this process of culinary skimming to physiological elimination: "As it is when we boil meat, the filth and skim that riseth up must be purged, lest the meat should be polluted with some excrements and filth: so at first by sweat, vomit, phlebotomy, purging, the humours heaped in the body must be removed, before they spread into the veins."[36] Spenser thus calls appropriate if unexpected attention to the technology of waste disposal:

> But all the liquour, which was fowle and wast,
> Not good nor serviceable else for ought,
> They in another great round vessell plast,
> Till by a conduit pipe it thence were brought:
> And all the rest, that noyous was, and nought,
> By secret wayes, that none might it espy,
> Was close convaid, and to the back-gate brought,
> That cleped was Port Esquiline, whereby
> It was avoided quite, and throwne out privily.   (2.9.31–32)

This notorious passage is perhaps less indecorous when we remember that the unsuccessful elimination of waste is the primary cause of illness in the Galenic regime. Although not as glorious as the front gate, the "back-gate" is no less necessary to the health of the individual. The heavy-handed pun on "privy" reminds us that the quotidian processes of elimination are a critical activity of the well-ordered self. That is why the urine flask came to represent the medical profession, and why almost all medical therapies in the period – particularly phlebotomy, purgation, and clysters – involve ridding the body of the excess fluids that cause disease. "Physicke," notes Robert Burton in *The Anatomy of Melancholy*, "is naught else but *addition and subtraction*."[37] A temperate, well-regulated body is not a classical immured structure but a dynamic and porous edifice continually producing "superfluous excrements" from the very matter which nourishes it, excrements which must be purged. As William Vaughan writes:

Natures providence hath devised and framed sundry passages needfull for the purging, conveiance and evacuation of all such superfluous humours: to wit, the Kidneyes and the Urine-pipes, the empty or fasting Guts ... the Bladder, Eares, and Pores, appointed for the avoydance expulsion of sweat. And in the most part of these, if obstructions should happen, all the whole filthy masse of noysome humours is thereby kept within the body, and then gives violent assault to some of the principall parts.[38]

Disease is a product not of flow but of obstruction. The "violent assault" that Vaughan asserts will be made by "noysome humours" is simply another version of the irruptive forces that Maleger and his troops represent, since such humors were the primary cause of the passionate excesses that the troops perform. The intricate processes of digestion, assimilation, and elimination portrayed within the Castle of Alma are thus intimately related to the heroic labor that Arthur accomplishes outside Alma's walls, and to Guyon's ultimate destruction of the Bower of Bliss. Rather than being an indecorous interruption of Spenser's ethical pattern, Port Esquiline supplies an absolutely essential component of it. As Carol Rawcliffe remarks of late medieval physiology, "However 'ignoble' they might appear, the bladder, anus and intestines were essential for survival, and thus 'principal' members in a way that the hands and feet, or even the eyes and ears, were not. This particular hierarchy was often headed by the stomach, in recognition of the cook's sterling work in feeding rich and poor alike."[39] The ejection of noxious material it accomplishes is psychologically, physiologically, and ethically necessary to Spenser's portrait of the temperate individual.

In his sustained and compelling account of the Castle of Alma, David Miller argues in a chapter entitled "Alma's Nought" that Freudian psychoanalysis can usefully "summon into representation what Spenser's poetic intentions necessarily exclude from view. What Spenser's intentions exclude are the genitals."[40] It is true that Spenser does not give a genitally based sexual identity to the Castle of Alma. The castle is not anatomically correct, in this or other regards. It is also true that Spenser seems to give the castle a deliberately hermaphroditic cast, even though the terms of that hermaphroditism involve conventional expressions of masculine superiority:

> The frame therof seemd partly circulare,
> And part triangulare, o worke divine;
> Those two the first and last proportions are,
> The one imperfect, mortall, foeminine;
> Th'other immortall, perfect, masculine. (2.9.22)

I would argue that here psychoanalysis, rather than providing us with a key to an earlier site of repression, encourages us to impose our own sense of the primacy of the genitals onto a culture where other forms of somatic activity – including, as we have seen, the alimentary tract – assumed equal if not greater importance in the formation of identity. Debora Shuger has recently called attention to the difference between "the modern definition of the body as the sexual body" and early modern conceptions, in which "sexual desire is an inflection of erotic longing, not its origin or essence."[41] We certainly are made to feel in the Bower of Bliss the intensity of this inflection, but it remains an inflection of the larger effort of self-control. It is not until Book 3, with its portrait of Britomart, heroine of the heterosexual marital desire that Spenser terms chastity, that the positive and procreative nature of sexual desire is given full voice. And even there, sexual desire overtakes one like a wound and a disease, continually threatening the health and sanity of the lover.

Indeed, as Michel Foucault has argued of the Galenic system that Spenser portrays, "it is a trait manifested by all Greek and Roman medicine to accord much more space to the dietetics of alimentation than to that of sex. For this medicine, the thing that matters is eating and drinking."[42] That is why for Spenser, the stomach rather than the genitals is at the narrative and conceptual center of the well-ordered self. Its careful processing of nutritive matter and elimination of noxious substances inspires not belly laughter but religious awe in the two knights:

> Which goodly order, and great workmans skill
> Whenas those knights beheld, with rare delight,
> And gazing wonder they their minds did fill;
> For never had they seene so straunge a sight. (2.9.33)

The seemingly unexpected turn that Arthur and Guyon make from the stomach to the brain (with a brief stop in the parlor of the heart), moreover, involves not the act of repressing genital sexuality that Miller posits – certainly the poet who conceived Ollyphant, that ambulatory penis, could deal with the genitals when he chose – but rather a logical anatomical progression, since, as Juan Huarte and other physiological writers assert, "albeit the stomacke abides so far distant from the braine, yet... the brain and the stomacke are united and chained together with certaine sinewes, by way of which they interchangeable communicate their dammages."[43] These mysterious sinews, canals that connect the stomach to the brain, explain an itinerary that seems so curious by modern physiological standards. The mental activity that ensues, moreover, involves a process of assimilation and discrimination that is akin to the process of digestion. Spenser prepares for this transition from physiological digestion to intellectual assimilation when he has his knights "fill" their minds with wonder. "Knowledge," suggests Huarte, must "have his due digestion... for as the bodie is not maintained by the much which we eat and drinke in one day, but by that which the stomacke digesteth and turneth: so our understanding is not filled by the much which we read in little time, but by that which by little and little it proceeds to conceive and chew upon" (p. 11). In the *Confessions*, Augustine terms the memory "a sort of stomach for the mind, and that joy or sadness are like sweet or bitter food."[44] The connections linking the stomach to the brain are at once conceptual and physiological. When Miller argues that "Digestion (Spenser's 'concoction') is a kind of sublimation through which the body assimilates nutriment from food; it is Spenser's most physical image of the movement from matter to spirit on which his fiction and his poetics are based," he is, I think, on target. But when he continues, asserting that "Reminders of the physical basis and origin of sublime allegorical figures are thus a structural embarrassment, an inopportune return of what should have been 'avoided quite'" (p. 179), he is, I think, employing a deeply anachronistic notion of embarrassment, one that depends on a separation of the physical from the sublime that Spenser would certainly not have endorsed, and might not have understood.

The prominence of digestive and defecatory technology in Spenser's portrait of the well-tempered individual thus underscores the fact that the regime of the self Spenser depicts entails hierarchies and distinctions very different from our own. After the tour of the stomach, Guyon and Arthur are brought into "a goodly Parlour," the heart, where they find

> A lovely bevy of faire Ladies sate,
> Courted of many a jolly Paramoure,
> The which them did in modest wise amate,
> And each one sought his Lady to aggrate...
>
> Diverse delights they found them selves to please;
> Some song in sweet consort, some laught for joy,
> Some plaid with strawes, some idly sat at ease;
> But other some could not abide to toy,
> All pleasaunce was to them griefe and annoy:
> This frownd, that faund, the third for shame did blush,
> Another seemed envious, or coy,
> Another in her teeth did gnaw a rush.   (2.9.33–35)

These disparate ladies probably represent, in the words of Jonson's marginal gloss on this passage, "the Passions of the minde."[45] As such, they depict the emotions or moods that energize life, but that require constant monitoring. They show their awareness of their proper place in the hierarchy through their deference to Alma: "Soone as the gracious Alma came in place, / They all attonce out of their seates arose, / And to her homage made, with humble grace" (2.9.36). Each knight, moreover, chooses a lady: Arthur is drawn to one who is "right faire and fresh as morning rose, / But somwhat sad, and solemne eke," whose name turns out to be "Prays-desire, / That by well doing sought to honour to aspire" (2.9.36, 39). Guyon, meanwhile, courts a lady who "was right faire, and modest of demaine, / But that too oft she chaung'd her native hew ... Unto the ground she cast her modest eye, / And ever and anone with rosie red / The bashfull bloud her snowy cheekes did dye" (2.9.40–41). Her bashfulness makes her seem "So straungely passioned," and involves a "strong passion [that] mard her modest grace" (2.9.41, 43). Guyon is puzzled, until Alma tells him that "She is the fountaine of your modestee; / You shamefast are, but *Shamefastnesse* it selfe is shee" (2.9.43). Guyon in response "did blush in privitee, / And turnd his face away" (2.9.44). It is telling that the embarrassment we would locate in the discussion of Port Esquiline or the suppression of the genitals is for Spenser manifested in the parlor of the heart, in a moment of self-recognition. This strange, almost surreal, encounter involves a wary affirmation of emotion in the well-regulated moral life. Where temperance could sometimes be imagined to entail the rejection of passion entirely,

Spenser here situates the passions at the heart of his temperate self, as spurs to the very virtue he depicts rather than as forces opposing it.

Indeed, in Thomas Wright's *Passions of the Minde*, a work dedicated to the proposition that "Passions, are not only, not to be extinguished (as the Stoicks seemed to affirme) but sometimes to be moved, & stirred up for the service of vertue," Wright invokes the two passions Spenser has his knights court to exemplify this principle:

The passion of shamfastnesse bridleth us of many loose afections, which would otherwise be ranging abroad. The appetite of honour, which followeth, yea, and is due unto vertue, encourageth often noble spirite to attempt most dangerous exploits for the benefit of their countries.[46]

Together, the two passions balance temerity against reticence, audacity against modesty. The one is a spur, the other a bridle, but both move to virtuous action.

Miller offers an astute comparison of the behavior of Shamefastness in the parlor of the heart to the elimination of waste via Port Esquiline:

It would be perverse, therefore, to point out that the words "close," "secret," and "privily," which occur together in stanza 32 [the stanza on waste disposal], occur together again in stanzas 42 and 44, where Guyon asks Shamefastnesse what "in the secret of your heart close lyes," and blushes "in privitee" when he finds out. The words have been cleansed... and so can have no relevance to the obviously strained interpretation of blushing as an unwelcome reminder of the personification's "person."[47]

I admire Miller's close reading here, but would argue that the echo works in just the opposite way. The point of the echo is not to suggest that the heart is a "cleaner" space than the anus, but to correlate their activities. It is not perverse to point out this link between visceral activity and social demeanor – only good Galenic physiology. Guyon's blush identifies his inner affinity with the passion he has addressed – an affinity which is physiological as well as psychological. As Thomas Wright observes,

the passions of our minde, are not unlike the foure humours of our bodies... for if blood, flegme, choller, or melancholy exceed the due proportion required to the constitution and health of our bodies, presently we fall into some disease: even so, if the passion of the Minde be not moderated according to reason (and that temperature vertue requireth) immediatly the soule is molested with some maladie.[48]

Passions function on the psychological plane as humors do on the physiological plane. Both require the imposition of due proportion by reason, or they threaten the health of the organism.

Passions, moreover, can influence physiology, as well as be altered by it:

What Maladies grow by cares and heavinesse, many can testifie, and few men there bee, which are not subject to some melancholy humour, that often assaulteth them, troubling their mindes, and hurting their bodies.[49]

Indeed, the effect of passions in the body is to aid and extend the technologies of digestion outlined in the description of the stomach:

> Pleasure and Delight, if it be moderate, bringeth health, because the purer spirits retyre unto the heart and they help marvellously the digestion of the blood, so that thereby the heart engendreth great abundance, and most purified spirits, which after being dispersed thorow the body, cause a good concoction to be made in all parts, helping them to expell the superfluities.[50]

The passions are thus part of a larger systemic ecology of digestion and expulsion that Spenser's verbal echoes cleverly identify. The passions, that is, not only produce Guyon's private blush but also aid in the "privy" expulsion of superfluous matter. Both the processing of food and the dispensation of the emotions participate in the discourse of organic inwardness made available by Galenic physiology.

Our attitude to this discourse grows problematic when the enforcement of the order on which it depends demands effort that is destructive rather than constructive, and destructive of a beautiful and deeply desirable landscape. When Spenser inaugurates canto 12's trajectory of ruin by announcing that "Now gins this goodly frame of Temperance / Fairely to rise," he reminds his readers that temperance is a "frame," a rational structure, at once aesthetic and ethical, imposed on the inherently unruly desires and beastly passions that inhabit all mortal bodies. The very title of Sir Thomas Elyot's immensely popular *Castel of Helthe* (1541) demonstrates the pervasiveness of the metaphor that underpins Spenser's Castle of Alma. Psychological, ethical, and physiological health is an edifice perpetually being constructed, and in need of continual maintenance. The self that Spenser endorses is a profoundly fabricated being, one that discovers individuation in regulating a repertoire of desires possessed in some degree by all. It is, moreover, a structure built in part on the ruins of those forces that threaten it.

The fetish of order and discipline that is the essence of this regime immediately arouses our suspicions of authoritarianism. The fact that Book 2 concludes with the violent destruction of a sensuous and beautiful landscape has done little to allay those suspicions. These suspicions have encouraged a kind of ideological enjambment between the self-control that Spenser articulates and the colonial domination in which the poem also participates. Spenser himself even provides the terms for the enjambment when he compares the forces of Maleger to "a swarme of Gnats at eventide" that "Out of the fennes of Allan do arise" (2.9.16). In this reference to insects from the bogs of central Ireland, Spenser suggests that defeating the forces that threaten the castle of the self is like conquering a dehumanized indigenous Irish population. Spenser, furthermore, describes Maleger's troops in terms that are, Thomas Healy suggests, "remarkably similar to Irenius's descriptions of Irish dress and manners recounted in *A View*":

> A Thousand villeins round about them swarmd
> Out of the rockes and caves adioyning nye,
> Vile caytive wretches, ragged, rude, deformd,
> All threatning death, all in straunge manner armd,
> Some with unweldy clubs, some with long speares,
> Some rusty knives some staves in fire warmd,
> Sterne was their looke like wild amazed steares,
> Staring with hollow eyes, and stiffe upstanding heares. (2.9.13)

The author of the *View of the Present State of Ireland*, moreover, reports of the typical Irish guerrilla warrior: "it is well known he is a flying enemy hiding himself in woods and bogs."[51] "Intemperance," remarks Richard McCabe in a wonderful essay on the way that Spenser's Irish experience suffuses his entire career,

was part of the stock racial profile of the "meare" Irish whose association with Acrasia may be inferred from Ruddymane's indelibly blood-stained hand, an oblique allusion to the Gaelic war cry, noted in the *Vewe*, "the Red Hand Forever, that is the bloddie hande which is Oneles [Oneal's] badge."[52]

The details of Book 2 frequently demand an Irish setting for their full comprehension.

But this does not mean that the discipline endorsed in Book 2 is delegitimated by its complicity in the strategies of colonial domination. In *Renaissance Self-Fashioning*, Stephen Greenblatt has extended the links between Spenser's experience as a colonial administrator and the portrait of temperance in Book 2 into a cogent interpretation of the Bower of Bliss. For Greenblatt, the Bower and its destruction represents the vehement unease of Western Christian culture towards sexual pleasure. Taking off from a passage in Freud's *Civilization and Its Discontents* – "Civilization behaves toward sexuality as a people or a stratum of its population does which has subjected another one to its exploitation" – Greenblatt sees the book's violent conclusion as revealing the covert violence on which Western civilization depends. "The Bower of Bliss," he argues, "must be destroyed not because its gratifications are unreal but because they threaten 'civility' – civilization – which for Spenser is achieved only through renunciation and the constant exercise of power."[53] It is I think significant that Greenblatt's account barely mentions the Castle of Alma, since that baroque presentation of regulated pleasure would complicate his compelling account of the apparently gratuitous destruction of the Bower of Bliss. Where Greenblatt frames his analysis of the Bower of Bliss in terms of an opposition between pleasure and control, Spenser frames his narrative in terms of an opposition between two kinds of pleasure: illicit, immoderate pleasure, which is to be resisted, even eradicated, and the salutary pleasure made possible by control, which is to be enjoyed, even relished. We need to remember that Alma's castle is not a site of ascetic self-denial; Alma's "bounteous banket" is rather "Attempred goodly well for health and *for delight*" (2.11.2; my italics). Gustatory pleasure as well as the more ineffable joys of good health are the goal of its bustling but carefully regulated activity. We need also to remember that it is the forces of Maleger, not the Castle of Alma, which inhabit a strangely disembodied state: "though they bodies seeme, yet substance from them fades" (2.9.15). Temperance involves a defense of the body, not a denial of it.

Part of the difficulty is the way in which Spenser needs his allegory to find external correlatives for the largely internal activities that temperance entails. This produces in the fiction as it comes to us a tension between the project of self-governance and governance of another. The swarm of gnats from the fens of Allan is meant to represent the internal assaults of emotion. As Spenser declares of the siege of Maleger and his troops:

> What warre so cruell, or what siege so sore,
> As that, which strong affections do apply
> Against the fort of reason evermore
> To bring the soule into captivitie:
> Their force is fiercer through infirmitie
> Of the fraile flesh, relenting to their rage,
> And exercise most bitter tyranny
> Upon the parts, brought into their bondage:
> No wretchednesse is like to sinfull vellenage.   (2.11.1)

To conquer such troops is to resist internal usurpation, not to participate in colonial domination. In *The Passions of the Minde*, Thomas Wright notes that "Inordinate passions rise up in a drunkard like a swarme of Bees, buzzing on every side."[54] In the turret of the brain, moreover, Guyon and Arthur enter the chamber of Phantastes, the imagination, and are confronted with a similar swarm of pests:

> And all the chamber filled was with flyes,
> Which buzzed all about, and made such sound,
> That they encombred all mens eares and eyes,
> Like many swarmes of Bees assembled round.   (2.9.51)

"What Spenser demonstrates" in the verbal parallels between this passage and the description of Maleger's troops, Thomas Healy argues,

Spenser's castle of moral health 69

is that uncontrolled phantasy lies close to the destructive savagery which lurks, similarly insubstantial and "dispersed thin" without. The maintenance of the castle is more than a concerted defence of the ordered interior against the disorderly exterior. The interior, too, contains elements which are potentially destructive.[55]

Self-governance in Spenser's world involves the imposition of order on swarms of ideas and emotions. The self is a seething mass of such infestations until properly constructed through the deliberate rigors of temperance. The figures over whom these rigors are allowed to exert control is not a colonized indigenous population but a series of forces already materially contained within the self.

Indeed, when fashioned by these rigors, the body assumes a remarkable aesthetic beauty which the pleasures of the beautiful Bower of Bliss would destroy:

> But in a body, which doth freely yeeld
> His partes to reasons rule obedient,
> And letteth her that ought to scepter weeld,
> All happy peace and goodly government
> Is setled there in sure establishment;
> There Alma like a virgin Queene most bright,
> Doth florish in all beautie excellent.   (2.11.2)

Through a heroic combination of immense moral effort and political consent, the body yields to the rule of reason, and achieves the thorough beauty Spenser describes.

The ideal of self-governance here is articulated in the language of political governance, but this does not make the two projects synonymous. Although the body was frequently deployed to defend hierarchical privilege, as in Agrippa's famous fable of the belly discussed in Chapter 1, the ideal of self-governance could compete with rather than extend political absolutism. I would argue, furthermore, that despite these obvious links between Spenser's own experience as a colonial administrator in Ireland and the assault on Alma, the sense of order that emerges from Book 2 is not a discipline necessarily complicit with colonial suppression, but something very different, potentially even opposite: a discipline intended to inculcate the internal stability that makes possible the subject's liberation from the passions that rage within all. It is not temperance but rather intemperance that Spenser portrays in terms of political violence and unjust subjugation: intemperance involves the physiological equivalent of the political violations of tyranny and usurpation, "When raging passion with fierce tyrannie / Robs reason of her due regalities, / And makes it servant to her basest part" (2.1.57). In his sonnet to Gabriel Harvey, Spenser describes his friend as one who "freely does, of what thee list, entreat / Like a great lord of peerless liberty."[56] This internal freedom from external and internal pressure is exactly what Spenser intends the precise and demanding disciplines of temperance to achieve. As Foucault argues in *The Use of Pleasure*, discipline is not necessarily complicit with political domination: "in classical Greek thought, the 'ascetics' that enabled one to make oneself into an ethical subject was an integral part – down to its very form – of the practice of a virtuous life, which was also the life of a 'free' man in the full, positive and political sense of the word."[57] Freedom emerges within the parameters of discipline rather than being opposed to it.

Greenblatt's account of Guyon's destruction of the Bower of Bliss as an act of colonial violence, then, leaves little room for the positive aspects of the self-regulation Spenser here endorses. Guyon, moreover, is not out to colonize the Bower, but to avenge Mordant's death, and to liberate those trapped there. When considering the role that Ireland might play in the discipline of Book 2, it is worth noting that the teeth in Alma's well-fortified mouth are made of stone "more smooth and fine, / Then Jet or Marble far from Ireland brought" (2.9.24). The very material that guards the castle gates is compared favorably to marble from the country that ostensibly breeds those who attack them.

Guyon destroys "all those pleasant bowres and Pallace brave, . . .with rigour pittilesse" (2.12.83). His act of destruction is comparatively brief, but Spenser is careful to record the extensive nature of the damage to the pleasing landscape he has lovingly described:

> Ne ought their goodly workmanship might save
> Them from the tempest of his wrathfulnesse,
> But that their blisse he turn'd to balefulnesse:
> Their groves he feld, their gardins did deface,
> Their arbers spoyle, their Cabinets suppress,
> Their banket houses burne, their buildings race
> And of the fairest late, now made the fowlest place.   (2.12.83)

It is difficult to see how the "tempest" of his wrath is an appropriate expression of the "temperance" he represents, but that is exactly what Spenser asks of us, even as he reminds us of the "goodly workmanship" that is thereby destroyed. Spenser has even allowed "the secret signes of kindled lust [to] appeare" in Guyon's face, as he pauses from his mission to watch two naked women wrestle in a fountain (2.12.63–69), in order to show the compelling nature of the desires the Bower stirs. Spenser depicts Acrasia's love as one that does not edify but rather liquefies the carefully constructed self, and makes what should be a morally alert being sleep drowsily:

> And oft inclining downe with kisses light,
> For feare of waking him, his lips bedewd,
> And through his humid eyes did sucke his spright,
> Quite molten into lust and pleasure lewd.   (2.12.73)

Acrasia's over-heated love melts the stone from which a self is composed. The castle of the self is swept away in a lava flow of passion, a flow that also accomplishes the separation of body from spirit whose miraculous conjunction is the subject of much of the book. The young man, moreover, has discarded his armor, demonstrating his failure to sustain the fortified moral self the Castle of Alma represents (2.12.80).

After Guyon and the Palmer capture Acrasia in "A subtile net," and destroy the Bower, their final task is the liberation of all those whom Acrasia, like Circe, has transformed into animals. The Palmer tells Guyon that

> These seeming beasts are men indeed,
> Whom this Enchauntresse hath transformed thus,
> Whylome her lovers, which her lusts did feed,
> Now turned into figures hideous
> According to thier mindes like monstruous. (2.12.85)

Jonathan Sawday argues that "Acrasia's sexuality is all mastering, able to transform the rational masculine intellect into a world of beast-like appetite associated with the feminine."[58] Earlier we are told that Acrasia,

> with vaine delightes,
> And idle pleasures in her Bowre of Blisse,
> Does charme her lovers and the feeble sprightes
> Can call out of the bodies of fraile wightes:
> Whom then she does transforme to monstrous hewes,
> And horribly misshapes with ugly sightes,
> Captiv'd eternally in Yron mewes,
> And darksom dens, where Titan his face never shewes. (2.5.27)

Yet the gloss that Ben Jonson provides on these lines in his personal edition of *The Faerie Queene* demonstrates the source of the metamorphic power: "excesse of pleasur enervats the body and exanimates the strongest."[59] The Palmer's suggestion that their beastly appearance is "According to their mindes like monstrous," and Guyon's subsequent commentary – "Sad end (quoth he) of life intemperate" – indicate that it is not so much Acrasia's all-mastering sexuality, as the innate beastliness of humanity at a moment of moral relaxation, that their metamorphoses exemplify.

Indeed, the notorious Grill, the character with whom the book ends, prefers to remain a hog, even after the Palmer has changed them all back into men. He represents essential, unregulated, and unreconstructed humanity, or in Guyon's words,

> the mind of beastly man,
> That hath so soone forgot the excellence
> Of his creation, when he life began,
> That now he chooseth, with vile difference
> To be a beast, and lack intelligence. (2.12.87)

Grill is the negation of the ancestral memory that is read in Alma's turret. He is not so much the victim of Acrasia's powerful magic as of his own forgetting; he is the beast that all are capable of becoming in a moment of moral relaxation. In the myth of the Promethean creation of humanity that Guyon reads – "how first Prometheus did create / A man, of many partes from beasts deryv'd" (2.10.70) – Spenser suggests the immense effort that is required to keep from sliding back into the congenital bestiality Grill embodies. Laurentius describes the internal processes by which the original and essential animality of humans can be unleashed through faulty ethical conduct:

when a man by his malicious will becomming an apostate and revolt, defaceth the ingraven forme of the Deitie, and commeth by the filth of sinne to defile the holy temple of God, when through an unruly appetite, he suffereth himselfe to be carried in such headlong wise after his passions, either of choler, envie, or gluttonie, as then he becommeth more outragious then a lyon, more fierce then a tyger, and more filthie and contemptible then a swine.[60]

Grill is just such a swine, transformed by his failure to control his own passions, and trapped by his wish to remain in this state. His wish to remain a beast represents the willed lack of freedom that for Spenser issues from the indiscriminate following of one's desires.

Richard McCabe links Grill to those English colonists who adopted Irish customs, and cites Sir John Davies on how these colonists "became degenerate and metamorphosed . . . like those who had drunke of Circes Cuppe, and were turned into very Beasts, and yet tooke such pleasure in their beastly manner of life, as they would not returne to their shape of men again."[61] But the fact that the discipline Grill repudiates can be aligned with an ideology we would disavow does not invalidate the larger project of constructing a self through the rigorous exercise of such discipline. "If [a man] give himself to do evill," remarks one of the interlocutors of Bryskett, *A Discourse of Civill Life*,

forsaking the light of reason, he becommeth a bruite beast, and looseth the divine gift of his libertie: for thenceforth doth he work no more freely of himself, but yeeldeth his minde, which ought to be the Lord of our libertie, slave to the two basest parts of the soule, and then reigneth no more the reasonable soule, but the brutish, which maketh him abandon the care of the minde, and onely to attend the pleasures of the body, as brute beasts doe.[62]

Rather than opposing the shackles of self-restraint, liberty and humanity emerge from them. What separates humans from animals in this regime is the capacity for self-control. "Let Grill be Grill," remarks the Palmer in the book's penultimate line, suggesting that what appears to be a magical metamorphosis from a man to a beast is in fact a simple act of predication.

Spenser, then, imagines the self as a fragile and unstable edifice, eternally under construction, and assailed on all sides (including the inside) by insurgent passions. Humanity is the product of this construction, and beastliness the issue of its ruin. In *Hamlet*, the prince proposes a materialist account of human frailty that emphasizes not so much the capacity of the moral agent to fashion himself as it does the shaping of behavior by physiology: "oft it chances in particular men," remarks Hamlet, listening to the carousing at the Danish court,

> That for some vicious mole of nature in them,
> As in their birth, wherein they are not guilty
> (Since nature cannot choose his origin),
> By their o'ergrowth of some complexion
> Oft breaking down the pales and forts of reason . . .   (1.4.23–28)

Hamlet, in contrast, praises Horatio as one of those "whose blood and judgment are so well co-meddled, / That they are not a pipe for Fortune's finger / To sound what stop she please"; he is "not passion's slave" (3.2.69–72). In the next chapter, we will attend to Shakespeare's exploration in the Sonnets of the ways that desire assaults "the pales and forts of reason" which Spenser spends so much time erecting. We will explore the lyric utterances of one who is passion's slave, and pay particular attention to a sonnet which lauds the temperate equanimity that Hamlet admires in Horatio. Although their emphases are different, both Spenser and Shakespeare imagine the self as a fragile construction barely containing the physiological and psychological pressures of desire. Where Shakespeare offers a lyric portrait of the desiring subject's self-destructive affection, Spenser provides an epic blueprint of the constitutive nature of self-discipline. We should remember that Spenser's declared purpose for the entire epic in the letter to Ralegh is "to fashion a gentleman or noble person in virtuous and gentle discipline."[63] Identity is achieved not, as we might imagine, in the discovery of a hidden self buried deep beneath the encrustations and inauthenticities of civility; rather, it is achieved through discipline, through the forceful imposition of rational order on energies that tend naturally to the twin poles of tyranny and anarchy. The temperance Spenser portrays throughout the book is not "The dull shore of lazy temperance" mocked by Lord Rochester ("The Disabled Debauchee"), but something actively opposed to this: a dynamic, even frantic maintenance of order in the face of perpetual insurrection. If Spenser's portrait of the temperate subject has more traffic with the conduct of the colon than with the suppressions of colonialism, and finds the entrails to be a more significant locus of identity than the genitals, confronting such a seemingly alien formation of the human subject can perhaps remind us of the implicit strangeness of our own models of self.

3 The matter of inwardness: Shakespeare's Sonnets

> Soul is only a word for something about the body.
>
> Friedrich Nietzsche[1]

In *The Book Named The Governor*, Sir Thomas Elyot employs an image strikingly like that used by Spenser to delineate the materials of the well-tempered self. For Elyot, the attraction of comparing the self to stony materials is their capacity to depict the virtue of constancy that is at the center of Shakespeare's Sonnet 94, "They that have powre to hurt, and will doe none":

> In building of a fortress or other honourable mansion, it ought to be well considered that the cement wherewith the stones be laid be firm and well binding. For if it be brokle [fragile] and will moulder away with every shower of rain, the building may not continue, but the stones, being not surely couched and mortared, falleth away one after another, and finally the whole house is defaced, and falleth in ruin. Semblably, that man which in childhood is brought up in sundry virtues, if either by nature, or else by custom, he be not induced to be alway constant and stable so that he move not for any affection, grief, or displeasure, all his virtues will shortly decay, and, in the estimation of men, be but as a shadow, and be soon forgotten.[2]

Both Spenser and Elyot envision the self as an edifice needing not only meticulous care in construction but also continual vigilance in maintenance. Strikingly, the stability of the constructed self, as well as its social reputation, depends on its capacity to be unmoved by "any affection, grief, or displeasure." In Spenser's portrait of temperance, the moment of greatest dissonance occurs when the exemplar of this virtue is moved by anger to an act of destruction. In Shakespeare's depiction of the vagaries of lyric desire, by contrast, dissonance will emerge from Shakespeare's praise of those with the capacity to remain "as stone, / Unmooved, could" (Sonnet 94, lines 3–4).

In this chapter, I will attempt to read Sonnet 94 against the pathologies of desire explored in the other sonnets. I will argue that this poem has been particularly troubling for twentieth-century criticism because it idealizes a kind of imperturbable self-containment like that articulated by Elyot, an unmoved stability which seems oppressively chilly if not deeply hypocritical to twentieth-century sensibilities. The poem is most frequently read as an ironic epitome of pathological repression rather than a praise of self-mastery. When viewed against the endorsement of self-control and the suspicion of unregulated desire that epitomizes some early modern accounts of the self – accounts that locate pathology not in suppressing desire but in surrendering to it – the poem's vexations can be understood as part of a larger cultural confrontation between the urgent demands of the body's various appetites and the classical ideal of absolute self-control. This confrontation restages the collision between the Christian validation of properly directed emotion and the classical suspicion of all emotion that we witnessed in Spenser's portrait of the temperate self in Book 2 of *The Faerie Queene*. Close attention to this atypical yet pivotal sonnet allows us to view the larger collection not just as remarkable articulations of a desiring subject but also as impressive discussions of the textured subjectivity that can emerge from the fastidious regulation of desire.

Amid the contemporary appetite for discovering in the Renaissance prefigurations of modernity, Shakespeare has proven a particularly tempting site. Although the plays, and *Hamlet* in particular, have provided the primary evidence, the Sonnets have played a part in this conversation.[3] In this chapter I intend not to forward my own set of claims for the signal modernity of the Shakespearean subject but rather to highlight some of the considerable differences and surprising similarities that exist between the early modern language of interiority and our own, and to show some of the interpretive dissonance that has been generated by our inability to apprehend these differences and to clarify these similarities. I particularly want to call attention to the profound medical and physiological underpinnings of Shakespeare's acute vocabulary of psychological inwardness. Shakespeare turns so frequently to physiological terminology because the job of the doctor, like that of the playwright and poet, is to intuit inner reality via external demeanor. Lyric poet and medical doctor, then, are both students of inwardness. The Renaissance cult of melancholy – marked by a plethora of books defining, diagnosing, and curing this phenomenon – attests to the widespread search for physiological explanations and treatments for an extensive psychological phenomenon.[4] Perhaps significantly, the Shakespearean play that is most frequently cited in arguments seeking a moment in which to inaugurate "modern subjectivity" – *Hamlet* – is itself drenched with this vocabulary. The Sonnets, by contrast, invoke this vocabulary only glancingly, but nevertheless they ask its principles of regulation to underpin their ideal of the well-balanced self, and to underscore their portrait of desire as a disease that threatens the physical and mental health of this self.

The form of the sonnet itself seems to contain something of the contrary forces between passion and reason, between order and desire, with which Sonnet 94 vibrates. A deliberately taut and rigid structure, the sonnet demands the formal confinement of a vocabulary of extravagant longing. Where Spenser's stanzas may go on and on, a Shakespearean sonnet (with one exception) concludes in fourteen lines, carefully arranged into three quatrains and a concluding couplet. In *The Art of Shakespeare's Sonnets*, Helen Vendler has recently demonstrated with great force the various formal resources of the Shakespearean sonnet, focusing in particular on the quatrain as a unit of poetic meaning. Shakespeare, argues Vendler, learned in the Sonnets "to find strategies to enact feeling in form, feelings in forms, multiplying both to a superlative degree through 154 poems."[5] I would agree, and hope in the following chapter to exacerbate the tension between feeling and form by linking it to larger cultural tensions between Stoic apathy and Christian affect. I hope, moreover, to render visible the physiological underpinnings of the parameters of psychological depth – the very depth that has led subsequent readers to value these formal utterances as the source of something uniquely modern.

Two poems that do make explicit reference to the humoral vocabulary of Renaissance medicine are Sonnets 44 and 45. These poems exploit the conventional linkage between the four elements (earth, air, fire, and water) and the four humors (melancholy, blood, choler, and phlegm) that is mapped out in the illustration from Walkington's *Optick Glasse of Humors*. They do so not just to explore the relationship between humanity and its environment but also to confront rather playfully an issue that animates and haunts the Sonnets: the status of desire when distance separates one from the object of desire. The speaker of Sonnet 44 wishes that "the dull substance of my flesh were thought" so that when he thought of his beloved he would be with him.[6] Separated physically from his beloved by the elements of "earth and water," the speaker is left in despair. Although "nimble thought can jumpe both sea and land," thought is not flesh. The speaker of Sonnet 45 sends his "thought" and his "desire," which he likens to the other two elements of "slight ayre, and purging fire," to be with the beloved, only to discover that "My life, being made of foure [elements], with two alone / Sinkes downe to death, oppresst with melancholie." Together, the two poems provide a playfully physiological explanation for the sadness that afflicts one when separated from the object of desire. Stephen Booth's note to this sonnet suggests that "Shakespeare's primary attention is to the tenor of his statements not to their vehicle – the technical details of traditional physics and medicine." He bases this claim on the perception of medical inaccuracy, since earth and water would produce not melancholy but the far less appropriate phlegm (*Shakespeare's Sonnets*,

p. 207). But as the chart from Walkington (Figure 1) demonstrates, earth could be aligned with melancholy alone, making the poem's diagnosis accurate within the noted inconsistencies of Galenic medicine. Flesh is not thought, then, but thought is afflicted by the material claims of the flesh.

A more solemn model of body–soul relations emerges in Sonnet 146 ("Poore soule the center of my sinfull earth"), but a similar conceptual pattern linking physiology and psychology emerges. Rather than wishing that his flesh were thought so that he could possess the remote object of his ardent desire, the speaker of 146 aggravates the tension between body and soul, finding ethical comfort in the distance between flesh and thought that the speaker of 44 wished to close. Sonnet 146 deploys a conventional image to demonstrate the eternal tension between the demands of the body and the aspirations of the soul that is dictated by classical and Christian ethics, and that underpins the imperturbability idealized in Sonnet 94.[7] In 146, the soul is imagined as "the center of my sinfull earth," a comparatively impotent monarch surrounded by "these rebbell powres that thee array." This particular image of the self as a fortress under siege, moreover, familiar from the Castle of Alma in Book 2 of Spenser's *Faerie Queene* and its various medieval precedents, deliberately confuses inward urging and external temptation in order to argue a politically contestatory model of body–soul relations. (It is, I think, significant that a poem filled with such commonplace notions includes one of the unresolvable textual cruces of the sequence, since the repetition of the phrase "my sinfull earth" at the beginning of line 2 itself indicates a compositor's unthinking repetition of familiar material. Suggestions for the elided phrase include "Pressed by," "Lord of," "Thrall to," and "Feeding."[8]) The poem resolves the respective claims of body and spirit by reversing typical siege tactics, urging the besieged soul to starve the body in order to banquet itself:

> Then soule live thou upon thy servants losse,
> And let that pine to aggravat thy store;
> Buy tearmes divine in selling houres of drosse:
> Within be fed, without be rich no more. (lines 9–12)

Outward fasting is inward feasting.[9] This moralized anorexia, familiar from medieval mystical writings as well as early modern health manuals, is designed to re-establish a hierarchy between body and soul that the urgent, quotidian hungers of the flesh would deny. As Nicholas Culpepper observes in the delightfully titled *Health for the Rich and Poor, by Diet, without Physick*, to indulge in "ill Diet" is "to make thy soul a slave to the Flesh, a Servant to his Vassal." In *The Passions of the Minde*, Thomas Wright observes: "he that pampereth his body, feedeth his enemie, and hee that will feed it with dainties, cannot but find it rebellious.... And he that will mortifie his passions, and let his body flow with delicates, doth like him which will extinguish fire by adding more fewell."[10] The sonnet's concluding couplet – "So shalt thou feed on death, that feeds on men, / And death once dead, ther's no more dying then" – renders even the mundane mystery of consumption, by which life is sustained by feeding on dead matter, an extension of this restored hierarchy, and a premonition of the end of time. In a sense, we feed on death at every meal.

But in the subsequent sonnet, 147, this comparatively simple opposition between the hungers of the body and the aspirations of the soul receives nightmarish complication. Rather than starving the body to feed the soul, the speaker behaves like the misguided figure who attempts to "extinguish fire by adding more fewell." The speaker of 147 articulates a desire which is evinced in its yearning for what at once precipitates and prolongs the illness:

> My love is as a feaver longing still,
> For that which longer nurseth the disease,
> Feeding on that which doth preserve the ill,
> Th'uncertaine sicklie appetite to please:
> My reason the Phisition to my love,
> Angry that his prescriptions are not kept
> Hath left me, and I desperate now approove,
> Desire is death, which Phisick did except.
> Past cure I am, now Reason is past care,
> And frantic madde with ever-more unrest,
> My thought and my discourse as mad men's are,
> At random from the truth vainely exprest.   (lines 1–12)

The common root of "longing" and "longer" underscores the larger conceptual link between desire and the extenuation of illness that succumbing to desire breeds, a linkage stated with chilling simplicity: "Desire is death" (line 8). The medical terminology that underpins so many of Shakespeare's portraits of psychological inwardness here restructures the dualism that comprised the subject of the previous sonnet, but now the opposition is not between body and soul but rather between reason and desire. The desiring self is allegorized as a patient who refuses to follow the prescriptions of his frustrated physician, reason. The poem's stunning imagery of a divided self aligns desire, illness, and madness.

"If we are to understand Shakespeare," remarks Lily B. Campbell, "we must see fever as caused by the distemperature of the heart and hence as being both the potential cause and the possible result of passion." Although Campbell refers here to the drama, the insight holds true for the lyric Shakespeare as well. In *The Passions of the Minde*, Wright gives a fuller description of this psychobiological phenomenon: "When we are moved with a vehement passion, our soules are then, as it were infected with a pestilent ague, wch both hindereth the sight of our eies, and the tast of our tongues, that is, corrupteth the judgement, and perverteth the will."[11] Rather than following a regimen which might moderate if not cure this madness – a regimen which would likely include a kind of therapeutic fasting like that moralized in Sonnet 146 – the speaker of Sonnet 147 can only describe the maddeningly divided sensibility that his unregulated desire produces: "For I have sworne thee faire, and thought thee bright, / Who art as black as hell, as dark as night."[12] He is like the speaker of the final two sonnets (153 and 154), poems which employ the *deus ex machina* of the Anacreontic Cupid and the fact of venereal disease to depict the baffling and incurable phenomenon of amorous passion. The speaker of these poems is "sick," "a sad distemperd guest," and seeks a "sovereign cure" for "love's fire" in the "seething bath" which issued from the immersion of Cupid's brand in "a could vallie-fountaine." Shakespeare here plays with the idea that venereal disease, a malady of love often likened to fire (as in Sonnet 144), was thought to be ameliorated if not eradicated by baths, a kind of purge through the skin rather than the alimentary canal. The speaker of these sonnets, though, learns only that "Love's fire heates water, water cooles not love."[13] Desire is an infection which is spread by the very act of trying to treat it. At the bitter conclusion of Shakespeare's most cynical play, *Troilus and Cressida*, Pandarus tells the audience he will "sweat and seek about for eases, / And at that time bequeath you my diseases" (5.10.556–57). The speaker of the final sonnets likewise discovers bitterly that any ostensible remedy for erotic desire only provides an occasion for further contagion.

In Sonnet 151, a similar dualism is explored, as the depth and force of the speaker's desire leads him to "betray / My nobler part to my grose bodies treason." In this sonnet, that is, the "rebell powres" of the body have revolted successfully. In response, the soul offers the body a concession, telling him that "he may / Triumph in love." The flesh responds to this victory with lofty exaltation; "proud of this pride," it is ready to "stand in [the] affaires" of the beloved or to "fall by thy side." But in Sonnet 147, not even such brief phallic victories are allowed the speaker; rather, abandoned by reason, his "Phisition," for not keeping his "prescriptions," the speaker is "Past cure ... And frantick madde." His situation resembles that of the insane Lady Macbeth. When Macbeth frantically demands of the attending doctor

> Canst thou not minister to a mind diseas'd?
> Pluck from the memory a rooted sorrow,
> Raze out the written troubles of the brain,
> And with some sweet oblivious antidote
> Cleanse the stuff'd bosom of that perilous stuff
> Which weighs upon the heart?

– the doctor can only respond: "Therein the patient / Must minister to himself" (*Macbeth* 5.3.40–45).[14] Where the mad speaker of Sonnet 147 refuses to abide by the prescriptions of his physician/reason, Lady Macbeth is abandoned by her physician to a regime of self-ministration.

This account of erotic desire as an incurable disease provides a marked contrast to the model developed in Spenser's *Amoretti*. In Spenser's sequence, the speaker is certainly stirred up by his desire, but the overall effect is to be calmed rather than overheated to the point of madness by his beloved. Where the Sonnets descry in love the physiology of madness, the *Amoretti* articulate the experience of love as a "most goodly temperature." In Sonnet 8, for example, the speaker denies the Anacreontic origin of his desire, asserting that

> Thrugh your bright beams doth not the blinded guest
> shoot out his darts to base affections wound:
> but Angels come to lead fraile mindes to rest
> in chast desires on heavenly beauty bound. (lines 5–8)

Rather than the lover producing the kind of tortured, perjured inwardness that Shakespeare identifies, Spenser's speaker tells his lover that

> You frame my thoughts and fashion me within,
> you stop my toung, and teach my hart to speake,
> you calme the storme that passion did begin,
> strong thrugh you cause, but by your vertue weak. (lines 9–12)

Spenser's beloved calms the storms of passion that Shakespeare's dark lady causes. The dark lady poems, in contrast, seem to be composed by one who has succumbed to Acrasia's seductions but who, unlike Grill, knows with tortuous precision just how far he has descended the moral chain of being.

Behind the portrait of love's decidedly unhealthy diet in Sonnet 147 – "Feeding on that which doth preserve the ill" – is a larger meditation in the Sonnets on nourishment, appetite, and identity. This is in part a response to Galenic physiology, which, as we have seen, imagines the self as an inherently porous, necessarily unstable entity, in continual need of nourishment and purgation. "The matter wherof man is compounded," observes Juan Huarte,

> prooveth a thing so alterable, and so subject to corruption, that the instant when he beginneth to be shaped, he likewise beginneth to be untwined, and to alter, and therin can find no remedy.... For it was said, so soon as we are born, we faile to be.

Constancy assumes immense moral and therapeutic power when physiological instability is presumed to be the norm. Yet as Huarte continues, Galenic medicine also makes available strategies for manipulating this fungible humoral economy to the benefit of the well-regulated individual through the necessary processes of assimilation and excretion:

> Wherthrough nature provided, that in mans body, there should be 4 natural faculties, attractive, retentive, concoctive, & expulsive. The which concocting & altering the aliments which we eate, returne to repaire the substance that was lost, ech succeeding in his place.[15]

Properly managed, diet and excretion ameliorate the inherent instability of mortal existence.

In the Sonnets, though, Shakespeare develops the links between the corollary appetites for food and love not so much to provide strategies for rendering both salutary as to explore the relevance of the necessary periodicity of hunger to the ebb and flow of erotic desire. In Sonnet 56, for example, the speaker hopes that an apparently sated love will "renew thy force," so that it will be more like gastronomic "apetite, / Which but too daie by feeding is allaied, / To morrow sharpned in his former might." He is concerned that erotic "fulnesse" might "kill / The spirit of Love, with a perpetual dulnesse" rather than provide a moment of temporary satiation.

Throughout his corpus, Shakespeare investigates the nexus at which desire is satiated, and migrates into its opposite, disgust. In *Twelfth Night*, a play whose opening line asks "If music be the food of love," Orsino suggests that women's "love may be called appetite, / No motion of the liver, but the palate, / That suffer surfeit, cloyment, and revolt" (2.4.96–98). The speaker of Sonnet 75 articulates the bulimic patterns of his erotic life, telling the beloved that he is "to my thoughts as food to life":

> Some-time all ful with feasting on your sight,
> And by and by cleane starved for a looke,
> Possessing or pursuing no delight
> Save what is had, or must from you be tooke.
>   Thus do I pine and surfet day by day,
>   Or gluttoning on all, or all away.   (lines 9–14)

In *Venus and Adonis*, Adonis distinguishes love from lust precisely by recourse to its inability to experience such gluttonous satiation, even temporarily: "Love surfeits not, Lust like a glutton dies" (line 803). Shakespeare's Cleopatra, on the other hand, is famously distinguished from "other women" who "cloy / The appetites they feed" by "mak[ing] hungry / Where most she satisfies" (*Antony and Cleopatra*, 2.2.239).

The speaker of Sonnet 118 juxtaposes contemporaneous culinary practice with contemporaneous medical theory in order to delineate a different strategy for sustaining desire in the face of satiation:

> Like as to make our appetites more keene
> With eager compounds we our pallat urge,
> As to prevent our malladies unseene,
> We sicken to shun sicknesse when we purge.   (lines 1–4)

He links the Renaissance fashion (largely imported from Italy) for bitter salads as appetizers to the paradox inherent in the central therapeutic procedure of Renaissance medicine: inducing a symptom of illness – vomiting – in order to rid a patient of the excess humors that would make him or her truly sick. Eating something bitter to be hungry is like vomiting one's way to health; the poem explores the uneasy nexus of sickness and health that such practices assume. In a brilliantly ambiguous phrase, the speaker describes himself as "full of your nere cloying sweetnesse"; here "nere" means both "never" and "near," either denying the possibility of satiation or confessing it, because in this regime both produce the death of desire.[16] In response, the speaker turns to "bitter sawces" to whet his palate. Declaring himself "sicke of wel-fare" – that is, at once tired of, and ill because of, a particularly unsatisfying form of health – the speaker makes himself "diseas'd ere that there was true needing." The poem's exploration of the parallel perversions of medical and dietary therapy culminates in the suggestion that "a healthfull state," rephrased as the oxymoronic "rancke of goodnesse," would "by ill be cured." In the poem's concluding lines, the speaker only discovers that "Drugs poyson him that so fell sicke of you," that what he imagined as inducing a cure of the excess that precipitates disease is functioning in fact as an agent of illness. Dissolving into oxymorons that repeat the paradoxes about appetite with which it began – sickness is health, and cures are poisons – the poem deconstructs the critical difference between health and illness. In doing so, it opens a space for the damning paradoxes of the dark lady poems.

In Sonnet 129, Shakespeare explores with clinical precision and pathological disgust the madness pervading the available physiology of sexual desire and corporeal satisfaction. Where most erotic poetry since Petrarch had been premised on the unavailability of the love object, Shakespeare in Sonnet 129 writes about exactly what happens when you get what you say you want, and demonstrates that it is not a consummation devoutly to be wished, but rather a nightmare that cannot be avoided. In this poem, the imagined physiology of sexual intercourse underpins a visceral disgust with the entire enterprise of corporeal hunger and physical satiation:

>   Th' expence of Spirit in a waste of shame
>   Is lust in action, and till action, lust
>   Is perjurd, murdrous, blouddy full of blame,
>   Savage, extreame, rude, cruell, not to trust,
>   Injoyd no sooner but dispised straight
>   Past reason hunted, and no sooner had
>   Past reason hated as a swollowed bayt,
>   On purpose layd to make the taker mad;
>   Made in pursut and in possession so,
>   Had, having, and in quest, to have extreame,
>   A blisse in proofe and proud and very wo,
>   Before, a joy proposd behind a dreame.
>   All this the world well knowes yet none knowes well,
>   To shun the heaven that leads men to this hell.

The fact that in the act of orgasm a male was thought to expend his vital spirit and so to shorten his life becomes for Shakespeare a representation of the larger loss of self that unregulated desire involves. The often-noticed pun on "waste" and "waist" (buttressed by "shame," the English for *pudendum*, the Latin word for the genitals, meaning "the shameful parts") demonstrates the unproductive economy of the self that the poem finds essential to the act of sex. Erotic activity in the vicinity of the waist is a waste, an excremental expenditure of self that depletes rather than replenishes health. It is as if Port Esquiline, the canal for waste removal in the Castle of Alma, were conflated with the desires located in the genitals Spenser does not mention. Where the early sonnets encourage the young man to give himself away as a strategy of self-preservation via reproduction – "To give away your selfe, keeps your selfe still" (Sonnet 16) – this poem locates the self in an economy whereby it desires uncontrollably just what enfeebles and deranges it. Where Sonnet 1 accuses the young man of "mak[ing] waste in niggarding," Sonnet 129 depicts a sexual economy in which getting is spending, laying waste to our powers. Erotic attraction here is not an avenue to the divine, as it had been for Petrarch, but rather an alley to the hell of self-betrayal, a "swollowed bayt" that makes "the taker" insane, both in pursuit and in possession. Erotic desire is at once "proud" (the reading of the Quarto in line 11), evidence of the fleshly "pride" of erection explored in Sonnet 151, and "A bliss in proof, and proved, a very woe" (line 11; the reading of most modern editors), a testimony to the ephemeral natural of its pleasures. Like the unhealthy diet in Sonnet 147 – "Feeding on that which doth preserve the ill" – sexual appetite is imagined in alimentary terms. As Stephen Booth astutely observes, the poem's headlong meter and distorted syntax mimic the compulsion the poem records.[17]

It is amid such portraits of the deeply physiological and psychological dangers of desire that Sonnet 94 must be read. I want to argue that this poem, probably the most discussed of the Sonnets in the twentieth century, vexes us in large part because we unintentionally vex it with an anachronistic model of self and desire. We fail, that is, to see the premium that Shakespeare's own articulations of desire place on self-control, as well as the medical and moral culture from which they derive. In his compelling interpretation of the poem, Stephen Booth asserts that "throughout the poem the reader has to cope with conflicting reactions, impressions and systems of coherence."[18] I do not want to deny that there is conflict in the poem, but I do want to show that our sense of the occasion and depth of conflict is altered by the very different predispositions about self that we unintentionally import into the poem. The poem's urgent endorsement of cool stability can only be understood against the unstable, overheated self, susceptible to the insanities of insubordinate desire, that is depicted in the other sonnets, and that is a product of the period's medical, theological, and philosophical inheritance. Under this dispensation, modes of constraint we construe as unhealthy repression are coveted as acts of self-government necessary for the maintenance of self and the protection of others. In reading Sonnet 94, we need to remember the historicity of our own psychological theories, theories the poem predates and inadvertently challenges.

Like "Th'expence of spirit," "They that have powre" posits a general case rather than the particular desires of a yearning individual. It is fitting that this poem dedicated to the importance of being inscrutable is itself a critical conundrum. A common critical strategy has been to invest the general with a particular narrative meaning. Conceding that Sonnet 94 "has proved obscure to commentators," John Crowe Ransom, for example, argues that the poem "is clear if taken in context, as an imaginary argument against the friend's relation with the woman, or with any woman."[19] But what has most troubled contemporary readers of Sonnet 94 is not the imagined narrative situation of the poem's general sentiments but rather the apparent disparity between the emotional coldness of the figures being praised and the divine reward they are said to merit:

> They that have powre to hurt, and will doe none,
> That doe not do the thing, they most do showe,
> Who moving others, are themselves as stone,
> Unmooved, could, and to temptation slow:
> They rightly do inherit heaven's graces,
> And husband nature's ritches from expence. (lines 1–6)

It has proven particularly difficult for modern readers to see how being unmoved can be imagined as an avenue to heaven.[20] Critics of the poem sometimes concede that it is good to be "to temptation slow," but not to be "as stone, / Unmooved, could." Edward Hubler, for example, reads the entire octave as "ironic," and announces that "It is preposterous on the face of things to proclaim as the inheritors of heaven's graces those who are 'as stone.'" William Empson's brilliant reading similarly refers dismissively to those the poem praises as "the cold people."[21] Empson intriguingly compares the poem's ideal of emotional aloofness to Angelo in *Measure for Measure*, a man, in Lucio's apt phrase,

> whose blood
> Is very snow-broth; one who never feels
> The wanton stings and motions of the sense. (1.4.57–60)

But Angelo's problem is not that he is unmoved, but that he is moved beyond his control. Angelo is not a study in repression but in failed suppression. In the course of the play he becomes one of those who has power to hurt and will do so. Being "cold" and "as stone" is a state to be preferred to the seething instability articulated in "My love is as a fever," and dramatized in Angelo's cruel abuse of power in the effort to satisfy a desire he fails abysmally to harness.

Booth supplies an apt paraphrase of the radically inconsistent positions the poem seems simultaneously to endorse: "Unmoved people who are cold as stone are unfeeling and unadmirable. Unmoved people who are slow to temptation are steadfast and admirable."[22] The disparate responses the poem fosters restage one of the central philosophical struggles of Renaissance culture, between the eradication of emotion that constitutes the Stoic ideal of *apatheia* and the proper direction of emotion that comprises Christian devotion.[23] Yet as Katharine Maus observes, the ethical goals of the Roman moralists often were in harmony with those of Christian devotion:

> The benefits of their rationality – tranquillity, security, joyfulness, harmony with God – as well as certain side-effects, like the moderation of sensual desire, resemble those described by Augustine as the benefits of the Christian faith. And neither camp gives favorable publicity to vices like gluttony, lust, anger, envy, and avarice. But the Roman moralist and the Augustinian Christian employ radically different strategies both to obtain these spiritual benefits and to avoid these spiritual pitfalls.[24]

J. H. Salmon describes the popular *Constancy* (1584) of Justus Lipsius, one of the founding texts of Renaissance Neostoicism, as "a system of practical ethics that adapted Stoic assumptions to an undogmatic Christianity." Dedicated to the virtue of being unmoved in a sinful world, *Constancy* offered both solace and survival tactics amid political flux.[25] Yet the adaptation of classical ideals to Renaissance culture was not always so seamless. As Lily B. Campbell remarks, "the Stoic attitude toward passion, that of complete rejection, met an objection in Christian teaching; it was pointed out that the passions could not be evil in themselves since the Scriptures attributed certain passions to Christ and to God himself."[26] In *A Treatise of the Passions and Faculties of the Soule of Man*, Edward Reynolds attacks the Stoic ideal

> which maketh Passion in general to be ... a Sicknesse and Perturbation, and would therefore reduce the Mind to a senselesse Apathie, condemning all Life of Passions, as Waves, which serve onely to tosse and trouble Reason. An Opinion, which, while it goeth about to give unto Man an absolute government over himselfe, Leaveth scarce any thing in him which he may command and governe ...
>
> There is more honour in the having Affections subdued, than in having none at all ... And therefore our Saviour himselfe sometimes loved, sometimes rejoyced, sometimes wept, sometimes desired, sometimes mourned and grieved.[27]

Although occasionally held in nervous suspension by Justus Lipsius and other Christian Neostoics, the Stoic emphasis on self-sufficiency and stasis pulled repeatedly against a Christian emphasis on dependence and affect. Sonnet 94 is poised uneasily on the precarious cusp that Christian Neostoicism aimed to inhabit, idealizing the cool self-control of classical Stoicism as a behavior appropriate to the Christian heaven.

By describing the ideal of constancy in terms of lifeless stone, Shakespeare knowingly deploys conventional anti-Stoic terminology. In the first edition of the *Basilikon Doron*, for example, the future King James I decried "that Stoic insensible stupidity that proud inconstant Lipsius persuadeth in his *Constantia*." In *Nosce Teipsum* Sir John Davies says of the passions: "Yet were these natural affections good; / (For they which want them blocks or divels be)."[28] Gabriel Powel, a Puritan, similarly attacked "that blockish conceit that would have men to be without affection, howbeit of late it hath been newly furbished by certain upstart Stoics."[29] Shakespeare invokes such denigrating terminology not to render the poem's larger claims for self-control ironic but rather to remind us of the liabilities of sustaining the ethical stability the poem demands.

We need to remember, moreover, that the imagery of stone possesses in other contexts a variety of positive connotations that may be as present as the negative ones modern critics tend to emphasize. The stone of Sonnet 94 is perhaps composed of the same material as that with which one of the virtuous characters in *The Faerie Queene*, Book 2, is rewarded. As we saw in the last chapter, the nymph is transformed into a stony fountain in order to preserve her virginity from Dan Faunus, who "Inflamed was to follow beauties chace"; she represents the particular kind of unmoved, monumental virtue that Sonnet 94 praises (2.2.7). As a reward and a protection from violation, Diana "Transformd her to a stone from stedfast virgins state" (2.2.8); the material correlative of the steadfastness she represents is stone. Read against the volcanic instability of unregulated desire articulated in "My love is as a fever" and exposed in the Bower of Bliss, the stony dispassion of Sonnet 94 assumes a profoundly positive valence. Moreover, amid the very religious discourses the poem repeatedly invokes, rock functions as a site of stability desired fervently by the tortuously erratic speaker of the Davidic Psalms. God has traditionally been defined as the unmoved mover, one who "moving others" is nevertheless "unmoved." In Matthew 16.18 – "thou art Peter, and upon this rocke I will buylde my Church" (AV) – Christ chooses a similar stability on which to found his church, punning in the process on the derivation of Peter from the Greek *petros*, rock. Perhaps the improbable bridge the poem asserts linking dispassionate demeanor to heavenly grace is composed of rocks noted more for their constancy than their coldness.

Matthew 16.18 was of course a central verse for Catholics, legitimating their claim to be the inheritors of Christ's true church. Richard Wilson and others have recently made convincing cases for longstanding links between Shakespeare and the Catholic nobility. Wilson has even argued that the characteristic self-effacement of Shakespearean drama may have emerged in part from the experience of strategic self-effacement required for survival amid a prosecuted religious minority.[30] It is possible that Sonnet 94's emphasis on the importance of maintaining control of one's facial expressions may derive from a similar imperative. Survival amid a persecuted religious minority would demand just the kind of strategic hypocrisy the poem advises.

Sonnet 94 also absorbs the tensions between two competing models of masculinity, a more psychological one which emphasizes dispassionate self-control, and a more physiological one which emphasizes the greater natural heat of men. Although heat was in this latter discourse frequently correlated with masculine vigor, it was not an unequivocal good, and always part of a network of contested relational concepts whose ideal involves balance and temperance, not instability and extremity.[31] As we saw in the last chapter, Spenser's Pyrochles exemplifies unbridled passion as a fire that burns uncontrollably.[32] In such a representational framework, the coldness Sonnet 94 praises could possess positive physiological and ethical significance, since it indicates that the individual has not allowed its agitated passions to overwhelm it. In *The Examination of Men's Wits*, a popular guide to the strategic uses of humoral psychology, Juan Huarte outlines the contrary opinions on the relative merits of cold and hot, playing Galen off against Aristotle:

Galen sayd, Coldnesse is apparantly noysome to all the offices of the soule; as if he should say, Cold is the ruine of all the operations of the soule, only it serves in the body to temper the naturall heat, and to procure that it burne not over-much: and yet Aristotle is of a contrary opinion... that that blood carrieth most forcible efficacie, which is thickest and hottest, but the coldest & thinnest hath a more accomplished force to perceive and understand; as if he would say, the thicke and hot blood makes great bodily forces, but the pure and cold is cause that man possesseth great understanding... such as are very hot brained [argues Aristotle], cannot discourse nor philosophise, but are giddie headed, and not setled in any one opinion.[33]

Thomas Wright similarly argues that the rashness of male youths is a direct result of their greater natural heat: "Young mens incontinency, bouldnesse, and confidence proceedeth of heat which aboundeth in them, and those, whose complexions are hottest, are most subject to these affections."[34] Laurentius argues in turn that bodies need cool organs in order to counter the heat of passion with cold reason and so to achieve the moral and physiological homeostasis that defines health:

The temperature of the braine must be cold, thereby to temper the spirits of sence and motion, to resist their aptnes to be wasted and spent, and to keep that this

88   Bodies and selves in early modern England

noble member (which is commonly imployed about so many worthie actions) should not set it selfe on fire, and make our discourses and talke rash and headie, and our motions out of order, as it befalleth them which are frenticke.[35]

The pun on "headie" underscores the crucial linkage between the physiological properties of an organ and the psychological conduct of the organism. The intrinsic coolness of the brain at once refrigerates a system whose natural heat threatens spontaneous combustion and restrains the forces of insurrection and entropy – themselves imagined as heat – which urge the subject to the wasteful expenditure that haunts the Sonnets.

Huarte also explains psychological instability by recourse to the humoral temperature of an individual: "the cause why a man is unstable, and changeth opinion at every moment, is for that he hath a hote braine: and contrariewise, his being stable and firme, springs from the coldnesse of his braine."[36] Ethical conduct, moreover, influences (and is in turn affected by) humoral physiology. "When the understanding overruleth," continues Huarte, "it ordinarily inclineth a man to vertue, because this power is founded on cold and drie: From which two qualities, bud many vertues, as are Continencie, Humilitie, Temperance, and from heat the contrarie" (p. 143). For Huarte, the pernicious moral effect of physiological heat on the brain offers the clearest refutation of the Platonic notion of the immaterial soul:

Plato held it for matter verie certain, that the reasonable soule is a substance bodilesse, and spirituall . . . yet for all this, Galen could never bring within his conceit, that it was true, but held it alwaies doubtfull, seeing a wise man through the heat of his braine, to dote, and by applying cold medicines unto him, he commeth to his wits againe.[37]

Far from indicating an inhuman dispassion, the coldness the sonnet counsels represents the victory of unruffled reason over insurrectionary desire.

Where the speaker of Sonnet 147 is "frantick madde with ever-more unrest," the speaker of 94 articulates a mode of conduct intended to apply the "cold medicines" prescribed by Huarte to the congenital madness and instability of the body. As is clear from the fact that our current word for mental health – sanity – is derived from the Latin term for corporeal vigor – *sanitas* – physical fitness and psychological stability are in this earlier medical regime two different sides of the same coin. In *The Anatomy of Melancholy*, Robert Burton contrasts the elite few who achieve successful self-governance – those who have power to hurt and will do none – with those many who fail to bridle their desires:

Some few discreet men there are, that can governe themselves, and curb in these inordinate Affections, by Religion, Philosophy, and such divine Precepts of meekenesse, patience, and the like: but most part for want of governement, out of indiscretion, ignorance, they suffer themselves wholy to be led by sense; and are so farre from repressing rebellious inclinations, ... they follow on, wheresoever their unbridled Affections will transport them, and doe more out of custome, selfe-will, then out of Reason.[38]

The result of this failure to allow reason to lead the passions is a vision of the self completely out of control, like that envisioned in Sonnet 129. Romans 7.15 ("For that which I do, I allow not: for what I would, that do I not, but what I hate, that doe I"; AV) underpins a portrait of the self shredded by the contrary vectors of its ethical knowledge and its desires:

this stubborne will of ours perverts judgement, which sees and knowes what should and ought to be done, and yet will not doe it. *Mancipia gulae*, slaves to their severall lusts, and appetite, they precipitate and plunge themselves into a Labyrinth of cares, blinded with lust, blinded with ambition . . . giving way to these violent passions of feare, griefe, shame, revenge, hatred, malice, &c. They are torne in peeces, as *Actaeon* was with his dogges.

Giving way to one's various passions is a loss of power over the self, a surrender of sovereignty to a vastly inferior jurisdiction. Torn apart by inevitably conflicting passions, the self loses any sense of its integrity, and disintegrates into its various undifferentiated appetites.[39]

Despite Freud's arguments to the contrary, we tend to discover identity in the object of desire – sexual identity, for example, is frequently constructed out of the sex of the object of desire. The Renaissance, however, seems to have imagined identity to emerge from the success one experiences at controlling a series of undifferentiated, and undifferentiating, desires. Giving way to one's various passions, moreover, is to yield the self to the kinds of inconstancy with which the Sonnets themselves continually battle on a variety of fronts. Indeed, if there is a theme that unifies this collocation of frequently disparate fourteen-line poems, it is their struggle with inconstancy and variability. Haunted by "the conceit of this inconstant stay," in the words of Sonnet 15, the poems aim to discover something that will abide (line 9). They aim, in the words of Sonnet 16, to "Make warre uppon this bloudie tirant time" (line 2). Where the early sonnets imagine progeny and poetry as corollary forms of reproduction that battle the inexorable ravages of time, other poems idealize a love marked by permanence, one that is "an ever fixed marke," and "alters not with [Time's] breefe hours and weekes" (Sonnet 116). Both the dark lady sonnets and many of the poems to the young man imagine inconstancy to be a harrowing betrayal. Sonnet 94 is part of this effort to locate a site of constancy amid inexorable flux within and outside the self, even if the rigid control it prescribes leaves little room for the emotional bonds of love that other poems postulate as effective bulwarks against the ravages of time.

Indeed, Shakespeare seems very aware throughout his career of the tension between self-control and emotional release that the poem exacerbates. Early in *The Merchant of Venice*, Nerissa offers an eloquent if conventional praise of moderation:

they are as sick that surfeit with too much as they that starve with nothing. It is no mean happiness, therefore, to be seated in the mean; superfluity comes sooner by whiter hairs, but competency lives longer. (1.2.5–9)

Portia responds with a kind of playful cynicism about the capacity of the reason to exert the requisite control over the emotions:

If to do were as easy as to know what were good to do, chapels had been churches, and poor men's cottages princes' palaces ... The brain may devise laws for the blood, but a hot temper leaps o'er a cold decree; such a hare is madness the youth to skip o'er the meshes of good counsel the cripple. (1.2.12–20)

The point of Shakespearean comedy is to find a way to direct such desire to socially approved ends.[40] The intention of the Sonnets, however, is to trace the excruciating gap between a hot temper and a cold decree, between the headlong extremity of emotional involvement with another and the rational self-control of moderation. The Sonnets as a whole, and Sonnet 94 in particular, ask a question stated with simple elegance by Martin Austin, the protagonist of a recent Richard Ford story: "How could you regulate life, do little harm and still be attached to others?"[41] While the Sonnets as a whole give several different, even contradictory, answers to this question, Sonnet 94 suggests that the regulation of life is the *sine qua non* of doing little harm and of being attached to others.

The poem presents difficulties to us, moreover, because it links the successful control of one's emotions with a social elitism we have for the most part abandoned. Those who control their demeanor are "Lords and owners of their faces," the poem declares, granting them titles far superior to those "others" who are "but stewards of their excellence." Self-governance, then, evinces social mastery, protecting one from the dangers of a "base infection" which would make "the basest weed out-brave his dignity." By "husband[ing] nature's riches from expense," moreover, the figures praised in Sonnet 94 avoid the entropy of self and vital energy entailed by the orgasmic waste of Sonnet 129, and so achieve resources befitting their exalted social and moral status. Hubler argues that this praise must be ironic, since "They are the owners of themselves, whereas throughout Shakespeare's work self-possession in the sense of living without regard for others is intolerable."[42] But Hubler's argument seems to misrepresent not only Sonnet 94 but also the virtue of self-possession throughout Shakespeare. Indeed, it is hard to imagine the rule of the detached, impenetrable, manipulative Henry V – in many ways Shakespeare's most effective monarch – without this virtue. In parts 1 and 2 of *Henry IV*, plays which are frequently invoked in discussions of this poem, the deployment of monarchical power depends on wily self-possession. In *The Castel of Helthe*, Sir Thomas Elyot suggests that self-control and social status are intimately related. Discussing "affects and passions of the mynde," he argues that "if they be immoderate, they do not onley anoy the body and shorten the lyfe, but also they doo appayre, and sometyme lose utterlye a mans estymation."[43] In *The Complete Gentleman*, Henry Peacham articulates well the ways that temperate conduct functions simultaneously as a moral virtue, a social asset, and an invigorating regimen. "The Principal means to preserve" reputation, argues Peacham,

is temperance and that moderation of the mind wherewith as a bridle we curb and break our rank and unruly passions, keeping, as the Caspian Sea, ourselves ever at one height without ebb or reflux.[44]

The self here is at once a beast needing to be curbed with a bridle and a sea whose propensity to tidal variations can be overridden by careful moderation. Self-control here is a critical element in the sustenance of social prestige.

Relatedly, accounts of the poem have foundered on the issue of the hypocrisy that the poem seems to endorse in its idealization of those "That doe not do the thing, they most do show," and who are "the Lords and owners of their faces." Empson, for example, argues that the poem provides an ironic comment on "the Machiavellian, the wicked plotter who is exciting and civilized and in some way right about life."[45] Other sonnets certainly obsess about the unknowable gap between the beloved's outer demeanor and his inner emotion. Sonnet 69, for example, contrasts the beloved's external beauty with "the beauty of thy mind" (line 9). Those who "measure by thy deeds" the beloved's inner reality, the speaker reasons, "To thy faire flow'r ad the rancke smell of weeds" (lines 10, 12). Developing the floral imagery that also inhabits the sestet of Sonnet 94, the speaker asks "why thy odor matcheth not thy show," and answers "The solye [soil] is this, that thou doest common grow" (lines 13–14). The constellation of poems that surround Sonnet 94, moreover, entail an explicit critique of concealed corruption: Sonnet 92 concludes with the fear that "Thou maist be falce, and yet I know it not," while Sonnet 93 warns the beloved that his enticing beauty will be like that of "*Eaves* apple . . . If thy sweet virtue answere not thy show" (lines 13–14). Sonnet 95 declares that the beloved's "sins" are "like a canker in the fragrant Rose" (lines 2, 4).

But Sonnet 94 is not about concealing corruption; rather, it is about exercising control over the self in order to ensure that the corruption that threatens all is not allowed to thrive. Where the octave praises the curiously unmoved nature of the absolute self-control the poem endorses, the sestet warns against "deedes" that expose one to the "base infection" that makes beauty at once repulsive and hypocritical. The poem, then, articulates two modes of disjunction between inner and outer, modes that are often confused in interpretations of the poem: the morally positive self-control that allows the virtuous to be "Lords and owners of their faces" and the morally negative capacity of "sweetest things" to "turn sowrest by their deedes" when they fail to exercise the self-control endorsed in the octave. The poem presumes an innate capacity for sin that must be continually harnessed so that they that have power to hurt will do none. The cunning and fastidious self-regulation that some construe as hypocrisy frequently functions for early modern England as the foundation of civility and of self. As George Herbert, the subject of the next chapter, observes:

>   Surely if each one saw anothers heart,
>   There would be no commerce
>   No sale or bargain passe: all would disperse,
>   And live apart.   ("Giddinesse," lines 21–24)

Social life, Herbert suggests, demands the salutary deceptions of civil conduct. Deliberately tracing the anxious continuum that conjoins a prized civility to a despised hypocrisy, Sonnet 94 addresses one of the central aporias of Western civilization.

The inherently unstable and unruly self presumed by Herbert and Shakespeare – the "giddinesse" of Herbert's title – makes it a necessary good for they that have power to hurt not to do the thing they most do show, particularly in a culture in which social prestige was marked in part by the weapons one was allowed to own and display. Indeed, passions were to be feared particularly in those who have power to hurt, both because they tempted the powerful to abuse that power, and because in doing so the powerful subsequently endangered that power. As Thomas Wright observes, it is particularly necessary for one in power "to conceale, as much as thou canst, thy inclinations, or that passion thou knowest thy selfe most prone to follow . . . therefore great prudence wise men account it, for grave and great persons, not to lay their passions open to the censure of the world."[46] A lesson in the tactical and moral importance of being cryptic, Sonnet 94 collapses the tension between the ethical fictions with which power was frequently dressed and the naked manipulation that is its essence.

Another apparent aporia in the poem is the leap from the inorganic imagery of the octave to the organic imagery of the sestet. The poem's theme, moreover, seems to alter, from the declaration of a desired stability to protection from a feared contagion. Both sections of the poem, however,

Shakespeare's Sonnets 93

are linked by the attention they devote to self-control, and by the way they imagine the social dimensions of such discipline. The purpose of the sestet is to demonstrate how the rigorous self-control the poem endorses not only delimits a superior's efforts to hurt others but also inoculates such a superior against harm from base infection. The sestet, that is, moves from the sturdy, inanimate world of stone to the delicate, ephemeral world of flowers in order to stress the hygienically prophylactic rather than the socially strategic uses of the imperturbable self-absorption the poem praises. Self-mastery, the poem suggests, is not only the evidence of social status but also a tactic of self-protection:

> The sommers flowre is to the sommer sweet,
> Though to it selfe, it onely live and die,
> But if that flowre with base infection meete,
> The basest weed out-braves his dignity:
>   For sweetest things turn sowrest by their deedes,
>   Lillies that fester, smell far worse than weeds.

In order to render this statement ironic, Hubler contrasts this ideal of self-enclosure with the early sonnets that encourage the young man to abandon his sterile self-absorption.[47] But even in those early sonnets, the young man is urged to give himself away in order cunningly to preserve himself through the techniques of heterosexual reproduction, not out of some ethical joy implicit in the virtue of giving. We need to coordinate this ideal of self-enclosure, moreover, with the attitudes articulated in those sonnets in which the speaker laments the processes by which he or his beloved have exposed themselves to an infectious commonality imagined not just as an overt injury of class but also as a contagious social disease. Sonnet 33, for example, "Full many a glorious morning," blames the sun for allowing "basest cloudes to ride, / With ougly rack on his celestiall face" (lines 5–6). Like the "base infection" and the "basest weed" in Sonnet 94, these clouds are guilty of an offense that is at once social and sexual.[48] The speaker of Sonnet 110, in turn, laments having "made my selfe a motley to the view, / Gor'd mine own thoughts, sold cheap what is most deare" (lines 2–3). The speaker of Sonnet 111 complains that his "name receives a brand, / And almost thence my nature is subdu'd / To what it workes in, like the Dyer's hand" (lines 5–7). In response to this stain, the speaker says that "like a willing pacient I will drinke, / Potions of Eysell gainst my strong infection" (lines 9–10). Playing on the various available meanings of "infection" – to dye, stain, tinge, color; to spoil or corrupt by noxious influence; to affect with disease; to taint with moral corruption – Shakespeare links the social stain of the dyer's hand to a medical and moral illness that requires bitter medicine.[49]

94   Bodies and selves in early modern England

The relationship between the sestet's language of disease and the emotional temperature that is the subject of the octave is clarified in the surmise of the speaker of Sonnet 144 that he will not be able to confirm his suspicions of sexual betrayal "Till my bad angel fire my good one out." Here, "firing out" is at once infusing another with desire and infecting another with venereal disease. Even venereal disease, moreover, was imagined to enter the desiring subject not as a contagious disease but rather as a moral and humoral imbalance:

This burning lust spendeth the spirits and balsame of life, as the flame doth waste the candle: Whereupon followes corruption of humors, rotting of the marrow, and the joynts ake, the nerves are resolved, the head is pained, the gowt increaseth, & of times (as a most just punishment) there insueth that miserable scourge of harlots, The french Pockes.[50]

It is the festering heat generated by such "base infection" that the solipsistic self-absorption of the "summer's flower" aims to avoid – not through the bitter homeopathy of sickening to shun sickness but rather through rigorous preventative measures. The initially perplexing invocation of the flowers likewise adjoins the poem's obsession with disease. When Sonnet 35 reminds us that "loathsome canker lives in sweetest bud," it is important to remember that a *canker* is not only "an eating, spreading sore or ulcer" from which our word *cancer* derives but also "a caterpillar or worm which destroys the buds and leaves of plants" (*OED* 1, 4). The phallic worm, and the desires it represents, are likened to disabling disease. As we have seen, the poem that immediately follows Sonnet 94 similarly compares the "shame" of "sin" to "a canker in the fragrant rose" (Sonnet 95, lines 1–3). The particular flower that Sonnet 94 invokes – the lily – is, notes Thomas Cogan in *The Haven of Health* (1584),

hoat and dry of qualitie, both the flowers, leaves and rootes are used in medicine, but not in the kitchen. The flowers are commended in the gospell for beautie, and preferred before the royaltie of King Solomon. They are a great ornament to a garden or in a house, yet the smell of them is discommended and accounted ill for the plague.[51]

A figure of ornamental beauty and fetid stench, a staple of medicine and an accessory to the plague, a biblical figure of purity (they are a frequent motif in Annunciations) and a source of heat, the lily epitomizes at once the comeliness of self-control and the moral stench that arises from the misdeeds of those who misuse their power to hurt. Where Spenser's Phaedria uses the lilies of the field to urge relaxation, Shakespeare uses them to describe the beauty of control, and the repulsiveness of those who relax. Assuming a world rife with contagion from without and putrefaction from within, the poem prescribes an uneasy combination of heroic self-control and hygienic solipsism as therapeutic measures for holding such inexorable forces at bay.

John Kerrigan's commentary on the poem emphasizes the impersonality of the poem's chosen mode: "For the first and almost the last time in the sequence Shakespeare writes impersonally, neither addressing the friend nor describing him explicitly as *he*, and scrupulously avoiding *I* and *me* and *my*."[52] This detached, sententious mode suits perfectly the cool inscrutability the poem praises. But its position in a sequence of poems whose first-person speakers intend the utterance of ardent emotion has encouraged modern readers to ironize the poem's praise of reticence. We need to remember Wordsworth's claim about the Sonnets that "with this key, / Shakespeare unlocked his heart," not to endorse its overt biographical romanticization but to treat it as a symptomatic response to the inwardness the poems seem to promise.[53] We should also remember Robert Browning's devastating reply: "If so, the less Shakespeare he." Where other sonnets express in manifold ways the involuted curves and wrinkles of the desiring self, Sonnet 94 offers a strategy for ironing out these curves and wrinkles, to the benefit of this self and those around it. Rather than depicting the overheated instability of erotic passion, it articulates a mode of self-discipline intended to dampen such passion. It inculcates a "care of the self," to borrow a phrase from Michel Foucault, a practice by which one can become master rather than slave of one's own pleasures and desires.[54] *Contra* Wordsworth, this is a poem not about unlocking hearts but about locking them up tightly. It views such an act, moreover, as a narrative not of bondage to societal norms but of internal liberation from insurgent passions. The discipline it idealizes entails not the repression but rather the constitution of a self.[55] The difficulty we have in reading this poem without ironizing its endorsement of self-discipline measures some of the distance separating the modern fetishes of desire and exhibitionism from the Renaissance fetishes of inscrutability and control. In confronting this difficulty, we learn something profound about ourselves, and about a writer in whom many still desire to find textual evidence of the birth of the modern self.

4 Devotion and digestion: George Herbert's consuming subject

> He that eateth my flesh, and drinketh my blood, dwelleth in me, and I in him.
> John 6.56 (AV)
>
> Obsession with food is the best proof that we have of the existence of the soul.
> Charles Simic[1]

Perhaps because of the intensely inward trajectory of *The Temple* – a trajectory marked by the progression from the social maxims of "The Church-porch" into the internal architecture of "The Church" – critics of George Herbert have focused on the spiritual and theological components of his poetry at the expense of its engagements with the material world. This focus has prevented our giving to such a palpable subject as food the degree of attention it merits. As this chapter will show, the subject of food consumed Herbert, providing him with a primal occasion and an apt medium for exploring the very inwardness that subsequent criticism has so valued. As food progresses from the external liturgies of sacred and secular consumption to the internal labyrinths of digestion, it traces for Herbert the inner contours of the devotional subject. The speaker of Herbert's "Pearl," as if addressing a tendency in himself and others to sublimate material to spiritual concerns, declares that "My stuffe is flesh, not brasse; my senses live."[2] Throughout his comparatively limited corpus, Herbert devotes a surprising amount of attention to the abundant concerns of this flesh, and the clamors of these vital senses. His devotional effort engages with the food that nourishes and tempts his flesh as well as with the theology that engages his mind. In the process, he reveals a series of profound if unexpected linkages between the digestive operations that sustain somatic existence and the salvation theology that promises eternal life. As we will see, the *Treatise of Temperance and Sobrietie* that Herbert translated shares with the poetic *Temple* of devotion he compiled a concern with the ways in which the inner self is constructed by regulating carefully the substances that enter and exit the physical body. Like Spenser, Herbert will find in the regimens of temperance a blueprint for constructing a self. Like Shakespeare, he will be torn between the wish to eradicate his desire and his longing to orient his desire to an appropriate recipient.

An apt place to begin our analysis of the centrality of food to the production of interiority for Herbert is the pair of poems that he entitled "The H. Communion" – poems that use the Eucharistic feast to consider the relationship between flesh and spirit. The version of "The H. Communion" that Herbert did not include in *The Temple* mocks the doctrinal quarrelling that surrounds the issue of Christ's presence in the Eucharist: "ffirst I am sure, whether bread stay / Or whether Bread doe fly away / Concerneth bread, not mee" (lines 7–9). Transubstantiation is similarly disposed of with the observation that "I am sure / That thou didst all those pains endure / To' abolish Sinn, not Wheat" (lines 19–21). Herbert even brings up impanation – an obscure medieval doctrine that imagines Christ's flesh becoming bread in a kind of reverse transubstantiation – a doctrine which he says makes sense only "If thou hadst dyde for Bread" (line 27). Mocking materialist explanations that turn bread into Christ or Christ into bread, Herbert views the Eucharist not as a moment of material transformation but rather as the occasion for discovering the wall that divides matter and spirit:

> Into my soule this cannot pass;
> fflesh (though exalted) keeps his grass
>   And cannot turn to soule.
> Bodyes & Minds are different Spheres,
> Nor can they change their bounds & meres,
>   But keep a constant Pole.   (lines 37–42)

Where Milton will imagine that angelic digestion can "corporeal to incorporeal turn" (*Paradise Lost*, 5.413; see Chapter 5), for the young Herbert the divide between matter and spirit, bodies and minds, cannot be bridged, even in the Eucharistic event that Milton would have forsworn.

This absolute separation between bodies and selves, however, is complicated in the very different poem entitled "The H. Communion" that Herbert chose to include in *The Temple*:

> Not in rich furniture, or fine aray,
>   Nor in a wedge of gold,
>   Thou, who for me wast sold,
> To me dost now thy self convey;
> For so thou should'st without me still have been,
>   Leaving within me sinne:
>
> But by the way of nourishment and strength
>   Thou creep'st into my breast;
>   Making thy way my rest,
> And thy small quantities my length;
> Which spread their forces into every part,
>   Meeting sinnes force and art.

> Yet can these not get over to my soul,
>   Leaping the wall that parts
>   Our souls and fleshy hearts;
> But as th' outworks, they may controll
> My rebel-flesh, and carrying thy name,
>   Affright both sinne and shame.
>
> Onely thy grace, which with these elements comes,
>   Knoweth the ready way,
>   And hath the privie key
> Op'ning the souls most subtile rooms;
> While those to spirits refin'd, at doore attend
>   Dispatches from their friend.
>
> Give me my captive soul, or take
>   My bodie also thither.
> Another lift like this will make
>   Them both to be together.
>
> Before that sinne turn'd flesh to stone,
>   To sinne, or sinne to smother;
> He might to heav'n from Paradise go,
>   As from one room t'another.
>
> Thou hast restor'd us to this ease
>   By this thy heav'nly bloud;
> Which I can go to, when I please,
>   And leave th' earth to their food.

This poem begins with an expression of wonder at the fact that God selects food rather than finery as the occasion for approaching his creatures; he comes "Not in [the] rich furniture, or fine aray, / Nor in a wedge of gold" that would suit such an exalted presence but rather "by the way of nourishment and strength / Thou creep'st into my breast." Unlike the grand entries staged by Renaissance monarchs, Herbert's God here humbly creeps; rather than burdening his subjects, he nourishes them. This monarch, furthermore, "for me wast sold," completely reversing the standard trajectory of economic relations between kings and subjects.

The entry of God into his mortal subject through the medium of food at once delineates the border between matter and spirit and proceeds benevolently to transgress it. If God had not chosen this particular medium, Herbert claims, "thou should'st without me still have been, / Leaving within me sinne." The pun on "without me" – meaning both "outside me" and "excluding me" – brilliantly enacts the assimilation of substance into self, and of self into community, that the Communion represents. Although the bread, the speaker concedes, cannot "get over to my soul, / Leaping the wall that parts / Our souls and fleshy hearts," it nevertheless is efficacious within him, functioning as "th' outworks" which "controll / My rebel-flesh." "Outworks" here designates any part of a fortification lying outside the parapet; it is thus a kind of military installation exerting power over the flesh it sustains.[3] As they enter the human subject in the Eucharistic feast, God's powers "spread their forces into every part, / Meeting sinnes force and art". As in Spenser's Castle of Alma, the self is imagined as a castle fortified against its own insurrectionary forces. Remarkably, though, the trip through the digestive tract here is made by God, not by knights who admire the divine handiwork responsible for such a wonderful system of corporeal assimilation.

Although flesh is an inherently rebellious medium, then, the Holy Communion is a meal that disciplines and blesses the flesh it nourishes. Herbert discovers in this sacred meal, moreover, a bridge between body and soul, since

> Onely thy grace, which with these elements comes,
>   Knoweth the ready way,
>   And hath the privie key,
> Op'ning the souls most subtile rooms;
> While those to spirits refin'd, at doore attend
>   Dispatches from their friend.

The Eucharist, Herbert asserts, is the ultimate repast for body and soul, achieving an amity between mortal and God that is at once corporeal and social. Herbert here invokes the contemporaneous architectural innovation of consecutive private chambers in order to represent the inner recesses of the self. Tellingly, an architectural pattern designed to make secular power less accessible to its subjects is here used to display the processes by which divine power freely enters the purportedly inaccessible spaces of its mortal subjects.[4] The tenor for devotional interiority is overtly political and physiological. In "Praise (I)," Herbert similarly imagines the interior spaces of the consuming self in architectural terms: "An herb destill'd, and drunk, may dwell next doore, / On the same floore, / To a brave soul." This physical process, whereby the material herb is allowed to inhabit space parallel to the soul, evokes the exaltation of the mortal subject that "The H. Communion" gestures toward: "exalt the poore, / They can do more."

Both Shakespeare and Herbert understand "spirit" to be a particularly rarefied form of blood. But where in Sonnet 129 Shakespeare is haunted by the "expence of spirit" that contemporary physiology understood to occur at the moment of ejaculation, in "The H. Communion" Herbert imagines the recipient of the Communion to be blessed by the capacity of "spirits" to mediate between the body and the soul. For Herbert, the spirits function as amicable porters decorously waiting outside the threshold of "the souls most subtile rooms." This is a task for which they are eminently well suited, since as Robert Burton observes in *The Anatomy of Melancholy*,

Spirit is a most subtile vapour, which is expressed from the *Blood*, & the instrument of the soule, to performe all his actions; a common tye or *medium*, betwixt the body and the soule.[5]

The stomach and liver were thought to refine food into "natural spirits," whose primary function was nourishment. Natural spirits were further refined, most frequently in the heart, into vital spirits, and vital spirits were refined yet once more in the brain into animal spirits, which cause motion and enable perception. As Levinus Lemnius remarks, "The Spyrite is the originall mainteiner and conveigher of naturall heate, whereunto moysture necessarily adhereth: and that the Soule (by the ministerye, and ayde thereof) perfourmeth her powers and faculties, and achieveth all her actions."[6] Where Milton's Satan will attempt to "taint / Th'animal Spirits that from pure blood arise / Like gentle breaths from Rivers pure" in order to "raise / At least distempered, discontented thoughts" (*Paradise Lost*, 4.804–6), Herbert's animal spirits await dispatches not from the fiend but rather "from their friend." Where Herbert imagines the self as gently entered by a beneficent deity, Milton envisages the self as being invaded by a maleficent devil. The aura of wonder that suffuses the Eucharistic feast, Herbert suggests, is an intensified version of the quotidian miracle of digestion. Indeed, the Elizabethan *Homilie Against Gluttony and Drunkennesse* makes good digestion dependent upon divine grace: "except GOD give strengthe to nature to digest, so that we may take profite by [our meats], either shall we filthily vomite them up again, or els shal they lie stinking in our bodies, as in a lothsome sinke or chanell, and so diversely infect the whole body."[7] At the center of Herbert's interior castle is a privy chamber where the threshold between matter and spirit is traversed by means of the refining processes of digestion, which are imagined as versions of the amicable dispatches of grace. As a result of this commensal commerce between matter and spirit, the feast the poem celebrates can inaugurate a restoration of prelapsarian traffic between God and human, when Adam "might to heav'n from Paradise go, / As from one room t'another." Significantly, the intimacy between God and human that was lost because of a dietary transgression – consuming the forbidden fruit – is restored by an act of eating. Just as the grace of the elements enters the innermost chambers of the consuming subject, penetrating the wall separating matter and spirit, so can the postlapsarian distance between human and God be spanned. The Eucharist, then, regains for humanity a sociability lost at the Fall, and so enables that intense communication between earth and heaven known as "Prayer," the original title of the separate poem that lines 25–40 formerly constituted. As food sustains spirit by nourishing the matter that encases it, so grace (if not God) can inhabit the bread that is consumed.

For Herbert, then, corporeality and spirituality are not separate realms but contiguous arenas with mysterious yet necessary communication between them. Franciscus Van Helmont's *Paradoxical Discourses* (translated into English in 1685) cultivates the Pauline metaphor of the body as a temple of God, and the necessity of heat to digestion, in order to describe the stomach not as a kitchen but rather as the altar on which inward sacrifices are burnt:

> Forasmuch as the Body of Man, according to the testimony of Scripture, is and should be the Temple of God. . . . And that in the Temple at Jerusalem, there was an Altar of Burnt-offering, upon which many Beasts, &C. was offered: and seeing that all the meat a man feeds upon enters into the stomach, might not the stomach be compared with the said Altar? And might it not properly be called an Altar in the Temple of God, on which all right and well ordered food for the life of man, is to be offered up?[8]

The religious subject is constructed not by sacrificing body for soul but by exploring the threshold that joins body and soul on the altar of the stomach. Eating is not just the assimilation of material nourishment but an act of spiritual sacrifice.

Indeed, in a Latin poem, "In Thomam Didymum," Herbert demonstrates his fascination with the body as a site where human and divine meet and intermingle. But in this poem on the resurrected Jesus's corporeal response to Thomas's skepticism, God takes on flesh in order to invite another to penetrate his body, rather than the mortal assimilating God through the medium of nourishment:

> The servant puts his fingers in you.
> Do you, Redeemer, permit this sign?
> For sure you are all love, and the pith of it.
> You make a shelter and a sweet rest
> For a grudging faith and a narrow mind,
> In which, luxuriating, they may conceal
> And wrap themselves
> As in a good inn or a strong fort,
> Before a roaring lion eats
> Them as they wander.[9]

Not as a Eucharistic Host, but rather as a genial host, Jesus offers his resurrected body as a refuge from a predatory and carnivorous world. The wounded Jesus hospitably invites another to experience the tactile truth of his inner corporeality in order to banish all doubt. Flesh here confirms rather than denies the reality of the spirit, bearing witness to the truth of the resurrection, and to the cordial love that it manifests. As in Herbert's poem

"The Bag," the painful wounds that humans inflict on Jesus become portals to the visceral authenticity of his profound love.

Herbert values the corollary experiences of pain and pleasure in part because their urgent sensations demand a dialogue between body and soul. In "Affliction (I)," Herbert imagines the ill health to which he was subject throughout his life, and which led him to attend scrupulously to matters of diet in search of a cure, to occasion the flesh's direct address to the soul: "My flesh began unto my soul in pain, / Sicknesses cleave my bones; / Consuming agues dwell in ev'ry vein" (lines 25–27). Herbert here portrays the flesh communicating with the soul because of a consuming disease rather than the consumption of food. The poem "Church-musick" begins in a moment "when displeasure / Did through my bodie wound my minde." The material body is in this poem the conduit both for this comparatively undefined suffering and for the distinct pleasure that the titular subject, church music, brings. In "The Crosse" the speaker complains that "One ague dwelleth in my bones, / Another in my soul," delineating a profound link between the sicknesses of the body and those of the soul. "It is a laborious and very difficult matter," remarks Lemnius,

> to restore the body that is fallen sick, where the conscience is polluted with the spots of sinns, where the Organs of the sense and the Spirits vitall and animall are vitiated. And it is no lesse troublesome, for a Church-man to give comfort to the soul, when the body is full of vitious humours; for by reason of the narrow consent and union of both parts, the vices of the mind fly upon the body, and the diseases of the body, are carried to the Soul.[10]

The osmosis between a polluted conscience and an ill body indicates that they are simply different media for the same phenomenon. The commerce between body and soul that Herbert explores throughout his poetry can be precipitated by nutrition or affliction.

The topic of the poem "Confession" is the opening up through speech of the inner spaces of the self. In this way, the poem unites the architectural vision of the interior subject portrayed in "The H. Communion" with a Galenic physiology whose therapeutic goal is the purgation of noxious internal matter. In "Confession," divine access to the inner chambers of the self is gained not by the corporeal feeding featured in "Holy Communion" but by the cruel communion of body and soul depicted in "Affliction (I)." In "Confession" Herbert emphasizes the deeply constructed nature of the self, comparing the delineation of interior space to a process of elaborate furniture-making:

> within my heart I made
> Closets; and in them many a chest;
> And, like a master in my trade,
> In those chests, boxes; in each box, a till.

The poem reveals such intricate compartmentalization, though, to be a mode of sinful evasion rather than aesthetic accomplishment. Where Spenser had imagined the architectural construction of a self to be an unequivocal good, Herbert expresses uneasiness with the illusions of artifice, autonomy, and privacy that such constructionism fosters.

Throughout *The Temple*, Herbert is divided between the effort to construct a self and a poem worthy of presentation to God and his conviction of the deep sense of sin that inevitably suffuses all human artifacts.[11] The poem "An Offering," for example, suggests that the proper gift for God is the organ of the heart, but then asks "but is it pure? / Search well and see; for hearts have many holes." Herbert then proceeds to portray a self in which "lusts" create "divisions" within the heart, and "passions . . . set partitions" which "parcell out thy heart" (lines 14–17). Before he can offer his heart, the speaker must find a medicine which can restore such divided hearts to wholeness:

> There is a balsome, or indeed a bloud,
> Dropping from heav'n, which doth both cleanse and close
> All sorts of wounds; of such strange force it is.
> Seek out this All-heal, and seek no repose,
> Untill thou finde and use it to thy good:
> Then bring thy gift. (lines 19–24)

Herbert suggests that the Communion blood is a panacea which "cleanses and closes" the internal corridors produced by lusts and passions.

The fragility of such self-constructions is similarly explored in "Giddinesse," the poem that follows "Confession"; "Man," Herbert says,

> builds a house, which quickly down must go,
>   As if a whirlwinde blew
> And crusht the building: and it's partly true,
>   His minde is so. (lines 13–16)

Here the chaotic mutability of the interior human subject blows down his brittle constructions, not the imposition of divine affliction. Man, Herbert suggests, "is some twentie sev'rall men at least / Each sev'rall houre" (lines 3–4). He finds in the possible exposure of this restless interiority not a desired sincerity but rather a bitter comedy:

> O what a sight were Man, if his attires
>   Did alter with his minde;
> And like a Dophins skinne, his clothes combin'd
>   With his desires! (lines 17–20)

Throughout Herbert's poetry, the artful production of interior space proves vain (in both senses), since God can penetrate the inner recesses of the self, either by means of the gently nutritious Eucharistic feast or by means of the ferocious tortures he skillfully applies to his mortal subjects.

In "Confession," Herbert suggests that God's response to the human effort to construct private interior space is the careful application of affliction:

> No scrue, no piercer can
> Into a piece of timber work and winde,
> As Gods afflictions into man,
> When he a torture hath design'd.
> They are too subtill for the subt'llest hearts;
> And fall, like rheumes, upon the tendrest parts. (lines 7–12)[12]

Where "Giddinesse" imagines the roiled interiority of humanity to be the product of human inconstancy, "Confession" suggests that it is God's afflictions that render unsound the internal spaces on which humans attempt to bestow an architectural integrity:

> We are the earth; and they,
> Like moles within us, heave, and cast about:
> And till they foot and clutch their prey,
> They never cool, much lesse give out. (lines 13–16)

Humans, Herbert suggests, are like mole-infested earth, seething with chaotic activity under a deceptively placid exterior.

Herbert maintains, moreover, that there is only one paradoxical way to get rid of such infestations:

> No smith can make such locks but they have keyes:
> Closets are halls to them; and hearts, high-wayes.
>
> Onely an open breast
> Doth shut them out, so that they cannot enter;
> Or, if they enter, cannot rest,
> But quickly seek some new adventure.
> Smooth open hearts no fastning have. (lines 17–23)

Just as God's grace held the "privie key" to "the souls most subtile rooms" in "The H. Communion," here God's afflictions have access to the most private recesses of the inner self. The only amelioration for such afflictions is the spiritual immunization of total confession. The effort to fashion a self, or to reserve any interior space separate from God, is only an invitation to further suffering: "fiction / Doth give a hold and handle to affliction" (lines 22–23). The speaker concludes by acknowledging his "faults and sinnes," and asking God in turn to "take thy plagues away" (lines 25–26). He promises a cleansing of his interior self so complete that "the clearest diamond . . . shall be thick and cloudie to my breast" (lines 29–30).

The domain of God, observes Levinus Lemnius in a paraphrase of Psalm 7, is the internal organs of the devotional subject. God is the tryer of the very hearte and reynes [kidneys]. That is to say, hee perfectly searcheth out and knoweth all thinges, findeth a way into the most secret corners and innermost places. And [David] bringeth in an example, taken from the intrayles that be fardest of. For there is nothing in mans body, inwarder then the heart and Reynes: in so much that the concocted meat must be conveyed by many crooked bywayes and windings, before it can be brought thither. Furthermore he specially nameth those partes, for out of them chiefly the thoughts and cogitations of the mynde, and all the licentious lustes and dissolute disyres, do proceede and springe, which bee not, nor cannot lye hyd, or unespyed of God.[13]

The labyrinthine corridors of the physiological self represent, for Lemnius and for Herbert, the inmost recesses of the psychological self. The interior territory that is traversed in "The H. Communion" by means of food is in "Confession" traversed by means of pain. In "The H. Communion," God enters the subject by way of nourishment; in "Confession," he enters by way of punishment. Both poems give a particularly organic reading to the locus of God in the human subject. "There is but joy and grief," Herbert remarks in "Affliction (V)," "If either will convert us, we are thine" (lines 13–14). Whether suffering consuming agues or consuming the fruits of divine suffering, the body is for Herbert the substance in which devotional interiority lives, and moves, and has its being.

Indeed, the speaker of "The Church-porch," Herbert's versified conduct book prefacing *The Temple*, recommends that "thy mindes sweetnesse have his operation / Upon thy body, clothes, and habitation," suggesting that inner purity could mull bodily odor (lines 371–72). Traffic between interior and exterior is urged, but the trajectory is exactly opposite to that described in "The H. Communion," moving from inward quality to outward manifestation. Similarly, in *The Country Parson*, a manual of conduct for rural clergy, Herbert describes how the parson's "apparrel [is] plaine, but reverend, and clean, without spots, or dust, or smell; the purity of his mind breaking out, and dilating it selfe even to his body, cloaths, and habitation" (p. 228). In Herbert's universe, cleanliness is next to godliness, because it advertises corporeally the spiritual purity of the subject.[14] It also announces the health of that subject. As Carol Rawcliffe observes,

The idea that infectious diseases were spread by airborne vapours and absorbed through the open pores of the body had, like humoral theory, a long classical pedigree; and it, too, continued to find advocates until the eighteenth and nineteenth centuries.... The enormous popularity of scented clothes and pomanders, as well as powders, incense and perfumes for use in the homes of wealthy men and women, was thus (as almost all the surviving plague treatises attest) not simply a means of camouflaging unpleasant smells but an important prophylactic measure, intended to combat infection.[15]

Herbert's fascination with smell – "sweet" is one of his favorite words – derives in part from his abiding concern with health.

Cleanliness, moreover, is correlated with the attainment of spiritual and social status. One of the hardest lessons that the country parson must learn is not to disdain "to enter into the poorest Cottage, though he even creep into it, and though it smell never so lothsomly" (p. 249). George's elder brother Edward, Lord Herbert of Cherbury, remarks in a peculiar passage in his so-called *Autobiography*: "It is well known to those that wait in my chamber, that the shirts, waistcoats, and other garments I wear next my body, are sweet, beyond what either easily can be believed, or hath been observed in any else, which sweetness also was found to be in my breath above others, before I used to take tobacco."[16] In the Renaissance, one could (in both senses) smell rank. One could, moreover, taste it. The first sumptuary laws regulated not just what one could wear according to one's status, but also what one could eat. Food, then, is at once the site of communion and the place of difference; it can eradicate or delineate the social hierarchy. Indeed, the word *Lord* is derived from an Old English word that means "keeper of the bread."[17] The *Outlandish Proverbs* Herbert collected record some of his abiding fascination with the social valences of food. One such proverb underscores the power of food to establish utilitarian social relations: "Who eats his cake alone must saddle his horse alone" (p. 333, no. 348). Noting the social indebtedness that consuming another's fare implies, another of these proverbs remarks cynically that "Anothers bread costs dear" (p. 332, no. 324). Exploring in turn the politics of benefaction rather than reception, another proverb observes that "The bit that one eates, no friend makes" (p. 325, no. 142). Herbert indicates here that food nourishes not just physical bodies but also social bonds. The logic of such a statement would drive one to a kind of social anorexia, whereby one chooses to feed others rather than to nourish oneself in order to make as many "friends" as possible.

"Providence" translates such stringent social lessons into the fecund ecology of the natural world. "The beasts say, Eat me," announces the speaker, transforming all creation into a banquet demanding to be consumed by the humans for whom it was made (line 21). Herbert praises his God for a hospitality that welcomes all comers: "Thy cupboard serves the world: the meat is set, / Where all may reach" (lines 49–50). Yet the apparent democracy of this seating pattern is belied by the way that consumption manifests hierarchical difference. The order of predation, we learn, is synchronized with hierarchical position: "The great prey on the lesse, they on some weed" (line 52). The great chain of being is manifested as a great chain of eating.

This vision closely resembles that of Herbert's poem "Man," where we are told that "The whole [of creation] is, either our cupboard of food, / Or cabinet of pleasure." In "Man," Herbert gives a particularly Paracelsian twist to the commonplace idea that man is a microcosm of the universe. Paracelsus had proclaimed that

> Everything external in nature points to something internal; for nature is both inside man and outside man.... All nature is like one single apothecary's shop, covered only with the roof of heaven.[18]

In "Man," Herbert suggests that "Herbs gladly cure our flesh: because that they / Finde their acquaintance there," and "All things unto our flesh are kinde," that is kind because they share an elemental kinship. Sympathy here is understood in social as well as scientific terms. Both "Providence" and "Man" imagine humanity as vibrating with the energy of the entire universe. Amid the wonders of this hierarchy, Herbert expresses awe at the frugal wisdom behind the enclosed ecological cycle whereby animal feces fertilize the food they in turn consume: "Sheep eat the grasse, and dung the ground for more" ("Providence," line 69). As Richard Todd decorously remarks, "even the more unsavory forms of symbiosis are actually to be interpreted as expressions of praise because they are frank responses to God's liberal husbandry."[19] Indeed, in *The Country Parson*, the parson's examination of "the wonderfull providence and thrift of the great householder of the world" extends to God's care over these and other creatures who are nourished by human refuse:

> there being two things, which as they are, are unuseful to man, the one for smalnesse, as crums, and scattered corn, and the like; the other for the foulnesse, as wash, and dirt, and things thereinto fallen; God hath provided creatures for both: for the first, Poultry; for the second, swine. These save man the labor, and doing that which either he could not do, or was not fit for him to do, by taking both sorts of food into them, do as it were dresse and prepare both for man in themselves, by growing them selves fit for his table. (p. 241)

For Herbert, God's miraculous introduction of low creatures such as pigs and chickens, who find nourishment in the crumbs and washwater humans shun, is the highest manifestation of providence.[20]

Humans, though, must choose their fare with much more care since, as the speaker of "The Church-porch" colorfully puts it, "the fly / That feeds on dung, is coloured thereby" (lines 233–34). Eating requires continual discrimination of nourishment from dung, of the pure from the impure.[21] Even edible and salutary items must be culled before they can be consumed: "He pares his apple, that will cleanly feed" (lines 62–64). "Look to thy mouth," observes the speaker of "The Church-porch," "diseases enter there" (line 127). The pollution and disease that are omnipresent in Herbert's world can be neutralized only by scrupulous adherence to the maxims of conduct that constitute "The Church-porch." Although this poem declares its own pedagogical strategy to be to "make a bait of pleasure," that is, to attract the appetite of the "sweet youth" addressed, it also warns, immediately and sternly, how the apparent pleasure of lust and drink "doth pollute and foul" (lines 1–7). Appetite is at once deployed and demeaned.

"The Church-porch" issues, moreover, in a poem – "Superliminare" – whose threshold position demands that the "sweet youth" turn upon himself the dialectic between purity and impurity established in "The Church-porch." He is invited to "approach, and taste / The churches mysticall repast" (lines 3–4). But in order to partake of this meal, he must pass an improbably strenuous test of purity. "Avoid, Profanenesse," reads the threshold admonition, reminding the impure mortal subject that "Nothing but holy, pure, and cleare, / Or that which groneth to be so, / May at his perill further go." Ultimately, the impure mortal's desire for purity wins out over the impossible demand for purity as the grounds for admission, but only at continuing risk to the impure subject. Herbert's poem "The Invitation" may issue an unconditional welcome to "all," even the glutton, the drunkard, the libertine, and the lover, but "Superliminare" invites an impossibly fit reader to its dangerously meaningful repast. In Stanley Fish's apt description, the poem "proposes conditions and then tells us that they cannot be met."[22] Like the food that is the vehicle of its central metaphor for the experience of reading, the subsequent poems involve an experience that is at once necessary and perilous.

Among the sins that "The Church-porch" addresses in its attempt to purify the subject in preparation for this dangerous venture, excesses in drinking alcohol are revealed to be particularly insidious, since alcohol not only admits something alien and impure into the subject but also releases an alienating impurity already lurking within the subject. "He that is drunken," observes Herbert, "all kinde of ill / Did with his liquour slide into his veins" (lines 31–34). Alcohol releases the beasts within us that the constructions of civility keep on leashes:

> He that is drunken, may his mother kill
> Bigge with his sister: he hath lost the reins,
> Is outlawd by himself: all kinde of ill
> Did with his liquour slide into his veins. (lines 31–34)[23]

Drink causes one to "lose thy hold" (line 41), initiating a profound surrender of the consuming subject's precarious power over self. Like Acrasia's cup in Book 2 of *The Faerie Queene* (2.12.56), and like Comus's cup of orient liquor, it does not so much alter the self as release the beasts that lurk within all. Indeed, Thomas Hobbes uses the effects of wine to buttress his definition of madness as "too much appearing Passion":

For the variety of behaviour in men that have drunk too much, is the same with that of Mad-men: some of them Raging, others Loving, others Laughing, al extravagantly, but according to their several domineering Passions: For the effect of the wine, does but remove Dissimulation, and take from them the sight of the deformity of their Passions . . . Passions unguided, are for the most part mere Madnesse.[24]

Tellingly, wine removes the "dissimulation" that keeps domineering passions in check, and blurs the self-consciousness that might allow one to glimpse "the deformity of [his] passions." As a result, alcohol must be consumed with extreme caution: "Drink not the third glass," declares the sententious speaker three times in twenty-two lines.[25] In "Miserie," Herbert locates the epitome of human dejection in the Epicurean fatalism that would reject the checks on consumption offered in "The Church-porch": "*Man is but grasse, / He knows it, fill the glasse*" ("Miserie," lines 5–6). But it is significant that even in the severe "Church-porch," Herbert avoids total abstinence, opting instead for closely regulated consumption.

Only by strict adherence to rules and regulations does the consuming subject avoid dissipating into its appetites:

> Who keeps no guard upon himself, is slack,
> And rots to nothing at the next great thaw.
> Man is a shop of rules, a well truss'd pack,
> Whose every parcell under-writes a law.
> ("Church-porch," lines 139–42)

Rules constitute rather than suppress the self; without them one "rots to nothing." Proper administration of the self, moreover, demands that one plan for and take account of its every action:

> Summe up at night, what thou hast done by day;
> And in the morning, what thou hast to do.
> Dresse and undresse thy soul: mark the decay
> And growth of it; if with thy watch, that too
>   Be down, then winde up both; since we shall be
>   Most surely judg'd, make thy accounts agree.
> (lines 451–56)

Scrupulous examination of past acts and painstaking enumeration of future tasks impose order on what is inherently unruly. The self – here appropriately compared to a watch, an instrument designed to impose order on the flux of temporality--is continually being prepared for presentation to the ultimate authority through the deliberate cultivation of inhibition.

The economic life that supplies the metaphor for self-examination, moreover, depends upon cultivating a disjunction between inner desire and outer presence, the "dissimulation" that Hobbes speaks of. As Herbert remarks in "Giddinesse," a poem at which we have already glanced,

> Surely if each one saw anothers heart,
> There would be no commerce,
> No sale or bargain passe: all would disperse,
> And live apart.

Social life demands the salutary deceptions of civil conduct. What we construe as self-expression and self-indulgence would have been understood by Herbert as a complete and terrifying surrender of self.

As Herbert advises in "The Church-porch," "Lose not thy self, nor give thy humours way: / God gave them to thee under lock and key" (lines 143–44). Herbert here imagines the self as a principle of rigid containment amid the humors, a series of fluid but deeply material influences on conduct. The Jonsonian comedy of humors contemporaneous with Herbert's devotional compositions continually exploits for comic effect the material basis of behavior that underpins this physiology. Herbert's poem "The Collar" is itself a kind of comedy of humors. Its title puns upon *choler*, the physical substance that produces in the speaker the rage the poem records, as well as upon the constricting collar of behavioral control that should keep such humors in bondage, and the etymologically related disease of cholera, whose symptoms were "bilious diarrhea, vomiting, stomach-ache, and cramps" (*OED* 2, from 1565). The ultimate resonance of the title involves the voice of the divine "caller" that restores order to the self and the poem: "Me thoughts I heard one calling, *Child!* / And I reply'd *My Lord*" (lines 35–36). Significantly, Edward Herbert remembers his brother George as susceptible to the choleric temperament the poem dramatizes; although "his life was most holy and exemplary," Edward remarks, George "was not exempt from passion and choler."[26] The pained question asked by the exasperated speaker of "The Collar" – "Have I no harvest but a thorn / To let me bloud?" – takes on added resonance when one considers that bloodletting was a common treatment for choleric dispositions. "Blood letting," notes Richard Allestree, "cheereth sad minds, and pacifies anger."[27] A spiritual temper tantrum from a poet who wrote two poems called "The Temper," the poem exemplifies the spontaneous and disturbing overflow of powerful passion that can inundate the human subject as a result of an improper balance of humoral fluids. The near free verse form of the poem represents formally the derangement of the self which fails to keep its humors under lock and key. If a sonnet resembles a well-ordered self, carefully parcelling emotion into rhymed metrical lines and stanzas, this poem's frantic meter and stuttering syntax represent one "Who keeps no guard upon himself" ("The Church-porch," line 139). That this poem's deliberately perverse form looks "natural" and "free" to us measures the immense distance separating the Renaissance fetish of order from our own fetish of liberation. Herbert intends what we term "free verse" to represent not a liberation from formal constraint but rather a self in bondage to the emotions embodied in its humoral fluids. It is the phenomenon of constraint, for Herbert and for his culture, that makes any prospect of freedom possible.

The humoral fluids, then, must be harnessed or purged because they threaten to corrode the walls of discipline from which the social self of "The Church-porch" emerges. In "The Church-porch," Herbert admonishes an England that is "full of sin, but most of sloth" to "Spit out thy phlegm" (lines 91–92). Herbert here is advising not frequent expectoration – itself a source of increasing disapproval in the courtesy books of the period – but rather a purgation of the phlegmatic disposition that he feels afflicts the English gentry. In the poem "Miserie," Herbert locates the suffering of the title in failures of temperance – man "will not lose a cup of drink for thee: / Bid him but temper his excesse; / Not he" (lines 8–10). As a result of human intemperance, the humors run roughshod over the subject who should rule them; man "lets his humors reigne; / They make his life a constant blot" (lines 62–64). Galenic physiology, then, puts immense social and spiritual pressure on the rituals of consumption. Indeed, the title of a work by John Downame demonstrates the close relationship between spiritual and physical health to which Herbert's poems appeal: *Spiritual physicke to cure the diseases of the soule, arising from the superfluitie of choller, prescribed out of Gods word* (London, 1600). Humoral theory transforms each act of consumption and excretion into an operation that determines the health of body and mind.

These intense physiological and moral pressures make a philosophy such as Stoicism that advances self-control enormously attractive, even though its emphasis on apathy tends to conflict with Herbert's dedication to the idea of passion properly directed to God. It is the maddening mutability of human emotion that makes constancy in particular such a sought-after virtue. As Herbert bemoans in "The Flower," the poem that records the blessedly maddening changeability of mortal existence: "O that I once past changing were" (line 22). In the poem "Constancie," Herbert praises a figure who manifests the Stoic traits of solidity and consistency that were such an important part of Shakespeare's Sonnet 94 explored in Chapter 3. Punning several times on "still" (line 2, and twice in line 35) meaning both constant and unmoved, Herbert praises a kind of moral automaton, composed largely of Stoic sententia, who "doth still and strongly good pursue," who "when great trials come, / Nor seeks, nor shunnes them," whom "neither force not fawning can / Unpinne," who "never melts or thaws / At close tentations" and "Who still is right, and prayes to be so still" (lines 2, 4–5, 11–12, 21–22, 35). Such unyielding self-control can seem oppressively chilly to a twentieth-century sensibility; one recent critic describes this aggressively static figure as "awful" and "a monstrous possibility."[28] But for Herbert, far greater monsters lurk in surrendering to passion than in dispassionately rejecting it. "Reason," remarks Herbert in one of the *Outlandish Proverbs*, "lies betweene the spurre and the bridle" (p. 345, no. 711). Two instruments of control, one for accelerating and one for halting motion, demarcate the territory of rationality. To accede to the internal pressure of desire is to forfeit rather than to find the inner self.

"Constancie," which significantly follows a poem entitled "Frailtie," suggests that one bulwark against the perpetual insurgency of internal passion is Stoic apathy. To remain unmoved requires a heroic exertion of individual will over undifferentiated passion. Reading this poem amid the voices of passionate devotion that constitute *The Temple*, we confront the same dilemma that emerged in the discussion of Shakespeare's Sonnets – that a poet valued for uttering ardent if properly directed emotion can express sincere admiration for a state of absolute apathy. Richard Strier has written compellingly of the "privileged indecorousness of genuine emotion" in *The Temple*, while Peter Sacks has recently suggested that "it is [Herbert's] unflinching examination of the heart that has made him so intimately sympathetic to his successors."[29] Like so many of his contemporaries, Herbert at once admires Stoic constancy and self-control and eschews the Stoic devaluation of passion. Perhaps including a pun on the *stoa*, the porch from which Stoicism derived its name, "The Church-porch" is rife with Stoic sentiment. Herbert there encourages what he calls "A mastring minde," which can be happy with little, "For wealth without contentment climbes a hill / To feel those tempests, which fly over ditches" (lines 104, 111–12). He advises that "constancie knits the bones, and makes us stowre, / When wanton pleasures becken us to thrall" (lines 117–18). The final couplet has a long history among Stoic writers, including Cato the Censor: "If thou do ill; the joy fades, not the pains: / If well; the pain doth fade, the joy remains" (lines 461–62). Yet Herbert also indicates that he believes not in the eradication but rather the redirection of emotion; he advises the youth to "Correct thy passions spite; / Then may the beasts draw thee to happy light" (lines 263–64). Here the beastly passions are imagined to supply the energy that one uses to move in the direction of virtue. In "Humilitie," Herbert envisions an insurrection by these beastly passions, but the poem concludes not by banishing them but rather by asking them "double gifts to bring / At the next Session-day." His frequent recourse to the image of stony heart softened or cut by God (see "The Altar" and "Love Unknown") indicates that the mineral stability counseled in Sonnet 94 is an ultimately inadequate orientation to the world. Continually Herbert prays that his "hard heart" will be made soft, or even broken, by God's suppling grace.

Yet in "The Familie," Herbert longs to be purged of unruly passions and "distemper'd fears" (line 19). He complains about "this noise of thoughts within my heart," and asks God to "Turn out these wranglers, which defile thy seat" (lines 1, 7). His ideal self is not one where passion rules but one where

> First Peace and Silence all disputes control,
>   Then Order plaies the soul
> And giving all things their set forms and houres,
>   Makes of wilde woods sweet walks and houres.
>   Humble Obedience neare the doore doth stand,
>   Expecting a command.
> (lines 9–14)

This, Herbert suggests, is the kind of interior rule that would encourage God "to make a constant stay" within him (line 24). Herbert's privileging of emotion remains in perpetual tension throughout *The Temple* with his rage for order. He can express beautifully the salutary effect that uttering fervent and frequently indecorous emotion might have upon God, but when he examines his interior spaces, Herbert seems to long for the imposition of order and control that would make "sweet walks" out of the "wilde woods" within.

Wonderfully encapsulating the explosive blend of physiology and psychology that underpins Galenic medicine, the phrase "distemper'd fears" indicates a connection between one's humoral temperament and the emotions the predominant humors produce. Rather than allowing such distemper to rule the self, Herbert hopes for a state in which "Order plaies the soul." Embedded in this simple line is a metaphor of the soul as a stringed instrument that needs to be tuned, a metaphor that derives from Plato, and that receives particular emphasis in "The Temper (I)." This poem marvelously translates the mutability that is so frequently opposed to order into an image of tuning that epitomizes harmony and order. The speaker opens by wishing that "what my soul doth feel sometimes, / My soul might ever feel!" This emotional mutability takes on cosmological implications in the next stanza:

> Although there were some fourtie heav'ns, or more,
>   Sometimes I peere above them all;
>   Sometimes I hardly reach a score,
>   Sometimes to hell I fall.

Herbert then translates these vast distances into the kinds of torture he frequently imagines his God employing upon him – "O rack me not to such a vast extent." But it is in the very image of God stretching his creature that the speaker achieves an image of the internal harmony advertised in the poem's title:

114   Bodies and selves in early modern England

>   Yet take thy way; for shure thy way is best:
>   Stretch or contract me, thy poore debter:
>   This is but tuning of my breast,
>   To make the musick better.

As steel is made stronger by going from the extreme of heat to cold – another available meaning of "temper" – so does the internal constitution of the devout subject develop tensile capacity by enduring the emotional extremes that Herbert's form of Christianity seems to demand.

Yet the resolution that is reached in this poem proves fragile and ephemeral at the beginning of the next poem, "The Temper (II)": "It cannot be. Where is that mightie joy, / Which just now took up all my heart." The very mutability that was understood as tuning itself demands that the resolution it achieved be temporary. This poem ends with a politicized version of "The Familie," asking God to be more constant, and so to bestow upon him the capacity for sustaining internal stability:

>   O fix thy chair of grace, that all my powers
>   May also fix their reverence:
>   For when thou dost depart from hence,
>   They grow unruly, and sit in thy bowers.
>
>   Scatter, or binde them all to bend to thee:
>   Though elements change, and heaven move,
>   Let not thy higher Court remove,
>   But keep a standing Majestie in me.[30]

This poem, whose original title in the Williams manuscript was "The Christian Temper," manifests at once the capacity to record the flashpoint changes of emotion that we so value in Herbert and the longing for a stability that such mutability precipitates. Whereas the point of the first poem entitled "The Temper" is to find meaning in the excruciatingly intemperate emotions of spiritual experience, the second "Temper" poem implores God to maintain a single stable residence, so "that all my powers / May also fix their reverence: / For when thou dost depart from hence, / They grow unruly, and sit in thy bowers" (lines 9–12). God's presence, Herbert hopes, will "temper" his emotional experience, and so bestow order upon an inherently unruly self, just as temperance would delimit the distressingly open-ended experience of eating. Both the byzantine demands of temperance and the deferential liturgies of reverence involve discursive systems intended to stabilize a fundamentally unstable self.

Rule and order thus become for Herbert bulwarks against the inevitable flux of human emotion. In "The Church-porch," he encourages the youth to "Slight those who say amidst their sickly healths, / Thou liv'st by rule" (lines 133–34). The point is that even health, if not subjected to "rule," is "sickly," always on the edge of swerving into disease. Throughout his career Herbert sought to remedy moral and spiritual ailments by regulating his consumption. In his notoriously unreliable *Life of Mr. George Herbert,* Izaak Walton records that Herbert cured a "quotidian ague," a particularly malicious fever that lasted for twelve months, by "forbearing Drink, and not eating any Meat, no not Mutton, nor a Hen, or Pigeon, unless they were salted; and by such a constant Dyet, he remov'd his Ague, but with inconveniencies that were worse; for he brought upon himself a disposition to Rheums, and other weaknesses, and a supposed Consumption."[31] Cruelly, Herbert's attempt to conquer his ague through control of his consumption only makes him more susceptible to consumption (so named because it seemed to eat away at the body of its victims), the pulmonary disease that would eventually kill him. If the story is to be believed, and its sense of Herbert's near-perpetual illness certainly suits the facts as we have them, Herbert's primary guide in this "constant Dyet" was probably Alvise Cornaro (although Herbert calls him "Luigi"), an Italian whose *Della vita sobria* (1558) Herbert translated into English as *A Treatise of Temperance and Sobrietie.* Devoted to the pragmatic benefits of the virtue of temperance within a Galenic regime, the treatise argues that all illness derives from the ingestion of something either excessive or bad.[32] "He which lives a temperate life," Cornaro promises, "cannot fall into diseases, and but very seldome into indispositions; because Temperance takes away the cause of diseases" (*Works,* pp. 299–300). Cornaro describes himself as one who formerly "followed my Appetite, and did eate meats pleasing to my taste"; as a result, he was "continually oppressed with pain and sicknesses" (p. 292). "By [intemperance], and my ill constitution, (having a most cold & moist stomack)," notes Cornaro, "I fell unto divers diseases, to wit, into the pain of the stomack, and often of the side, and beginning of the Gout, with almost a continuall fever and thirst" (p. 291). The image of the afflicted Dürer pointing to the pain in his side is appropriate to invoke here. "Fully perswaded, that all my griefs arose out of Intemperance," Cornaro reports that he "resolved to follow Temperance and Reason" in diet (p. 292). He subsequently (and, he argues, consequently) "was perfectly cured of all my infirmities," and lived vigorously into his eighties (p. 292). "Bodies," Cornaro remarks, are "kept in good order by a moderate Diet." Cornaro cites two Italian proverbs – "He that will eat much, let him eat little," and "The meat which remaineth profits more then that which is eaten" – which offer salubrious versions of the social advice given in the *Outlandish Proverb* cited above ("The meat which one eats no friend makes"; pp. 295–96). Eating little, it seems, is the way to make friends and influence people while living a long and healthy life.

Indeed, the essence of Cornaro's diet is "taking care never to rise [from the table] with a full stomach," a discipline which ensures the removal of the peccant abundance of humors: "all superfluities passing away without difficultie, and no ill humours being ingendred in the body" (p. 293). Cornaro reports, furthermore, that the benefits of such a regime are psychological as well as physiological: "having endured many heats & colds, and other like discommodities of the bodie, and troubles of the minds, all these did hurt me little, whereas they hurt them very much who live intemperately" (p. 294). This leads him to praise the "great power a sober and temperate life hath over our bodies and mindes," and to assert that "neither melancholie, nor any other passion can hurt a temperate life" (p. 294). The rigors of a temperate life ultimately demand a radical inwardness and individuality, at precisely the point where we might imagine that the need to order and discipline a self would suppress the qualities of individuality and inwardness. Cornaro writes that

> no man can be a perfect Physician to another, but to himself onely. The reason whereof is this, Every one by long experience may know the qualities of his own nature, and what hidden properties it hath, what meat and drink agrees best with it . . . there is a greater diversitie of tempers, then of faces. (p. 297)

Only through scrupulous attention to one's humoral temperament can one discover the "hidden properties" of the self, and respond with the proper diet. In this way, the dietary regimes that Herbert explored throughout his life were continuous with the spiritual inwardness Herbert mapped so brilliantly in his poetry. Both demand scrupulous self-examination.

Cornaro, though, was not the only figure whose advice about health and consumption Herbert endorsed. In *The Country Parson*, Herbert remarks that the parson should be a physician to his parish, and informs his audience that it is

> easie for any scholer to attaine such measure of Phisick, as may be of much use to him both for himself, and others. This is done by seeing one Anatomy, reading one Booke of Phisick, having one Herball by him. And let Fernelius be the Phisick Author . . . (p. 261)

Herbert here endorses the work of Jean Fernel, physician to Henry II of France, whose *Physiology* (1542) remained very popular into the seventeenth century. Fernel, remarks Charles Sherrington,

> treats mind as coming within physiology. It forms the theme of a full third of his "Physiology." . . . Fernel seems not to apprehend any difficulty about the spiritual and the corporeal (the material) interacting . . . Fernel had of course Galen's "spirits" to serve as mediators between the corporeal and incorporeal . . . The "natural" spirits were . . . a sort of half-way house between substance of soul and material of body.[33]

The spirits which served as porters between body and soul in "The H. Communion" were thus central to the physiology of one of Herbert's primary medical authorities. Fernel's *Physiology* also includes a long and detailed description of the stomach as a kind of internal oven, cooking and fermenting food in preparation for corporeal assimilation, and explores the processes by which ingestion determines "temperament," the psychological and physical balance of the four cardinal qualities: cold, warm, dry, and wet.[34] Fernel, furthermore, compares the elements of the temperament to notes in a musical chord, the concept which underpins the physiology of "The Temper (I)."

Indeed, the amount of attention the parson pays to corporeality, and to food in particular, is surprising to a culture that expects its spirituality to be divorced from materiality. The regulation of food, Herbert remarks, always has for the parson a "double aime, either of Abstinence a morall vertue, or Mortification a divine" (p. 267). Food is an occasion where morality and spirituality meet physiology. Indeed, defects in table manners are seen to entail moral and dietary transgressions: "he that eats offensively to the Company, either in his order, or length of eating, is scandalous and uncharitable" (p. 266). The remarkable opening of "The Collar" manifests spiritual rebellion as a deliberate breach of commensal decorum – "I struck the board, and cry'd, No more" – and depicts the moral transgression its angry speaker desires as a reaching for forbidden food: "but there is fruit, / And thou hast hands." In contrast, so concerned is the pragmatic speaker of Herbert's "Church-porch" about offensive table manners that he advises the cautious diner on what to do if his stomach growls: "Thou hast two sconses, if thy stomack call; / Carve, or discourse" (lines 129–30). Because conduct that offends others is at once socially indecorous and morally culpable, one has a duty to mask the clamor of a hungry stomach either by the noise of talking or by getting on with the meal in order to silence it.

Eating, moreover, involves a constant application of dietary casuistry, since it is, unlike the drinking of alcohol, necessary to survival, yet more difficult to quantify. Its sins are particularly insidious, always ones of degree rather than of kind. As a result, appetite must be checked repeatedly by rules. The parson warns his congregation "not to eate of all those dishes at table, which even their present health otherwise admits ... but to put bounds, and hoopes, to their joyes" (p. 280). Eating requires one continually to determine the borders of morality: "a man dining, eats at first lawfully; but proceeding on, comes to do unlawfully, even before he is aware; not knowing the bounds of the action, nor when his eating begins to be unlawfull" (p. 264). The consumer must be continually on the lookout for the moment "when the appetites of the body ... [become] sins of gluttony" (p. 230).

In response to this expressed need for such guidelines, Herbert fastidiously proposes a variety of "rules" that "generally comprehend the faults of eating ... men must eat neither to the disturbance of their health, nor of their affairs, (which being overburdened, or studying dainties too much, they cannot wel dispatch) nor of their estate, nor of their brethren" (p. 266). As if these precepts were not demanding enough in their anxious regulation of eating, Herbert proceeds to propose another "three rules" specific to parsons, which are in fact occasions demanding rigorous self-examination. In order to prevent them from eating "so as to disable themselves from a fit discharging ... of Divine duties," parsons should consider

first, the custome, and knowledg of their own body, and what it can well disgest [*sic*]: The second, the feeling of themselves in time of eating, which because it is deceitfull; (for one thinks in eating, that he can eat more, then afterwards he finds true:) The third is the observation with what appetite they sit down. This last rule joyned with the first, never fails. (pp. 266–67)

Eating demands acute self-scrutiny; the parson "hath considered how to carry himself at table about his appetite ... having studied, and mastered all his lusts and affections within, and the whole Army of Temptations without" (p. 278). Indeed, because temperance is a continuous and unending battle with internal forces rather than a one-time struggle with external power, Herbert suggests that the country parson should be more impressed by the "daily temperance" of the primitive martyrs than the courage they demonstrated when facing a tortuous death (p. 237). Proper commensal conduct demands intrepid vigilance: "knowing what one usually can well disgest, and feeling when I do to meat in what disposition I am, either hungry or not, according as I feele my self, either take my wonted proportion, or diminish of it" (p. 267). In order to eat well, one must keep a running tabulation of one's internal feelings, attending to one's occasional appetite as well as one's particular constitution. Self-control, and finally self-knowledge, are produced through fastidious attendance to the nuances of desire.[35]

Considering intently his particular constitution, Herbert writes that "an English body, and a Students body, are two great obstructed vessels.... And obstructions are the cause of most diseases" (p. 243). Under Galenic humoral theory, the body is a dynamic and porous edifice continually producing "superfluous excrements" which must constantly be evacuated or the organism will poison itself. As Lemnius writes:

God that made the body of man hath not in vain created so many wayes and passages to purge for the humours and to wash away the excrements, lest a man might be choked or oppressed by the abundance of them, or the vapours that arise from them.... They do well, who take care of their health, and keep the body and all its parts free from excrements.[36]

Constipation, then, is not just an annoyance in and of itself but also the source of most disease, since it blocks the necessary flow of excess substances from the body. Corporal flow flushes the system of excrements. "Crudities," remarks Leonard Lessius, whose *Hygiasticon* was published with Herbert's translation of Cornaro, are "the mother of all diseases."[37] Herbert's own continual ill health, apparently including the obstructions just described as well as the fevers and consumption that plagued him throughout his adult life, drove him to attend to matters of diet with a scrupulousness born of physical as well as moral urgency. Cornaro cites Galen to the effect that "immoderate heats and colds, and windes and labours did little hurt him, because in his meats and drinks he kept a due moderation" (p. 294). Herbert's own meticulous attention to consumption was an apparently futile attempt to protect himself from such internal afflictions.

This attention is manifested in Herbert's detailed descriptions of the parson's diet:

His fare is plain, and common, but wholsome, what hee hath, is little, but very good; it consisteth most of mutton, beefe, and veal, if he addes any thing for a great day, or a stranger, his garden or orchard supplyes it, or his barne, and backside: he goes no further for any entertainment, lest he goe into the world, esteeming it absurd, that he should exceed, who teacheth others temperance. (p. 241)

Tellingly, this is neither the Rabelaisian festivity identified by Mikhail Bakhtin as central to the Renaissance concept of eating nor the holy fast identified by Caroline Bynum as exemplary to medieval spirituality but rather a wary embrace of laudable temperance.[38] Deliberately rejecting the exotic and the lavish, Herbert's parson serves up a homely, carnivorous repast characterized by careful control of portion and of origin.

For Herbert, the way to taste the world is not absolutely to deny its pleasures but to control them, to make them avenues to or foretastes of heaven. As Terry Sherwood remarks, "The full physiological reality of tasting configures profound spiritual truths."[39] "Ungratefulnesse" declares that the Incarnation – itself a "box ... of sweets" resembling in structure the internal cabinetry that constitutes the interior subject in "Confession" – is intended to "allure us with delight," at once blessing the senses and adapting them to religious purposes. Herbert remarks in "Mans medley" that "as birds drink, and straight lift up their head, / So he must sip and think / Of better drink / He may attain to, after he is dead." Sense-experience is not absolutely negated, but it is kept tightly controlled, and always pointing at a higher good. "The Size" reminds us we should not be too concerned with exotic spices such as "cloves and nutmegs" and "cinamon," since we are "heir / To th' Isle of spices." Because heaven promises authentic pungency, terrestrial hunger assumes a moral valence: "To be in both worlds full / Is more then God was, who was hungrie here... Wouldst thou both eat thy cake and have it?" This emphasis on hunger as a condign state issues in a moralized portrait of the physiognomy that such a spare diet would produce:

> A Christians state and case
> Is not a corpulent, but a thinne and spare,
> Yet active strength: whose long and bonie face
> Content and care
> Do seem to equally divide.   ("The Size," lines 31–35)

The speaker of the poem "Home" pointedly asks: "What is this weary world; this meat and drink, / That chains us by the teeth so fast?" For Herbert, the salient issue is not so much to deny appetite as to govern it rather than to be governed by it. The speaker of "The Church-porch" even advises a kind of cultivated disgust as a check on hunger: "Look on meat, think it dirt, then eat a bit; / And say withall, Earth to earth I commit" (lines 131–32). The paraphrase in the final line of the Burial Office in The Book of Common Prayer reminds one of the dust from which even the finest food as well as the flesh it nourishes arises, and endows the diminishment of appetite with a moral and eschatalogical dimension.

In the poem "Conscience," though, it seems as if such moralizing attitudes are mocked rather than championed. The poem opens with a command intended to silence a spoilsport rather like the speaker of "The Church-porch" or "The Size":

> Peace pratler, do not lowre:
> Not a fair look, but thou dost call it foul:
> Not a sweet dish, but thou dost call it sowre.

The speaker declares to the pratler that he has "physick to expell thee," a medicine that is at once delicious and salubrious: "My Saviours bloud: when ever at his board / I do but taste it, straight it cleanseth me, / And leaves thee not a word." Remarkably, ingestion here purifies rather than pollutes, allowing Herbert to expel the truly tasteless pratler by consuming the spiritual emetic of Eucharistic wine. This "pratler," as Sidney Gottlieb astutely argues, is reviled for having the kind of palate that fulfills every high church stereotype of the seventeenth-century Puritan in his or her inability to appreciate anything gustatory.[40] Yet Herbert's own position amid theological controversy cannot be mapped as unequivocally as Gottlieb suggests. Herbert certainly identifies the prattler as a presence within himself rather than a theological other – an identification that links up with the other statements deprecating appetite throughout *The Temple* that we have tracked. Moreover, the way that Herbert continually uses the sweetness of the divine repast to criticize terrestrial excess echoes the Puritan repudiation of the lavish banquets, and the equally lavish high church communions, that would occur, in the words of "The Priesthood," on "the boards of those / Who make the bravest shows." Like Milton's bounteous deity, Herbert's God creates a bower of sensual bliss for his creatures, but it is a bower used to check rather than endorse the transience of terrestrial indulgence. Assimilating the language of theological controversy to the internal debates that the practice of temperance demands, "Conscience," as its title indicates, occurs within the individual subject.

In the poem "Lent," however, Herbert does assume an uncharacteristically polemical position on a controversial aspect of alimentary control – the practice of seasonal fasting. Where Conformist apologists supported the traditional "Christological cycle, with its judicious admixture of feasts, fasts and holy days, as one of the distinctive beauties of the English church," Puritans identified this cycle with the Catholicism that the Reformation was still busy undoing.[41] Herbert's "Lent" – a praise of the moral and physical rewards of denying the senses in obedience to the "laws of fasting" – deliberately locates dietary conduct at the nexus of personal and public control: "Welcome deare feast of Lent: who loves not thee, / He loves not Temperance, or Authoritie, / But is compos'd of passion." Because it is mandated by ecclesiastical authority yet practiced individually, fasting involves both the personal discipline of the passions and obedience to political authority. According to Herbert, command of the self is on this occasion synchronized with submission to external power.

The poem links ritual fasting with temperate discipline, and affiliates nonconformist non-participation with disobedience to secular authority and a surrender to one's own internal passion. It then steals the thunder of nonconformist polemic, identifying ritual abstinence with purity and pleasure while linking the refusal to fast, for whatever pretexts of doctrinal purity, with pollution and dyspepsia:

> Besides the cleannesse of sweet abstinence,
> Quick thoughts and motions at a small expense,
>   A face not fearing light:
> Whereas in fulnesse there are sluttish fumes,
> Sowre exhalations, and dishonest rheumes,
>   Revenging the delight.
>
>   (lines 19–24)

Economical as well as clarifying, abstinence is "sweet," while feasting only produces the "sowre exhalations" of indigestion. Abstinence, moreover, is "clean," in contrast to the "sluttish fumes" that feasting occasions, as if food sullies the interior of the very subject it sustains. In a Latin poem, *Lucus* 21, "In Gulosum" ("On the glutton"), Herbert indulges in conventional if colorful castigation of one who over-eats:

> While you shovel food
> In your swooping mouth
> And pick clean whole trays,
> You are weighted down within
> And without with a flood
> Of dirt. That deep hole –
> Don't just call it belly now,
> But cavern in which so many
> Fierce beasts have been packed together.
> You alone can take pleasure
> In a tomb's stench. He will visit you
> Who wants to be interred before his time.[42]

Over-eating produces intestinal broils within the body of the individual subject, Herbert suggests, just as violating the "laws of fasting" does within the body politic. As ritual abstinence became an issue of heated conflict in Herbert's England, so is over-indulgence the cause of internal disturbance in the individual subject.

Feasting, then, is understood to produce abiding discomfort rather than the gastronomic pleasure it promises. Fasting, in turn, is made the recipient of whatever pleasure feasting is reputed to have. The poem, we remember, opens by endowing Lenten fasting with the values embodied in feasting – "Welcome deare feast of Lent" – and proceeds to describe abstinence as "sweet." It concludes, moreover, by discovering in the morally authentic revelry of fasting a telling blend of personal abstinence and social action:

> Yet Lord instruct us to improve our fast
> By starving sinne and taking such repast
>   As may our faults controll:
> That ev'ry man may revell at his doore,
> Not in his parlour; banquetting the poore,
>   And among those his soul.

The economy of fasting makes more consumable resources available to the poor, those whose status makes hunger not a choice but a way of life. Like the Lady in Milton's *Comus*, Herbert imagines that the practices of temperance might actually produce a more equitable distribution of societal benefits. By starving sin corporeally, moreover, one banquets the soul, just as Shakespeare's Sonnet 146 suggested that the soul will thrive by denying the hungers of the body. In Herbert's poem, though, the soul is rewarded sensually – tasting "sweet abstinence" – by prohibiting the body sensual pleasure. The holy fast becomes the holiest of feasts.

In *The Country Parson*, Herbert similarly discusses fasting as a blend of corporeal and spiritual discipline, but fails to emphasize its sensual benefits: "fasting in Scripture language is an afflicting of our souls." As a result, "to eat little, and that unpleasant, is the naturall rule of fasting, although it be flesh" (p. 242). The central point of fasting for Herbert, then, is not that one eat fish rather than meat, but rather that one not have enough, and that one not enjoy it, whether fish or flesh. As a young college student, Herbert had in fact petitioned his stepfather Sir John Danvers for an advance on his annuity because

> I am fain ever and anon, to buy somewhat tending towards my health.... Now this Lent I am forbid utterly to eat any Fish, so that I am fain to dyet in my Chamber at mine own cost; for in our publick Halls, you know, is nothing but Fish and Whit-meats: Out of Lent also, twice a Week, on Fridayes and Saturdayes, I must do so, which yet sometimes I fast. (pp. 364–65)

The reason Herbert needed to eat beef rather than fish is because, in the words of a contemporary, "All manner of fish is cold of nature and doth ingender phlegm; it doth little nourish." A fifteenth-century schoolboy recorded his anguished response to the unrelentingly astringent diet of Lent: "Thou wilt not believe how weary I am of fish, and how much I desire that flesh were come in again, for I have ate none other but salt fish this Lent, and it hath engendered so much phlegm within me that it stoppeth my pipes that I can neither speak or breathe."[43] Herbert was "forbid utterly to eat any Fish," even during Lent, because his perennial pulmonary difficulties were aggravated by the phlegm that fish, because it was cold and moist like phlegm, was thought to engender. "It is certaine," adds Herbert in *The Country Parson*, "that a weak stomack being prepossessed with flesh, shall much better brooke and bear a draught of beer then if it had taken before either fish, or rootes, or such things; which will discover it selfe by spitting, and rheume, or flegme" (p. 242). For one suffering from the costive digestion that seems to have troubled Herbert, "there is nothing that is food, and not phisick, which doth lesse obstruct, then flesh moderately taken; as being immoderately taken, it is exceeding obstructive (p. 243)."[44] Herbert's anxiety about the parson's diet indicates he harbored deep suspicions about the wisdom of one of the proverbs he cites in "The Church-porch": "A good digestion turneth all to health" (line 358). It seems instead as if health depends on consuming only what one's particular digestion can handle.

The poems of *The Temple* betray an unexpected concern with the social and devotional meanings of the indigestion that underpins Herbert's praise of fasting in "Lent" and his redefinition of Lenten fasting in *The Country Parson*. Indigestion fascinates Herbert not simply because of his own ill health but also because it is an occasion where the very substance necessary to sustain life becomes a cause of illness and a medium of punishment, and where the body seems to turn upon itself in an act of civil war. As we will see in Chapter 5, for Milton indigestion is among the first physiological manifestations of the Fall. At times, Herbert locates its origins in his own failures of temperance, but on other occasions he points to the unnecessarily bitter purges and inexplicably disabling illnesses bestowed by a purportedly nourishing and healing deity. In "Affliction (I)," for example, God punishes the speaker by subjecting him to "consuming agues [which] dwell in ev'ry vein." Even when the speaker tries to achieve the severely limited unhappiness of enjoying his misery, "turning my purge to food," God thwarts him by "throw[ing] me / Into more sicknesses" (lines 27, 51–52).

In "Repentance," though, the speaker assumes some responsibility for his internal agony, pleading with his God to "Sweeten at length this bitter bowl, / Which thou hast pour'd into my soul; / Thy wormwood turn to health." The mention of wormwood links Herbert's deity to the angry god of Jeremiah 9.15 (AV), who declares to his stubborn people: "Behold I will feed them, even this people with wormewood." The biblical referent, moreover, allows Herbert to comprehend his gastric distress as a product of his own sin: "When thou for sinne rebukest man, / Forthwith he waxeth wo and wan: / Bitternesse fills our bowels." The bitter pun on bowels and bowls underscores Herbert's account of God's acute attention to mortal gastronomy, converting the very nourishment that normally signals favor into a substance that is at once a punishment and purgative for sin. In "The Churchporch," Herbert suggested that one must always be busy because "Slacknesse breeds worms" (lines 339), as if such creatures were spontaneously produced by the innate corruption of slothful flesh. Since the primary medicinal function of wormwood was as a vermifuge, a worm-killer, "Repentance" imagines that God's bitter medicine will expel the parasitical sin that is at once the cause and the product of the speaker's gastrointestinal distress. In "Sighs and Grones," unregulated consumption of the resources God makes available to his creatures likewise epitomizes human sinfulness – "I have abus'd thy stock, destroy'd thy woods, / Suckt all thy magazens: my head did ake, / Till it found out how to consume thy goods" (lines 9–11) – even as the prospects of God's punishment and his mercy are articulated in explicitly alimentary terms: "O do not fill me / With the turn'd viall of thy bitter wrath! / For thou hast other vessels full of bloud" (lines 19–21). The speaker reminds God that he is both "*feast* and *rod*, / *Cordiall* and *Corrosive*" (lines 27–28). At once an instrument of punishment and a source of nourishment, a medicine which invigorates the heart and a substance which eats away at organic tissue, God is a figure whose tender mercies and baffling torments frequently find alimentary expression.

The "Sighs and Grones" that Herbert utters to God, moreover, have a physiological as well as a psychological function. As Timothy Bright observes,

Sighing has no other cause of moving then to coole and refresh the heart, with fresh breath, and pure ayre, which is the nourishment and foode of the vitall spirites, besides the cooling which the heart it selfe receiveth thereby.[45]

Like the speaker of "Sighs and Grones," the speaker of "Even-song" blames himself rather than God for his own internal torments. He apologizes to his God for the fact that "thy diet, care, and cost / Do end in bubbles, balls of winde; / Of winde to thee whom I have crost, / But balls of wilde-fire to my troubled minde." Here, gastrointestinal disorder is linked to spiritual rebellion. Indeed, in Cornaro's *Treatise on Temperance*, we learn that the study of diet is really a meditation on

the power of order and disorder; whereof the one kept me well for many yeares; the other, though it was but a little excesse, in a few days had so soone overthrowne me. If the world consist of order, if our corporall life depend on the harmonie of humours & elements, it is no wonder that order should preserve, and disorder destroy. (p. 297)

As we saw in Spenser, the self is a physiological and moral battlefield between the forces of order and disorder. As Herbert writes in "The Knell" – a poem he did not include in *The Temple* – on the occasion of receiving the Eucharist:

> Now [is] the great combat of our flesh & reason:
>   O help, my God!
>   See, they breake in,
> Disbanded humours, sorrows, troops of Sinn,
>   Each with his rodd.

The self is in a state of perpetual insurrection, a state which eating pushes to the point of crisis, since even the most rigorous diet inevitably allows insurrectionary reinforcements to enter. The poem "Nature" describes a "natural" mortal subject, who is, in every sense of the phrase, "Full of rebellion." The speaker pleads with God to "tame my heart" since "It is thy highest art / To captivate strong holds to thee." The speaker compares his innate insurrectionary impulses to a "venome" that "lurk[s]" within him, which will without divine intervention

>   in suggestions fume and work,
> My soul will turn to bubbles straight,
>   And thence by kinde
>   Vanish into a winde,
> Making thy workmanship deceit.

God's curing the speaker's indigestion will also involve his reclaiming the speaker's inner spaces – by "nature" sites of turmoil and rebellion – as his own.

In the poem "The Rose," Herbert addresses a traditional image of secular pleasure and of Christian iconography not in order to show how the latter supersedes the former but rather in order to allow the medicinal use of roses as purgatives to supersede both secular and Christian meanings.[46] "The Rose among all Nations and in all countries," asserts Lemnius,

is accounted a most gallant, beautiful, and sweete smelling flower, comfortable both for the braine and also the hart.... The juice, decoction or infusion thereof is reckoned among the kindes of gentle and soft medicines: for it mildly looseth and openeth the bellie, purgeth downward yellow Choler, openeth the obstructions of the liver, strengthening and cleansing the same ... without any danger maketh the bellie soluble, and purgeth all such cholerike excrements.[47]

Herbert's rose thrives in a climate totally different from that of Phaedria's lilies. It is an instrument of rigorous self-examination, not an example of reckless negligence. "The Rose" is in many ways spoken by the ascetic "pratler" of "Conscience" as a rejoinder to the eudaemonic voice that dominates that poem: "Presse me not to take more pleasure / In this world of sugred lies." Where the speaker of "Conscience" warns the prattler that "I have physick to expell thee," the speaker of "The Rose" discovers physic in a symbol of the sensual pleasure he is being urged to experience – the rose.

Asserting that "there is no pleasure here," just "Colour'd griefs" and "Blushing woes," the speaker of "The Rose" denies the possibility of authentic pleasure in this world. Then he turns to "this gentle rose," a symbol of the pleasure he denies, in order to clinch his point by invoking its medicinal uses:

> What is fairer then a rose?
>   What is sweeter? yet it purgeth.
> Purgings enmitie disclose,
>   Enmitie forbearance urgeth.
>
> If then all that worldlings prize
>   Be contracted to a rose;
> Sweetly there indeed it lies,
>   But it biteth in the close.
>
> So this flower doth judge and sentence
>   Worldly joyes to be a scourge:
> For they all produce repentance,
>   And repentance is a purge.

The fact that a rose is beautiful, aromatic, and yet a medical purgative provides Herbert with a model for the role of pleasure in the construction of a spiritual and moral self. The biochemistry of pleasure, according to Herbert, demands that "it biteth in the close."[48] Synchronizing the physical rhythms of consumption and purgation with the moral rhythms of indulgence and repentance, the rose epitomizes the illusory assets and all-too-real debits of pleasure. In the speaker's moral ledger, the choice is not between indulgence and restraint but between the "health" of temperate refusal and the unpleasant "physick" that intemperance inexorably demands.[49]

Indeed, throughout his career Herbert turns to the rose for its telling blend of emblematic and therapeutic uses. In the poem "Providence," God's creative wonders include the fact that "A rose, besides his beautie, is a cure" (line 78). Likewise, in one of the more pragmatic discussions in *The Country Parson*, Herbert tells us that among the "home-bred medicines" available to parsons are "damask or white Roses" for "loosing," that is, for a laxative (p. 261). In his *Diary*, Ralph Josselin records that he "tooke above 2 ounces sirrup roses which wrought very kindly with mee, gave me 9 stooles brought away much Choler, I went to bed, with a persuasion after seeking of god, that he would rebuke my distemper." By being beautiful and by serving as an emetic, roses purge the desire they produce. In doing so, they teach that the proper use of pleasure is to make one relinquish it.[50]

The final utterance in *The Temple*, "L'Envoy," seems to petition the "King of Glorie" to direct the punitive gastritis he has often inflicted upon his devout creature towards "Sinne," a predatory monster who desires to "devour thy fold" and who brags "that thy flesh hath lost his food":

> Choke him, let him say no more,
> But reserve his breath in store,
> Till thy conquests and his fall
> Make his sighs to use it all,
> And then bargain with the winde
> To discharge what is behinde.

Herbert's last words on sin coordinate the physical, social, and spiritual aspects of digestion we have been exploring. Where "for Luther, the Devil dwells in excrement," for Herbert, Sin experiences eternal flatulence.[51] At once immoral and indecorous, Sin is to be afflicted with an ailment that is both physically painful and socially repugnant.[52]

Despite (or perhaps because of) the immense anxiety that surrounds the encounter between inner and outer, between self and other, that is ingestion, eating nonetheless offers Herbert a scenario for profound community between heaven and earth. "The extrasensory *taste* of God," remarks William Kerrigan, "had approximately the emotional centrality for Herbert that the similarly extrasensory *vision* of God had for Milton."[53] Prayer is, in the remarkable sonnet by that name, "the Churches banquet." "Affliction (V)" links the prelapsarian sociability described in "The H. Communion" with the incarnation, conveying the two central moments in Judeo-Christian history in gustatory terms: "As we at first did board with thee, / Now thou wouldst taste our miserie." "Longing" describes a god whose pity for his creatures assumes nutritive and maternal forms: "From thee all pitie flows. / Mothers are kinde, because thou art, / And dost dispose / To them a part: / Their infants, them; and they suck thee / More free" (lines 13–18). The same speaker imagines God as a great householder, whose "board is full, yet humble guests / Finde nests" (lines 53–54). In "The Agonie," "Love" is imagined as "that liquour sweet and most divine, / Which my God feels as bloud; but I, as wine." *In vino, veritas.* What God experiences as corporeal suffering makes possible a morally authentic taste of corporeal voluptuousness. A mysterious synesthesia links divine suffering and human joy.

Because of the importance of alimentary imagery, the mouth – that anxious orifice where diseases are always ready to enter, but also the place from which words of praise emerge – becomes the site of traffic with God. "The Odour" compares the utterance of "*My Master*" with the power of "Amber-greese" to leave "a rich sent / Unto the taster... An orientall fragrancie,... [a] curious broth, / This broth of smells, that feeds and fats my minde." Divine praise, Herbert suggests, is an oral experience with a fragrant aroma and a delicious aftertaste. Miraculously, it nourishes the mind that produces it. In "The Glimpse," the capacity of some foods to generate but not to satiate desire offers a model for devotional longing: "Thy short abode and stay / Feeds not, but addes to the desire of meat," remarks the speaker to his far too ephemeral deity (lines 11–12). Like Shakespeare's Cleopatra, who "makes hungry / Where most she satisfies," Herbert's God increases the appetite he pleases.[54]

"The Invitation" welcomes "All, whose taste / Is your waste" and "whom wine / Doth define" to food and drink where God is "prepar'd and drest, / And the feast, / God, in whom all dainties are." Here, as Strier remarks, Herbert "presents the Eucharist as the ideal fulfillment of the passions involved in sinning."[55] Herbert endorses a spiritual capaciousness whose highest rewards are the alimentary activities whose excesses it condemns. The subsequent poem, "The Banquet," adds a twist to such hospitality, inviting the divine meal into the body and being of the speaking subject: "With me, in me, live and dwell." It celebrates, moreover, a feast whose sensual "delight / Passeth tongue to taste or tell." Speaking and tasting, the activities of the mouth highlighted in "The Odour," meet their match in this transcendently delightful feast. The violence implicit in eating, and in the sacrifice this meal commemorates, is translated into a process of accenting the aromatic qualities of the meal:

> But as Pomanders and wood
>   Still are good,
> Yet being bruis'd are better sented:
> God, to show how farre his love
>   Could improve,
> Here, as broken, is presented.

The synesthetic link between suffering and sensuousness established at the end of "The Agonie" is here asserted with a vengeance. As with a ball of pomander, the full taste of Christ demands his being bruised and broken so his scent may be released.

The poem "Faith" conveys the mystery of its titular subject in gustatory terms:

> Hungrie I was, and had no meat:
> I did conceit a most delicious feast;
> I had it straight, and did as truly eat,
>   As ever did a welcome guest.

Appetite is here likened to spiritual yearning, and spiritual satisfaction to corporeal satiety and social welcome. The Country Parson's experience of consummate spiritual satisfaction is, Herbert tells us, "when ... the Angels minister to us their owne food, even joy and peace; and comfort" (p. 280). In his single direct biblical translation, "The 23d Psalme," Herbert significantly selects an occasion where food provides a medium of gracious exchange between mortal and divine: "The God of love my shepherd is, / And he that doth me feed ... He leads me to the tender grasse, / Where I both feed and rest" (lines 1–6). Even at this moment of nourishment and comfort, Herbert signals the orderly disposition that accompanies God's bountiful care: "if I stray, he doth convert / And bring my minde in frame" (lines 9–10). Herbert chooses a similar moment of nourishment, divine ministration, and mortal rest to constitute the final lyric of "The Church" – "Love (III)" – a poem which brilliantly expresses at once the delicate rhythms of Renaissance table manners and the immense anxiety that for Herbert suffused situations of consumption.[56] The breaking of the most fearful of taboos regarding eating in Western culture – cannibalism – is demanded by divinity as the occasion of a literal consummation of the relationship between God and human: "You must sit down, sayes Love, and taste my meat: / So I did sit and eat." In deliberate contrast to "L'Envoy," "Love (III)" exhibits the most rarefied forms of commensal conduct; where "L'Envoy" sentences devouring sin to eternal flatulence, "Love (III)" welcomes a courteously reluctant soul to a heavenly banquet. Both salvation and damnation occur as alimentary processes.

Perhaps, as Yeats claims, "the poet is never the bundle of accident and incoherence that sits down to breakfast."[57] But for Herbert, who would have rejected the post-Romantic privileging of the poet as well as the post-Galenic separation of the creative self from the material body that underpin Yeats's claims, the devotional poet is in large part constituted by the food he eats and the way he sits down to it. Pressured by religious injunction and medical theory, the devotional subject of *The Temple* emerges from the endeavor to impose order upon the accidents and incoherence of consumption. In one of the central New Testament discussions of the importance of self-discipline, St. Paul had asked, "Knowe yee not that yee are the Temple of God?" (1 Cor. 3.16; AV). Herbert's *Temple* of poetic devotion is constructed in part on the principles of temperance. The unruly body is made a temple fit for divine habitation by subjecting it to the rules of temperance. Assimilating the Renaissance literature of dietary control to the lessons of Christian conduct, Herbert transforms the ambivalences that suffuse eating into the punishments and rewards of the Christian dispensation.

In "The Collar," Herbert's speaker imagines the moral transgression the excess of humoral choler leads him to contemplate as the seizure of a tempting fruit: "But there is fruit, / And thou hast hands." In the next chapter, I will explore the works of John Milton, a writer whose lifelong engagement with issues of self-regulation will provoke him to re-enact throughout his career similar scenes of gastronomic temptation. It will also induce him to value temperance, the virtue whose rigorous deployment would defeat the urges such temptations present. In the confrontation with culinary temptation, Milton will discover a radical form of inwardness, at once dependent on God and independent of the world, in which the material transformations of digestion provide a model for ethical and spiritual transcendence. Rather than achieving spirituality by turning away from materiality, Herbert and Milton deliberately map corporeal and spiritual concerns onto one another in a lifelong attempt to construct a Christian social practice. Food nourishes the devotional imagination of Herbert and Milton by offering them a kind of radium isotope that could trace, when consumed, the inner lineaments of the Christian devotional subject. But where for Herbert the Eucharistic feast is at the center of the process by which God blesses mortal appetite, for Milton the Eucharist is just another meal whose supposed miracles pale before the quotidian miracle of digestion. Herbert imagines God entering humanity through the digestive tract, while Milton imagines humanity transformed by a digestive process into divinity. Herbert's abiding attention to consumption was in essence an exploration of the mutually constitutive processes of social and devotional subject formation. For Herbert, the Incarnation graced the unruly flesh Herbert wishes to regulate, while the Holy Communion sanctified the food that nourishes that flesh. Jesus himself, Herbert argues in *The Country Parson*, "rather made food miraculously, then suffered so good desires [as hunger] to miscarry" (p. 267). Choosing to enter his creature "by the way of nourishment and strength," Herbert's God graciously ratifies the restrained appetites and disciplined bodies of his mortal subjects.

5 Temperance and temptation: The alimental vision in *Paradise Lost*

> The allegory of Adam and Eve eating of the tree of evil, and entailing upon their posterity the wrath of God, and the loss of everlasting life, admits of no other explanation than the disease and crime that have flowed from unnatural diet.
> Shelley, *Queen Mab* (1813)[1]
>
> A well-behaved stomach is a great part of liberty.
> Montaigne, "Of Experience"[2]

In *The Origin of Table Manners*, Claude Levi-Strauss identifies two primary functions of the widespread cultural regulation of conduct in the presence of food, functions that delineate

> the total opposition between the reasons for good manners believed in by so-called primitive people and ourselves.... Whereas we think of good manners as a way of protecting the internal purity of the subject against the external impurity of beings and things, in savage societies, they are a means of protecting the purity of beings and things against the impurity of the subject.

Levi-Strauss finds in this difference not a narrative of the superior "civilizing processes" of Western culture but rather "a lesson in humility" in the dietary practices the West has with misplaced pride forgotten, teaching "that sound humanism does not begin with oneself, but puts the world before life, life before man, and respect for others before self-interest."[3] In *Paradise Lost*, John Milton discovers a similar lesson in the central Judeo-Christian myth linking the origin of human history to conduct before food. He attempts to justify the ways of God to men and women by suggesting that humans, not God, introduce into the world through their past and present behavior toward food the contagions and impurities from which they continue to suffer. The regulation of conduct before food becomes for Milton the primary physiological and moral strategy for coping with the impurity we bring to, and confront in, every meal. Exploring both the physiology and the ethics of consumption and purgation, Milton in his epic of the Fall makes food a central site of pre- and postlapsarian morality.

The social, physical, and moral consequences of consumption preoccupied Milton throughout his career. As early as his schoolboy exercises,

Milton had valued the salutary and moral aspects of temperance, contrasting those "worthless fellows" who "give themselves up to gluttony, to drinking like whales, and to spending their nights in gaming and debauchery" to those who aim to "live modestly and temperately, and to tame the impulses of headstrong youth by reason and steady devotion to study, keeping the divine vigor of our minds unstained and uncontaminated by any impurity or pollution."[4] As both a physiological and an ethical phenomenon, eating fascinated Milton. Physiologically, Milton finds the processes of digestion to exemplify the principles of material transformation that animate his hierarchical yet meritocratic and monist universe. Ethically, he discovers in eating an experience whereby the choice he so values in all arenas must be exercised frequently and rigorously. From the Latin Elegies and *Comus* through *Areopagitica* and *Paradise Regained*, Milton focused his attention on eating because it encapsulates a central paradox of human existence: that food, the substance that sustains life, can seduce one into moral decadence and physiological death. Every meal is a moral test, a temptation to transgress what the Archangel Michael will call the "rule of not too much." Like Herbert, Milton was led by ill health to a deep personal engagement with the quotidian regimes of temperance. Like Herbert, Milton links the highest of spiritual aspirations with the most mundane physiological operations, and imagines indigestion as a moral and physiological state. Like Spenser and Shakespeare, Milton explores the ways that the demands of passion and reason collide in the individual, and articulates compellingly the pulls of both. Like all three writers, Milton discovers in the discourse of physiology a supple and profound discourse of psychological inwardness.

Throughout his career, Milton embraced the scenario of temptation – what W. B. C. Watkins felicitously calls "trial by food" – because it demands close attention to the physiological ramifications of the inner choices of the individual agent.[5] If Milton were to rewrite the Lord's Prayer, he would ask "Lead us into temptation," since temptation is for him so necessary to the moral life of the individual. As Milton asserts in a famous passage from *Areopagitica*,

I cannot praise a fugitive and cloistered virtue, unexercis'd & unbreath'd, that never sallies out and sees her adversary.... Assuredly we bring not innocence into the world, we bring impurity much rather: that which purifies us is triall, and triall is by what is contrary. That vertue therefore which is but a youngling in the contemplation of evil, and knows not the utmost that vice promises to her followers, and rejects it, is but a blank vertue, not a pure; her whitenesse is but an excrementall whitenesse. (p. 1006)

Milton here suggests that virtue without temptation is superficial, untested; but he also means for us to hear the other available meaning of "excrement," undigested and potentially noxious matter. That which transforms apparent virtue into authentic nutriment is temptation. As digestion separates nutriment from dross, so does trial distinguish true virtue from its mere appearance. Fascinated by the necessary blend of purity and impurity that constitutes postlapsarian existence, Milton embraces temptation as a winnowing experience intimately related to, and sometimes identical with, digestion. Censorship is rejected because it robs one of the occasion for exercising the virtue inherent in the separation of noxious from nutritive material.

For Milton, the political liberty to which he devoted so much effort is manifested most meaningfully and extensively in the quotidian regulation of appetite that temperance demands:

How great a vertue is temperance, how much of moment through the whole life of man? yet God committs the managing so great trust, without particular Law or prescription, wholly to the demeanour of every grown man. . . . For those actions which enter into a man, rather then issue out of him, and therefore defile not, God uses not to captivat under a perpetuall childhood of prescription, but trusts him with the gift of reason to be his own chooser. (pp. 1005–6)

Paradise Lost will tell the story of humanity's progress from the "perpetuall childhood of prescription" that is prelapsarian dietary experience to an anxious adulthood of consumption, whereby all meals become a battlefield between temperance and temptation.[6] Before the Fall, Adam and Eve must obey only "This one, this easy charge, of all the trees / In Paradise that bear delicious fruit / So various, not to taste that only Tree / Of Knowledge" (4.421–24). Their diet is clearly prescribed. But after the Fall, eating becomes a terribly anxious pleasure demanding the continual application of reason to the clamors of appetite. In *Paradise Lost*, Michael declares that the purpose of "so many and so various laws" under the Old Dispensation is not so much to elicit obedience as "to evince [the] natural pravity" (12.282, 287–88) of those who are subject to it. By the same token, the function of the complex Levitican dietary laws that Christianity would subsequently suspend was not so much to disclose the impurity of certain foods as to reveal the impurity that humans bring to the table. Under the Christian regime as Milton construes it, eating becomes a far more complicated moral action than it is under the intricate dietary strictures of Leviticus, since food is excluded not by decree but by an unending series of ethical interrogations of self and appetite. As a result, the consuming subject must exercise relentless dietary casuistry in order to determine the crucial moment when sustenance becomes indulgence, and thus threatens its moral and physical well-being. This casuistry demands ultimately, as it does for Herbert, a periodic and profound introspection. Although labori-

134   Bodies and selves in early modern England

ous, such introspection will also make possible the discovery of the essence of that Paradise from which humans were expelled amid the inner chambers of the sinful human subject.

More than just the arbitrary occasion for the exercise of obedience, then, eating provides a central opportunity for the exercise of virtue and vice in Milton's universe. The virtue imagined to control appetite – temperance – extends of course to other appetites besides food. In *On Christian Doctrine*, Milton defines temperance widely, as "the virtue which regulates our appetite for the pleasures of the flesh."[7] As we saw in the chapter on Spenser, numerous dissonances emerge when the language of temperance is applied indiscriminately to the realms of food and of sex, since food is a physiological necessity, while sex is not, and since sex is particularly troubling to Christian ethical practice, while food is not. Although the principle of self-regulation amid temptation remains the same for sex and food, then, the practical parameters of the virtue can alter dramatically. When Milton in *Areopagitica* praises Spenser's depiction of temperance in Book 2 of *The Faerie Queene*, the temptations that Guyon experiences are not commensal but acquisitive in the Cave of Mammon, and erotic in the Bower of Bliss. For Milton Spenser is

> our sage and serious Poet ... whom I dare be known to think a better teacher then Scotus or Aquinas, describing true temperance under the person of Guion, brings him in with his palmer through the cave of Mammon, and bowr of earthly blisse that he might see and know, and yet abstain. (p. 1006)

Although Milton forgets that the Palmer does not accompany Guyon in the Cave of Mammon, he remembers vividly the central point of Spenser's portrait of "true temperance": that it is in fact a portrait of continence, depicting in the most compelling terms possible the insurgent desires that Guyon must experience and conquer. Although both *Comus* and *Paradise Regained* will focus on protagonists apparently immune to temptation, *Paradise Lost* will emphasize the direction rather than the eradication of passion.

The confusion produced by the parallel between a temperate sexuality and a temperate diet runs throughout *Paradise Lost*. When Eve succumbs to Satan, and when Adam accepts the fruit from the fallen Eve, dietary transgression is imagined in terms of illicit sexuality. Where Eve is "deflowered" by Satan, Adam is "fondly overcome with female charm." After both have eaten the forbidden fruit, "Carnal desire" is inflamed; Adam says to Eve, "Now I see thou art exact of taste," addressing her as if she were just another tender morsel (9.1013, 1018). Then they make passionate love. But where Spenser could imagine temperate consumption far more easily than he could envision temperate sexuality, Milton views eating as a more insidious temptation than eros, because the moral hazards of consumption issue directly from its deceptive blend of physiological necessity and sensual attraction. Every meal is for Milton a quotidian trek through a bower of dietary bliss, a bower which can never be destroyed, and can never be rejected absolutely. In *Paradise Lost*, as in *Areopagitica* and *The Faerie Queene*, one is not allowed to take the comparatively easy way of avoiding potentially contaminating contact with pleasures and passions, or of obeying a few simple edicts. Rather, one must aspire through a heroic blend of humble obedience and gustatory discrimination to separate good from bad, salutary matter from noxious, and so to turn the excremental material of error into the site of nutritious virtue.

Milton's exploration of the ethical aspects of consumption appeals to the deeply embodied psychology we have been tracing throughout this book. For Milton, the moral battle between reason and passion occurs most intensely on the plane of the corporeal. As William Kerrigan, one of the critics most attentive to the central role of materiality in Milton's imagination, remarks, "Including passions and appetites, 'flesh' is a diagnostic category in the pathology of the will; the body as a thing belonging to an alien world of things becomes, not the dead fact against which the soul is known, but a symbol in moral psychology."[8] Flesh, then, is not a realm opposed to Milton's spiritual and ethical aspirations, but its necessary medium. From the unmoved Lady of *Comus* and the unruffled Son of *Paradise Regained* through the Adam and Eve who eat what they should not and the Samson who achieves "calm of mind" through the violent expenditure of passion, Milton locates the ethics of choice in a physiology of ingestion and purgation.

In *Paradise Lost*, the regulation of ingestion very literally determines the patterns of individual and human salvation. As Watkins observes,

Milton from beginning to end is preoccupied with eating – literal and figurative ... we must read *Paradise Lost* and its great companion poems several times to realize how constant is the taking of food. Neither the denizens of Paradise nor of Heaven miss a meal, invariably described with unabashed enjoyment.[9]

In comprehending the story of Adam and Eve as primarily a narrative of dietary transgression, Milton of course draws on a vast exegetical and popular tradition extending from Genesis. But Milton deliberately alters the emphasis of the story, from a condemnation of appetite *per se* to a condemnation of unregulated appetite. The Abbot Nilus articulates well the conventional interpretation, observing that "It was the desire of food that spawned disobedience; it was the pleasure of taste that drove us from paradise."[10] The Elizabethan *Homilie Against Gluttony and Drunkennesse* similarly demeans appetite in its account of the Fall: "If our first parents

136   Bodies and selves in early modern England

Adam and Eve had not obeyed their greedy appetite in eating the forbidden fruit, neither had they lost the fruition of GODS benefites which they then enjoyed in paradise."[11] In *Paradise Lost*, though, Milton embraces appetite and pleasure with cavalier gusto as potential moral as well as sensual goods.[12] By making his angels actually eat and praise material food – something no writer before him had done – Milton legitimates terrestrial hunger and consumption, even as he legitimates the corollary appetite for sex by having Adam and Eve, and the angels, participate in its deeply embodied pleasures. Tellingly, we never see Satan and the fallen angels experience these sensual pleasures.[13] Indeed, if we were to map Book 2 of Spenser's *Faerie Queene* onto Milton's moral landscape, we would see that Paradise is a Bower of true Bliss, and Satan, rather than the exemplar of temperance, its destroyer. While he foregrounds the ethical and spiritual importance of food, though, Milton at the same time rejects for theological reasons two central occasions for exploring the religious significance of eating: the Eucharistic feast, and the holy fast.[14] In the last chapter we saw the importance that these held for Herbert's religious imagination. In place of these devotional and liturgical practices, which for Milton would have been tainted by their association with Catholicism, Milton rewrites the classical virtue of temperance as the product of a truly reformed Christian religion. What Catholicism claims to do institutionally – transform bread into flesh – is for Milton the quotidian prerogative of individual digestion. Milton here gives a particularly materialist emphasis to the prototypically Protestant doctrine of the priesthood of all believers.

Throughout *Paradise Lost*, Milton bestows upon food an even more central role than do his biblical sources, representing the highest social occasion imaginable as a terrestrial feast shared by angel and human, and portraying Sin and Death as unmannerly and repulsive diners. Indeed, Milton's ideal of mortal consumption is carefully plotted against two extra-human examples of table manners: the incestuous cannibalism of Sin's children, and the angelic banquet described by Raphael. In the *Christian Doctrine*, Milton terms the Mass "a banquet of cannibals," and suggests that transubstantiation should be renamed "anthropophagy."[15] Sin, the ultimate *alma mater*, tells Satan that her children "when they list, into the womb / That bred them . . . return, and howl and gnaw / My bowels, their repast" (2.797 –800), invoking just the cannibalistic imagery that Milton associates with the Catholic Eucharist.

The heavenly banquet Raphael describes is in deliberate and decorous contrast to this indecent and incestuous cannibalism. The "sweet repast" to which the heavenly angels "turn / Desirous" manifests a sumptuousness that might surprise those who expect bleak asceticism from a poet wedded to the regimens of temperance:

> Tables are set, and on a sudden pil'd
> With Angels Food, and rubied Nectar flows
> In Pearl, in Diamond, and massie Gold,
> Fruit of delicious Vines, the growth of Heav'n.   (5.632–35)

Blending the control of civility and the release of festivity in a humanist fantasy of disciplined surfeit, the angels

> On flours repos'd, and with fresh flouerts crownd,
> They eate, they drink, and in communion sweet
> Quaff immortalitie and joy, secure
> Of surfet where full measure only bounds
> Excess, before th' all-bounteous King, who showrd
> With copious hand, rejoycing in thir joy.   (5.637–41)

Sounding remarkably like the royalist feasts Milton repeatedly censured, the heavenly banquet is characterized by desire, excess, and fullness.[16] Particularly surprising is the bejeweled sumptuousness of heavenly plate and cutlery. The dishes sound more appropriate to the Cave of Mammon than the Castle of Alma. But that is Milton's point. Categories that in the moral and physiological discourse about appetite invariably denote sin, corruption, excess, and disease are here used to celebrate the plenitude of the creator, a truly gracious host. In contrast to the sensual delights produced by divine bounty, the figure of Sin unwillingly provides only the unsavory and unsatisfying – albeit Eucharistic – meal of her own body.

When he portrays the terrestrial dining experience, Milton is no less lavish with sumptuous detail. Our first vision of Adam and Eve is of their eating together:

> to thir Supper Fruits they fell,
> Nectarine Fruits which the compliant boughes
> Yielded them, side-long as they sat recline
> On the soft downie Bank damaskt with flours:
> The savourie pulp they chew, and in the rinde
> Still as they thirsted scoop the brimming stream.   (4.333–36)

The remarkable attention to sensual detail, even to the experience of chewing, is matched by the description of the care with which Eve "prepared / For dinner savory fruits, of taste to please / True appetite" when they get ready to host a heavenly visitor (5.303–5). The sumptuous details serve to dignify the material reality of food, while the adjective "true" honors the passionate reality of appetite. Even constructing the menu entails decisions that are at once ethical and Epicurean; Eve determines

138   Bodies and selves in early modern England

> What choice to choose for delicacy best,
> What order, so contriv'd as not to mix
> Tastes, not well joynd, inelegant, but bring
> Taste after taste upheld with kindliest change.
> . . . .
>   fruit of all kindes, in coate,
> Rough, or smooth rin'd, or bearded husk, or shell
> She gathers, Tribute large, and on the board
> Heaps with unsparing hand; for drink the Grape
> She crushes, inoffensive moust, and meathes
> From many a berrie, and from sweet kernels prest
> She tempers dulcet creams.   (5.333–47)

Milton's vocabulary here brilliantly fuses the political and the aesthetic, allowing the virtues of temperance and choice to find their culinary counterparts. In noting that human and angel are able to discourse at leisure since there is "No fear lest dinner cool" (5.395), Milton playfully sets the opposition between the raw and the cooked against itself, allowing a distinction which can delineate the differences between civil and uncivil society to designate the heightened civility of prelapsarian society.[17] In this consummately urbane but uncooked meal, discursive concerns take precedence over the demands of culinary presentation. From the brutal exigencies of cannibalizing Sin to the baroque elegance of heavenly table manners, eating encompasses the highest and lowest possibilities of the existences it sustains in Milton's universe.

In heaven, it seems, there is no worry about over-eating. The angels are "secure / Of surfet," because angelic constitutions can consume heavenly excess freely, without the physiological and ethical recriminations that will afflict postlapsarian diners. The fact that indulgence does not precipitate surfeit in heaven, though, brings up the possibility that it might do so on earth, even before the Fall. In their prelapsarian after-dinner conversation, Raphael responds to Adam's "desire / Of knowledge" with a lesson based on the experience of digestion that depends on the ancient topos linking the reception of food with the ingestion of ideas:

> But Knowledge is as food, and needs no less
> Her Temperance over Appetite, to know
> In measure what the mind may well contain,
> Oppresses else with Surfet, and soon turns
> Wisdom to Folly, as Nourishment to Winde.[18]

Remarkably, intestinal gas is neither an exclusively postlapsarian nor an exclusively terrestrial experience, or the comparison has no meaning for either party. Surfeit in knowledge and food is marked by the process whereby what should nourish turns to the insubstantial and troubling winds of flatulence. Knowledge, says Juan Huarte in *The Examination of Men's Wits*, must

> have his due digestion ... for as the bodie is not maintained by the much which we eat and drinke in one day, but by that which the stomacke digesteth and turneth: so our understanding is not filled by the much which we read in little time, but by that which by little and little it proceeds to conceive and chew upon.[19]

As the forbidden fruit would impart knowledge and indigestion at once, so is knowledge here compared to the effect of callow fruit on digestion.

Throughout the poem, and throughout his life, Milton pays what seems like an inordinate amount of attention to digestive matters. So intense and pervasive is Milton's concern with the material processes of existence that his Garden of Eden is in many ways a Garden of Eating. Its hospitability to its human inhabitants is defined by its edibility. At the terrestrial meal shared by Adam and Raphael, human and angel eat until "with meat and drinks they had suffic't, / Not burd'n'd Nature" (5.451–52). The very wording suggests the possibility of their burdening nature through overeating, and indicates that an ethical decision, however unpremeditated and easy, is being made in order to exercise temperance amid the plenitude of Paradise. When Raphael reassures Adam that the food they have offered is indeed attractive to an angelic constitution, he describes the processes of angelic digestion in terms that make digestion the central moral and physical phenomenon of the universe. Both angels and humans, Raphael observes,

>   contain
> Within them every lower facultie
> Of sense, whereby they hear, see, smell, touch, taste,
> Tasting concoct, digest, assimilate,
> And corporeal to incorporeal turn.
> For know, whatever was created, needs
> To be sustaind and fed; of Elements
> The grosser feeds the purer, Earth the Sea,
> Earth and the Sea feed Air, the Air those Fires
> Ethereal, and lowest first the Moon;
> Whence in her visage round those spots, unpurg'd
> Vapours not yet into her substance turnd.
> Nor doth the Moon no nourishment exhale
> From her moist Continent to higher Orbes.
> The Sun that light imparts to all receives
> From all his alimental recompence
> In humid exhalations, and at Even
> Sups with the Ocean.   (5.409–25)

Explaining the craters on the moon as unpurged and undigested vapors, and imagining an ecological hierarchy of exhalations and assimilations culminating in the Sun's evening supper with the ocean, Raphael locates in digestion the animating principle of the universe. Milton's philosophical commitment to materialism conspires here with his dedication to ethical transformation, leading him to imagine the Great Chain of Being as a Great Chain of Digestion and Secretion.[20]

The narrator, moreover, assures the reader that digestion is meant literally. "Nor seemingly" does the angel eat, he declares,

> nor in mist, the common gloss
> Of Theologians, but with keen dispatch
> Of real hunger, and concoctive heat
> To transubstantiate; what redounds, transpires
> Through Spirits with ease.   (5.435–39)

Here Milton aggressively disagrees with all previous commentators on angelic behavior in order to establish the legitimacy of "real hunger," and to explain the processes by which, as Raphael had articulated it, "corporeal to incorporeal turn[s]."[21] By using the term "transubstantiate," Milton reveals angelic digestion to be a far greater miracle than the transubstantiation at the center of the Catholic Mass. Indeed, Milton proceeds to compare the digestion of matter to the purification of ore by heat that is the essence of alchemy:

> nor wonder; if by fire
> Of sooty coal the Empiric Alchemist
> Can turn, or holds it possible to turn
> Metals of drossiest Ore to perfet Gold
> As from the Mine.   (5.439–43)

Like the fire used to purify metals in the Cave of Mammon, and the cauldron stewing nutritive material in the stomach of the Castle of Alma, angelic digestion is engaged in a process of heated transformation via separation and purification. Rather than turning bread to flesh or coal to gold, though, angelic digestion transforms matter to spirit by purging dross. For Milton, the ubiquitous alchemy of daily existence far surpasses the mystifications of Catholic theological doctrine. What Catholicism claims to do institutionally – transform bread into flesh – is instead the prerogative of individual digestion – a transubstantiation fully available to a priesthood of all eaters. The philosophical consequence of denying that the Eucharist occasioned a miracle of any sort was, argues Kerrigan, to "make all eating a creator-centered sacrament of transubstantiation."[22]

As the alchemical comparison indicates, the marvel of angelic digestion seems to demand some possibility of waste products, as postlapsarian human digestion certainly does: "what redounds, transpires / Through

Spirits with ease." Milton here theorizes that whatever is excessive or cannot be digested (the *OED* glosses "redound" as "to overflow, superabound; to be in excess") passes through the body like a kind of sweat ("transpire" is glossed in the *OED* as "to emit or cause to pass in the state of vapour through the walls or surface of a body; [esp. to give off or discharge (waste matter, etc.) through the skin" and "to perspire"]). He thus makes angelic digestion a more graceful version of postlapsarian mortal defecation. As Jonathan Richardson remarks on this passage, "This Artfully Avoids the Indecent Idea, which would Else have been Apt to have Arisen on the Angels feeding, and withal gives a Delicacy to These Spirits, which Finely distinguishes Them from Us in One of the Most Humbling Circumstances relating to our Bodies."[23]

But the digestive technologies available to the first two humans in Paradise are less well spelled out. Indeed, it is one of the more puzzling aspects of the epic that, as Kerrigan aptly observes, "evacuation is the one everyday function of the body whose Edenic exercise Milton has not seen fit to tell us about directly."[24] In *Christian Doctrine*, Milton allows a very material concern with waste to mock the issue of transubstantiation, declaring: "Whereas if we eat his flesh it will not remain in us, but, to speake candidly, after being digested in the stomach, it will be at length exuded.... Then, when it has been driven through all the stomach's filthy channels, it shoots it out – one shudders even to mention it – into the latrine."[25] In *Paradise Lost* Milton manages to record the malodorous phenomenon of waste disposal in order to negate its appropriateness to Paradise when he compares Satan to "one who long in populous City pent, / Where Houses thick and Sewers annoy the Aire," and who escapes to the country where he "from each thing met conceives delight" (9.445–48). Paradisal air is certainly not burdened with the smells of sewage that suffused Milton's London.

The absence of a concern with defecation in Paradise is particularly troubling simply because the purgation of noxious matter is such a necessary principle of physiological and ethical discrimination for Milton. Even Aquinas, who thought unlike Milton that food would be unnecessary in heaven, imagines a place for prelapsarian defecation:

Some say that in the state of innocence man would not have taken more than necessary food, so that there would have been nothing superfluous. This, however, is unreasonable to suppose, as implying that there would have been no faecal matter. Therefore there was need for voiding the surplus, yet so disposed by God as not to be unbefitting.[26]

Aquinas, then, imagines paradisal digestion as needing to get rid of surplus material, but he does not suggest what comely procedure God might have chosen. Perhaps Milton assumes prelapsarian digestion is so efficient, and prelapsarian food so pure, that fecal evacuation is rendered unnecessary. But this would imply that human bodies possess digestions superior to those of the angels, whose own redounding matter is transpired, excreted through the skin as a kind of perspiration.

Part of the problem, though, is our exclusive definition of excrement as fecal matter, since the medical literature of the period conceived of a whole range of corporal effusions as excremental. As Thomas Venner observes in the *Via Recta ad Vitam Longam,*

> For in every concoction some excrements are ingendred, which residing in the body condense and oppilate, and so become the roots of divers diseases. Now the thicker sort of excrements which arise from the first and second concoction of the stomack and liver, are avoided by sensible evacuation, as by Stoole and urine; but the thinner that come of the third concoction in the limbs are wasted by transpiration, and purged forth by exercise, which causeth sweat in those which wish to live in health.[27]

Sweat, in other words, is classified as an excrement like feces, only thinner in substance, and escaping through pores all over the body rather than a specific channel. It is joined in the category of excrement by earwax, tears, fingernails, mucus, and hair.

Although there seems to be no defecation in Paradise, there is perspiration, a terrestrial version of the transpiration by which angels excrete what they cannot digest. Indeed, Adam awakes from his creation drenched in sweat:

> As new waked from soundest sleep
> Soft on the flowery herb I found me laid
> In balmy sweat, which with his beams the sun
> Soon dried, and on the reeking moisture fed. (8.253–6)

It is deeply significant to Milton's alimental vision that the first thing the first human does, even prior to consciousness, is sweat.[28] It is as if in this poem obsessed with firsts, the primal corporeal activity is excretion. Adam explains the evaporation of this balmy sweat as the sun feeding on excremental moisture, receiving "his alimental recompense / In humid exhalations" (5.424–25). Adam shows he has assimilated Raphael's lesson in the universal digestive tract of assimilation and excretion. Sweat, of course, will be part of the biblical curse that humanity receives for its dietary transgression: "In the sweat of thy face shalt thou eat bread" (10.205). Here, sweat serves as a synecdoche for the hard labor that produces it, but it is not cleaned of its excretory connotations.

Hair, too, is categorized as an excrement of sorts, and one that receives a lot of attention in *Paradise Lost*. As Juan Huarte remarks in *The Examination of Men's Wits*, "the material cause whereof the haire consisteth, the

Phisitions say, is a grosse vapour, which ariseth from the digestion, that the brain maketh at the time of his nourishment."[29] For Huarte, hair is excrement from the brain. But does hair grow in Paradise? If so, what does that suggest about the gender distinctions it is supposed to underpin, when Adam's "Hyacinthin Locks / Round from his parted forelock manly hung / Clustring, but not beneath his shoulders broad," while Eve wears "as a vail down to the slender waste / Her unadorned golden tresses" (4.301–5). Is this a product of nature or of culture? In *Samson Agonistes*, Milton places great weight on the way that Samson's strength returns as his hair grows back. The silence in *Paradise Lost* is meaningful only because Milton is a poet so deeply committed to the material basis of spiritual reality.

A related issue emerges with the question of waste management in Paradise. Although they almost certainly do not exude fecal matter, Adam and Eve do express a frequent anxiety about what to do with the extraneous material produced by this inherently lush garden. Adam, for example, suggests that the wildly growing plants "mock our scant manuring" (4.628). Here Milton takes a word which could refer to excremental waste – manure – and returns it to its Latin root, *manus*, "to work by hand." Adam laments not the plants' failure to grow, which would engage the excremental meaning (a failure to grow would mock their efforts to fertilize), but their over-growth, which mocks their efforts at pruning by hand. Adam continues, complaining that the trails in Paradise seem to become over-grown faster than they can clear them: "Those blossoms also, and those dropping gums, / That lie bestrewn unsightly and unsmooth, / Ask riddance, if we mean to tread with ease" (4.630–32). The question is both aesthetic and practical, since the excess here is at once unsightly and inconvenient. Where are they to dispose of this waste material? Does it rot? Even their delightful song of praise describes the garden as "this delicious place / For us too large, where thy abundance wants / Partakers, and uncropt falls to the ground" (4.729–31). Are we to imagine a Paradise strewn with over-ripe fruit? Does the fruit rot, or will it just continue to pile up until decay is introduced into the world almost as a relief? It is as if Comus's vision of a nature over-burdened by its own bounty, and needing gluttonous consumers, conveys an unexpected truth about Paradise.

When Milton describes the original act of creation, moreover, excretory processes play an essential role in the process:

> on the watrie calme
> His brooding wings the Spirit of God outspred,
> And vital vertue infus'd, and vital warmth
> Throughout the fluid Mass, but downward purg'd
> The black tartareous cold Infernal dregs
> Adverse to life. (7.234–39)

Milton here suggests that the act of creation also entails the act of defecation, a kind of downward purging of the dregs of the matter from which God made the universe.[30] Raphael's account of the universe as a vast digestive system needs to be heard behind this passage, since it seems difficult for Milton, or anyone, to conceive of an act of digestion that does not produce waste matter. Hell is composed of the excrement of the universe, the material that cannot (or refuses to) partake of that vast ecology of assimilation and secretion.

Behind Milton's portrait here is a particularly Paracelsian vision of physiology, best characterized by Alan Debus:

The physiology of the body is ruled over by archei acting more or less like internal alchemists in the different organs. The most important of these is the archeus of the stomach which separates the pure from the impure parts of the food, distributes the valuable portions to those parts of the body where they are needed, and discards the poisons. If the archei fail to act properly, poisons can accumulate within the body instead of being eliminated and when this happens disease can result. A good example may be seen in Paracelsus' theory of tartaric disease which included such afflictions as are associated with the building up of stony precipitates in the body (e.g., the calculus, tartar of the teeth, or the calcifying material built up in the lungs in a case of tuberculosis).[31]

Centered in the stomach like the Galenism it aspired to replace, Paracelsian medicine located the cause of disease in indigestible matter termed "tartareous." John Rogers astutely remarks that "the terms Milton employs for that which is excreted in the purgative step of this process – tartar and dregs – are the standard names in the period's natural philosophy for the inassimilable elements purged from the system in the process of digestion."[32] Rogers proceeds to ask a very important question: "why it is that Milton's Creation requires this act of digestive purgation at all." As Rogers points out, Paracelsus himself did not believe that there was any such residue at Creation. Rogers's ingenious and largely persuasive response is to argue that

the theologically irreconcilable figure of the "dregs" constitutes a relic of those political anxieties that trouble Milton's final political writings... the irrational, unspiritualized dregs had established themselves as permanent and untransformable members of the body politic. (pp. 137, 141–42)

Milton, then, is translating the spiritual and political recalcitrance of his countrymen into his physiological account of the unregenerate dregs of the matter from which the universe was made.

Another way of putting the question, and one that does not demand the sublimation of material to political concerns, would be to ask why Milton unconventionally chooses to include these dregs in his account of creation but leaves them out of his otherwise unconventionally material account of Paradise. Perhaps he does so in order to emphasize the way that the Fall tragically invites tartareous dregs, and the indigestion and disease they precipitate, into human existence. But he also wants the digestive principle of separating good from bad to constitute the essential structure of his universe. The inconsistency here involves perhaps the central ontological paradox in Milton's thought – how to account for the existence of unregenerate matter in a monist universe created by an all-good divinity.

Raphael himself forgets the lesson of the tartareous dregs of primal matter that he will soon give, telling Adam that God

> one Almighty is, from whom
> All things proceed, and up to him return,
> If not deprav'd from good, created all
> Such to perfection, one first matter all,
> Indu'd with various forms, various degrees
> Of substance, and in things that live, of life;
> But more refin'd, more spiritous, and pure,
> As nearer to him plac't or nearer tending
> Each in thir several active Sphears assignd,
> Till body up to spirit work. (5.469–78)

As Rogers explains, "Raphael reveals here the gradualist chain of all things that ties the barely spiritualized matter of gross substance to the ethereal, rarefied matter of pure spirit."[33] The hierarchy, however, betrays a deep philosophical tension between a principle of digestion, which separates nutrition from dross, and monism, which imagines all matter as coming from and returning to a good God. The passage certainly emphasizes the latter, but in acknowledging the possibility of being "depraved from good" it makes room for the former.

Expurgation of the unassimilable dregs is of course only one part of digestion; the other side involves a process of upward assimilation that also assumes great ethical importance in Milton's universe. For Raphael, finally, the desirable trajectory of body to spirit is best described by the technologies of digestion, through which the very material aspiration of vegetable life-forms, expressed in fruit and flowers, is transposed into a higher edible form. As such, they presage for Raphael the potential translation of human bodies into a higher, more spiritual sphere:

> So from the root
> Springs lighter the green stalk, from thence the floure
> Spirits Odorous breathes; flours and thir fruit
> Mans nourishment, by gradual scale sublimed
> To vital Spirits aspire, to animal,
> To intellectual, give both life and sense,
> Fansie and understanding, whence the Soule

> Reason receives, and reason is her being . . .
> Wonder not then, what God for you saw good
> If I refuse not, but convert, as you,
> To proper substance; time may come when men
> With angels may participate, and find
> No inconvenient diet, nor too light fare;
> And from these corporal nutriments perhaps
> Your bodies may at last turn all to spirit . . . (5.479–99)

At the core of digestion, Raphael suggests, is a principle of material conversion. Just as an angel can be nourished by terrestrial food, and just as humans can be nourished by life-forms below them, so may humans find their own corporal beings turning to the rarefied matter that Milton terms "spirit." It is as if the metamorphic dynamic of digestion would spread to the entire organism, and catalyze its transformation upwards.

But the term that Raphael uses to describe the digestive transformation of matter to spirit – "aspire" – is also the term repeatedly used throughout the poem to depict sinful ambition (see, for example, 1.38, 3.39, 4.526, 6.132, 6.383, 6.793, 6.899, 9.169, 12.64, 12.560). The processes of digestion license the conceptualization of a material aspiration that contradicts the poem's emphasis on patient obedience. Indeed, it is to just this conceptual aporia surrounding food that Satan successfully appeals. The temptation of Eve demonstrates that the hierarchical transformations promised by the processes of digestion could be bent to very different purposes from the patient and obedient aspiration for heaven that Raphael intends to inculcate. Where Raphael had suggested that the day may come when "men / With angels may participate," Satan asks, "And what are gods that man may not become / As they, participating godlike food?" (5.499–500, 9.716–17).

In the dream that Satan prompts in Eve's ear, the tempter/angel describes the fruit he offers as "able to make gods of men" (5.70), suggesting an alimentary metamorphosis similar to that envisaged by Raphael. Indeed, Satan's temptations continually depend on just the physiological link between mind and body that Raphael is at such pains to articulate. The narrator explains the effect of Satan's words on the sleeping Eve in terms borrowed from faculty psychology:

> Assaying by his Devilish art to reach
> The Organs of her Fancie, and with them forge
> Illusions as he list, Phantasms and Dreams,
> Or if, inspiring venom, he might taint
> Th' animal Spirits that from pure blood arise
> Like gentle breaths from Rivers pure, thence raise,
> At least distemperd, discontented thoughts
> Vaine hopes, vaine aimes, inordinate desires
> Blown up with high conceits ingendring pride. (4.801–9)

The stunning thing is that Milton allows Satan's words to have a direct influence on the sinless but sleeping Eve, yet that is precisely what is demanded by his sense of the necessary commerce between angels and humans. "Good and ill Angels," remarks Levinus Lemnius in T*he Touchstone of Complexions,*

> which being intermingled with the humours and spirits, cause sondry changes and mutations in mens myndes.... As Spirites be without bodyes, they fitly and secretly glyde into the bodye of man, even much like a fulsom stench, or as a noysome and ill ayre, is inwardly drawn into the bodye.[34]

In order to envision a good angel dining on terrestrial food with a human, Milton must be able to describe the capacity of a bad angel to glide into the body of a human. The yoking of "distempered" and "discontented" demonstrates the explosive fusion of physiological and psychological elements, as does the wonderful phrase "Organs of her fancy." The glorious interchange of material and psychological phenomena licenses the ethically transformative power of material reality in positive and negative directions.

In the temptation scene, this power is exploited to turn humans away from God when the serpent presents himself to Eve as one who has altered his diet in a course of self-improvement. Before he ate of the forbidden fruit, he was "of abject thoughts and low, / As was my food, nor aught but food discerned / Or sex" (9.572–74). As Donald Friedman suggests, it is typical of Satan to devalue the very appetites whose right use Milton is at such pains to legitimate.[35] But after eating, Satan claims he noticed "Strange alteration in me, to degree / Of reason in my inward powers, and speech / Wanted not long" (9.599–601). Satan appeals here to the idea, present in Raphael's discourse and still very much with us, that we are in some sense what we eat, and that an alteration of diet can alter one's physiological and intellectual essence.

Eve's response demonstrates that she has assimilated the monist continuum between matter and spirit that Raphael has described; she characterizes the fruit as "intellectual food," a repast that will "feed at once both body and mind" (9.768, 779). Like the meal shared by Adam and Raphael, then, the forbidden fruit purports to absorb the values of that epitome of Renaissance civilization, the humanist convivium, in which body and mind are nourished by the twin oral experiences of food and words.[36] Eve is, moreover, physically hungry (like Jesus in *Paradise Regained* at the moment of temptation), since it is almost noon, a time which "waked / An eager appetite" (9.739–40). As Milton announces in *Areopagitica* and *Paradise Regained*, it is no virtue to abstain if one is not hungry. Satan, though, knows well that "hunger and thirst" are "Powerful persuaders" (9.586–87). The sensory qualities of the fruit, too, are fully complicit in the temptation;

Eve's appetite is "raised by the smell / So savory of that fruit, which with desire, / Inclinable now grown to touch or taste, / Solicited her longing eye" (9.740–43). It is as if the fruit itself, like one of those hospitable creatures in Jonson's "To Penshurst," is begging to be eaten. Part of the psychological force of the temptation, furthermore, must involve a contrast between Eve's social position in the previous scene of eating with an angel and her situation here. With Adam and Raphael, Eve had silently served her purported superiors. Here, she is courted and served by an inferior, and told that the way to sustain such an exalted position is to eat. She is promoted, albeit briefly, from silent servant to honored guest.[37]

Eve endows the fruit with medicinal properties, as if it were a particularly efficacious version of one of the many plants described in Renaissance herbals: "Here grows the cure of all, this fruit divine" (9.776). She offers here a perverse twist to the "beneficent properties and allegorical attributes of plants" exhibited in Milton's Paradise; the fruit is, of course, not the cure, but rather the source, of all illness.[38] What might need to be cured in prelapsarian existence, moreover, she fails to specify. As Tobias Whitaker, a Norwich physician, relates, the need for medicine was traditionally imagined to derive from the moment of the Fall:

for had Adam never sinned, yet must his body have been preserved and maintained by diet, which is part of physick. But after his fall so violated his equall temper that as then he became subject to mortalitie and naturall decay. Then came in the necessity of medicine . . .[39]

As we will see, the Archangel Michael will become the first terrestrial physician, applying to Adam's eyes a medicine that will cure their bleared vision, and recommending a regimen of temperance for the health of his patient.

After eating, Eve's subjective experience of the effects of the fruit tells her the serpent did not lie when he promised that the fruit would have profound physiological and psychological effects. Indeed, she proposes to stay on this diet faithfully "Till dieted by thee I grow mature / In knowledge, as the gods who all things know" (9.803–4). When she offers the fruit to Adam, Eve repeatedly assures him of the wholesome effect the fruit has had on her – "not Death, but Life / Augmented, op'nd Eyes, new Hopes, new Joyes" – and adds praise of its unequalled flavor – "Taste so divine, that what of sweet before / Hath toucht my sense, flat seems to this, and harsh" (9.984–89). In one of the multitude of bitter ironies that infiltrate mortal discourse at the moment of and just after the Fall, Adam remarks that "Much pleasure we have lost, while we abstained / From this delightful fruit, not known till now / True relish, tasting" (9.1022–24). They have indeed lost pleasure, not by abstaining but by tasting. So far from the "true appetite" that Eve had pleased by carefully mixing tastes in the meal she prepared for Raphael, Adam and Eve falsely think they experience "true relish" in the taste of "that false fruit." Some of the delusive qualities of this apparent exaltation of intellect and sense, however, are betrayed by the physical manner of their eating. While "Greedily" Eve "engorged without restraint" (9.791), "Adam took no thought, / Eating his fill" (9.1004–5). Aptly, sin is correlated with bad manners; thoughtless transgression displays its immorality through its tactless indiscretion. Whereas the participants in the heavenly banquet were "secure of surfeit" amid divine excess because the moral vocabulary of dietary excess was irrelevant to heavenly experience, Adam and Eve in the moment of falling render that vocabulary fully operable as they ungraciously stuff themselves.

The forbidden fruit, moreover, has several immediate effects on Adam and Eve that are unaccounted for in Eve's praise of it, and that explore brilliantly the nexus of physiology and morality on which Milton's materialism rests. It gets them mildly drunk, and in the process stirs sexual desire, as certain foods and wines were thought to do:

> As with new wine intoxicated both
> They swim in mirth, and fansie that they feel
> Divinitie within them . . . but that false fruit
> Far other operation first displayed,
> Carnal desire inflaming, hee on Eve
> Began to cast lascivious Eyes, she him
> As wantonly repaid; in Lust they burne.   (9.1008–13)

The fruit, that is, affects them on both a psychological and a physiological plane, spreading the contagious fires of lust throughout their bodies. The imagery of fire that Shakespeare had used to such profound effect to depict the self-consuming nature of erotic desire is here imagined by Milton to be a direct result of the forbidden fruit on the constitutions of the first man and woman. Perhaps the mysterious "gumms of glutenous heat" (line 917) with which Comus traps the Lady in her chair derive from a pun on "gluttonous," since this would link the heat of sexual passion with the heat of over-eating as Milton does in Paradise.[40] It is, moreover, Sabrina's "chaste palms moist and cold" (line 918) that counteract their effect, as if a kind of humoral balance had to be achieved between Comus's heat and Sabrina's coldness before the Lady could be liberated. In *The Doctrine and Discipline of Divorce*, Milton had imagined that a properly managed diet could reduce the carnal lust that Adam and Eve experience at the Fall: "for that other burning, which is but as it were the venom of a lusty and over-abounding concoction, strict life and labour, with the abatement of a full diet may keep that low and obedient."[41] In the Galenic regime, over-

150   Bodies and selves in early modern England

eating literally produces a physiological over-heating, a spontaneous combustion of erotic desire which precipitates the fires of lust. Milton here explores the aphrodisiac function of food; an act of symbolic disobedience, eating the fruit actually invites into the body a substance that alters its conduct. Fusing Plato and Galen, medical prescription and moral admonition, philosophical materialism and Judeo-Christian myth, Milton's characterization of the Fall demands that one imagine body and soul as continuous, the same phenomena in different media.

Milton had in *Comus* shown himself interested in the process by which sin might affect the physiological body of the sinner. The Elder Brother describes well the mysterious process by which sin works morally and materially at once. The "lewd and lavish act of sin," he says,

> Lets in defilement to the inward parts,
> The soul grows clotted by contagion,
> Embodies, and imbrutes, till she quite loose
> The divine property of her first being.   (lines 464–68)

In a work whose primary drama is whether a young woman can be made to consume a liquid against her will, sin is imagined as an act of ingestion that increases the specific gravity of the material soul. Sin, that is, entails a transgressive consumption that invites moral contagion into the inner spaces of the human subject. That is why, for the fallen angels, the Fall is very literally a fall, a headlong plunge from heaven. Once "Spirits of purest light," they have grown "gross by sinning" (6.660–61), and must be purged from heaven, just as the tartareous dregs were purged from the first matter. What Milton does here is reverse the predominant trajectory of Galenic materialist physiology. Where Galen and others had imagined that the material composition of the body would affect the behavior of the subject, that the manners of the soul would depend on the temperature of the body, Milton emphasizes how the behavior of the subject alters the material composition of its body. As in Spenser, the act of sin allows something defiling into a self that should be fortified against such incursions, something that allows the innate beastliness (thus the verb "im*brute*") of undisciplined humanity to emerge.

Using appropriately alimentary imagery, Milton suggests that Adam and Eve take "thir *fill* of love and love's disport" (9.1042). Afterwards, they fall asleep, and discover that the heat produced by the fruit has other effects besides inflaming carnal desire. "The unsatiable feeder," remarks the *Homilie Against Gluttony and Drunkennesse*, "never sleepeth quietly, such an unmeasurable heate is kindled."[42] After their transgressive meal, Adam and Eve experience the first terrestrial case of sleep troubled by indigestion:

> Soon as the force of that fallacious Fruit,
> That with exhilerating vapour bland
> About thir spirits had played, and inmost powers
> Made erre, was now exhal'd, and grosser sleep
> Bred of unkindly fumes, with conscious dreams
> Encumberd, now had left them, up they rose
> As from unrest . . .   (9.1046–52)

One of the bitterest jokes suffusing Milton's portrait of the first dietary transgression is the fact that it causes indigestion, as if the body rejects in part the assimilation of its own corruption. At the Fall, humanity not only troubles its own house but also inherits the wind. The effects Milton identifies are those linked to over-eating and to drunkenness; as Lemnius observes, "ye mynd also with fulsome and unpleasant exhalations and sents is oftentymes greatlye annoyed and encumbered, even as ill naughty wyne bringeth to the brayne affects both hurtful and daungerous."[43] Milton never specifies the variety of fruit they consume, but if he is imagining an apple, as most writers and artists had, he may also be playing with the supposed effects of apples since, as Thomas Venner notes, "Apples are of a cold and moist temperature, abounding within a superfluous, crude, and windie moisture."[44] This unrestful sleep troubled by windy moisture is in stark contrast to Adam's rest before the Fall, which "Was Aerie light from pure digestion bred, / And temperat vapors bland" (5.3–4). In *Of Education*, Milton had declared the importance of good digestion to the life of the mind. Not only should his scholars be versed in "the tempers, the humors, the seasons, how to manage a crudity" (i.e., a bout of indigestion), but they also should be exposed to music, "which woud not be unexpedient after meat to assist and cherish nature in her first concoction, and send their mindes backe to study in good tune and satisfaction."[45]

After the Fall, moreover, Adam and Eve experience internal tempests, which represent at once the overthrow of inner reason by appetite, the introduction of disorder into the natural world, and the physiological gastritis that unregulated appetite produces:

> They sate them down to weep, nor only Teares
> Raind at thir Eyes, but high Winds worse within
> Began to rise, high Passions, Anger, Hate,
> Mistrust, Suspicion, Discord, and shook sore
> Their inward State of Mind, calm Region once
> And full of Peace, now tost and turbulent:
> For Understanding rul'd not, and the Will
> Heard not her lore, both in subjection now
> To sensual Appetite, who from beneathe
> Usurping over sovan Reason claimd
> Superior sway.   (9.1121–31)

Physiology here supplies a discourse of psychology and of politics. Ethical transgression is manifested in the "high winds" of extreme passion. The usurpations of appetite over reason produce internal disorder, literally and metaphorically. The language of physiological disease is turned to moral aims: Adam's "distempered breast" (9.1131), like Eve's cheek in which "distemper flushing glowed" (9.887), offers in its pun on dysfunctional temperance both a cause – a failure to exercise temperance over appetite – and an effect – the disease of distemper that results from improper balance of the humors – of the Fall. The discourse of temperance makes intemperate consumption the source of moral and physiological illness.

This portrait of the indigestion that ensues from the Fall is all the more poignant because, as William Kerrigan points out, "Milton certainly believed that digestive failure was the efficient cause of his blindness."[46] Kerrigan cites Milton's letter to Leonard Philaris, in which Milton had explained in detail the loss of his sight in the hope that Philaris might consult with a French physician about his case:

It is ten years, I think more or less, since I noticed my sight becoming weak and growing dim, and at the same time my spleen and all my viscera burdened and shaken with flatulence.... Certain permanent vapors seem to have settled upon my entire forehead and temples, which press and oppress my eyes with a sort of sleepy heaviness, especially from mealtime to evening.[47]

Milton's letter to Philaris is the epistolary equivalent of the *Self-Portrait of the Sick Dürer* discussed in Chapter 1, a drawing that also accompanied a description of symptoms addressed to a physician. Both locate the source of their agony in the belly, and particularly the spleen, the source of melancholy. Milton's linkage of his indigestion with his blindness makes sense within the medical regime he inherits. As Thomas Venner notes in his *Via Recta ad Vitam Longam*:

For the keeping of those ordinary and daily excrements, is very offensive to the body by reason of the noysome fumes that ascend from them, which of all other parts do chiefly annoy the head, causing dimnesse of the sight, dulnesse, heavinesse, head-ach, inflammation of the head; and not these only of the head; but the mind it selfe is oftentimes hereby disturbed, and malancholikly affected.[48]

Here blindness is explicitly linked to vapors rising from a stomach in which the excrements are not flowing adequately. These vapors would ascend to the eyes and brain via the very same channels that allow Guyon and Arthur to go from the stomach to the head in their tour of the Castle of Alma. Aubrey tells us that Milton "Seldome tooke any Physique, only sometimes he tooke Manna," a famous laxative, recommended by Sir Thomas Elyot and others, that would address just the obstructions Venner describes.[49] It is deeply significant that Milton portrays as direct effects of the Fall the two afflictions – blindness and gastritis – which he complains of in the letter to Philaris. As we will see, they are both afflictions for which the Archangel Michael will offer remedies – an ointment that temporarily alleviates the blindness that dims postlapsarian sight, and a temperate dietary regime to ameliorate the various physiological afflictions that issue from the Fall.

What Adam and Eve experience internally, moreover, is felt by the body of creation as a whole. Milton in fact alters the standard relationship between microcosm and macrocosm, between the inner passions of a human and the outer meteorological world, by making the world not the cause of an inward passionate disturbance but the effect of it. Sympathy and influence flow from the human subject to the astronomical and meteorological world rather than the other way around.[50] The Fall alters the world, rather than the world altering humanity. At the moment when Adam and Eve eat, "Earth trembl'd from her entrails, as again / In pangs, and Nature gave a second groan; / Skie lowr'd, and Muttering thunder" (9.1000–2). As Kerrigan remarks, "representations of digestive illness surround the crisis. At each disobedience nature suffers the cramps of a bellyache."[51] The earthquakes that occur at moments of unspeakable human crime in Christian history – the Fall and the crucifixion – are imagined as macrocosmic versions of the indigestion produced by that first act of transgressive eating. The astronomical heavens respond to that first commensal transgression with an abhorrence befitting the most repulsive meal imaginable: "At that tasted Fruit / The Sun, as from Thyestean Banquet, turn'd / His course intended" (10.687–89). Where Sin unwillingly feeds her offspring with her flesh, the effect of Original Sin is likened to Thyestes's unwitting consumption of his children – a suitable image for the congenital suffering that issues from this sin. The sun that "at Even / Sups with the Ocean" (5.425–26) before the Fall now turns away in disgust from the planet where such congenial meals occurred.

The effects of the Fall are translated on the earth into an altered astronomy and meteorology whose dynamics in turn echo the indigestion produced by that first meal; the skies are marked by "sideral blast, / Vapour, and Mist, and Exhalation hot, / Corrupt and Pestilent" (10.693–95). With the phrase "Corrupt and Pestilent," we see how the contagion that originates with humans produces the meteors that will in turn corrupt and infect the original source of corruption – humanity. Moreover, where once "vernal aires, / Breathing the smell of field and grove, attune[d] / The trembling leaves" (4.264–66), now a series of discordant climatological phenomena are released. "Bursting their brazen Dungeon, armd with ice / And snow and haile and stormie gust and flaw" (10.697–98), the virulent winds produce "outrage" (10.707) on the earth. This misguided liberation of armed marauders will make humanity perpetual hostage to the whims of meteorology. These winds echo the internal winds of passion that Adam and Eve release when they invite the forbidden fruit into their bodies.

Before the Fall, Milton intentionally dampens the actual violence of eating, not only by emphasizing the paradisal plenty that renders competition for resources irrelevant but also by making all creatures vegetarians, so that they pluck fruits rather than rend flesh. The Fall, however, invites carnivorous consumption, and the violence it entails, into the food chain:

> Beast now with Beast gan war, and Fowle with Fowle,
> And Fish with Fish; to graze the Herb all leaving,
> Devourd each other; nor stood much in awe
> Of Man, but fled him, or with count'nance grim
> Glar'd on him pasing. (10.710–14)

Threatened by the very animals that were originally made to serve them, humans now inhabit a precarious and vulnerable spot at the top of the food chain.

God, moreover, explains the necessity of the Expulsion in terms derived from the same physiological processes that Milton tracks in the human body:

> Those pure immortal Elements that know
> No gross, no unharmoneous mixture foule,
> Eject [man] tainted now, and purge him off
> As a distemper, gross to aire as gross,
> And mortal food, as may dispose him best
> For dissolution wrought by Sin, that first
> Distemperd all things, and of incorrupt
> Corrupted. (11.50–57)

Thus, as Michael Lieb argues in his erudite discussion of *Paradise Lost* amid Levitican dietary prohibition, "when Adam and Eve do violate God's command, they contract the uncleanness of the fruit itself, thereafter to be reproached as both 'unclean' (9.1097) and 'impure' (10.735)."[52] Humans are not just carriers of disease but humanity itself is an actual disease, a distemper to the pure world which it inhabits, and which was built for it. The puns on "distemper" show how much Milton interprets the Fall as a failure of temperance. In Leviticus 28.25, God announces, "The land is defiled: therefore I do visit the iniquity thereof upon it, and the land itself vomiteth out her inhabitants." Satan and the rebel angels are similarly thrown from heaven into "the wasteful Deep" (6.862), and can never return to heaven because "th' Ethereal mould / Incapable of stain would soon expel / Her mischief, and purge off the baser fire / Victorious" (2.139–42). Adam and Eve are in the same manner excreted from Paradise like some noxious and indigestible matter from a sickening body.[53]

Although in Paradise before the Fall the disposal of waste matter was the source of some anxiety, divine providence has already provided for an appropriately repulsive creature to clean up the plethora of excrement that will issue from the Fall. With the acute senses of a scavenger, Death "snuffed the smell / Of mortal change on earth" and is "lur'd / With scent of living Carcasses design'd for death" (10.273-74, 277-78). A "blind mouth" like the bad shepherds of *Lycidas* (whose sheep are "not fed" but "rot inwardly" and are "swollen with wind"), Death is a creature who lives to experience the oral gratifications of unregulated appetite. In a perverse way, a tamed Death might have made a useful pet in prelapsarian Paradise, a garbage disposal cleaning up those burgeoning piles of uneaten fruit. Tellingly it is the offspring of Sin who are the first carnivores in Milton's universe. When Eve eats the forbidden fruit, we are told, she "knew not eating Death" (9.792). As Diane McColley has recently argued, the phrase "eating Death" perfectly characterizes Death as a machine of unregulated consumption.[54] This is for Milton how a true belly god would be represented.

For Death, moreover, the impurity of the Fall that causes Adam and Eve to be expelled from Paradise is perversely a further enticement to appetite: "such a sent I draw / Of carnage, prey innumerable, and taste / The savour of Death from all things there that live" (10.267-69). In a parody of the providential bounty with which God surrounded Adam and Eve before the Fall, Death will have plenty of "ravin" to consume. Death, though, proves unsatisfied, even with the postlapsarian plenitude of carnage and rot: "though plenteous, all too little seems / To stuff this Maw, this vast unhidebound corpse" (10.601-2). Like a thoughtful host, though, Sin reassures Death that there will be more:

> on these Herbs, and Fruits, and Flowers,
> Feed first, on each Beast next, and Fish, and Fowle,
> No homely morsels, and whatever thing
> The Sithe of Time mowes down, devour unspar'd,
> Till I in Man residing through the Race,
> His thoughts, his looks, words, actions all infect
> And season him thy last and sweetest prey.   (10.603-9)

Sin sardonically imagines nature as an extended appetizer, and humanity as the main course, carefully seasoned by the products of its own transgressive consumption. In its own way, her menu is as carefully planned as that delightful mixture of tastes which Eve had prepared for Adam and Raphael.

From the divine perspective, though, Sin and Death are not the gourmands they fancy but rather the "Dogs of Hell," "Hell-hounds," who "lick up the draff and filth / Which mans polluting Sin with taint hath shed / On what was pure" (10.616, 630-32). Regina Schwartz describes well the narrative irony of this moral economy: "Those sent by Satan to pollute are ultimately employed in the divine service to clean."[55] Although Sin and Death seem insatiable, moreover, the end of time is imagined as the moment when Death will finally experience a kind of surfeit, and when the impurity deriving from the Fall will finally be purged from creation. Death will continue to eat, God tells the Son,

>   till cramm'd and gorg'd, nigh burst
> With suckt and glutted offal, at one sling
> Of thy victorious Arm, well-pleasing Son,
> Both *Sin* and *Death*, and yawning *Grave* at last
> Through *Chaos* hurld, obstruct the mouth of Hell
> For ever, and seal up his ravenous Jawes.
> Then Heav'n and Earth renewd shall be made pure
> To sanctitie that shall receive no staine. (10.632–39)

Like that first act of greedy engorgement, which inadvertently invited Sin and Death to feast upon the world, Death's final meal will be fittingly indecorous, a moment of gluttonous surfeit. In what God appropriately terms the "fullness of time," Death's own mouth will be crammed full, and he will in turn be used to obstruct the mouth of Hell. Having appropriately purged and purified heaven and earth, "God shall be all in all." Creation will again become a vast banquet, an interdependent system of excretion and nourishment like that described by Raphael in which there is in fact no defecation, no waste, just mutual feeding. In contrast, Hell will be obstructed, a stopped-up mouth, a dysfunctional alimentary system. The suffocating flatulence that Herbert in "L'Envoy" longed to inflict on Sin is transformed in Milton's cosmology into gluttonous constipation. Both link the patterns of eschatology to the rhythms of scatology.

Michael Lieb has argued adroitly that Satan is identified with faulty digestive processes throughout the poem. Lieb suggests that Satan's journey through Chaos in Book 2 has a scatological dimension: "entering Chaos' 'Furnace mouth,' which belches forth its innards (888–89), Satan becomes part of the 'crude consistence' (941) that characterizes Chaos' 'intestine broils.'"[56] His voyage is in certain ways a low comic parody of the tour of the alimentary tract that Guyon and Arthur take in Book 2 of *The Faerie Queene*, but where Arthur and Guyon ascend to the head, Satan becomes part of the waste material that must go through Port Esquiline. In his Limbo of Vanity, Milton likewise directs the winds of indigestion to the purposes of deflating an opponent, when he imagines that various monks are made "The sport of winds" emitted by "the backside of the world" (3.493–94). Even the landscape in Hell seems to partake of the gaseous internal turbulence that the Fall entails. The Lake of Fire in Hell is compared to the volcanic Mount Aetna,

The alimental vision in *Paradise Lost*

> as when the force
> Of subterranean wind transports a Hill
> Torn from Pelorus or the shatter'd side
> Of thundering Ætna, whose combustible
> And fewel'd entrals thence conceiving Fire,
> Sublim'd with Mineral fury, aid the Winds,
> And leave a singed bottom all involv'd
> With stench and smoak. (1.230–37)

It is as if the failure of Hell to provide Satan with sure footing is a product of the kind of roiled internal state the Fall – of which Satan is a prime mover – precipitates.

Temperance is in turn the virtue that restores stability to the individual subject. As we saw in Spenser, it involves a moral architectonics by which agents construct sturdy selves out of dynamic but unruly forces. The virtue that disciplines in particular the consumption of food, temperance is a central subject of the two angelic conversations that frame morally and socially the moment of transgressive eating that is the Fall: Raphael's convivium with Adam, and Michael's stern vision of future history. It speaks volumes about the differences between these two social events that Adam eats with Raphael but Michael does not eat with Adam. As the narrator declares at the beginning of Book 9, "No more of talk where God or Angel Guest / With Man, as with his Friend, familiar us'd / To sit indulgent, and with him partake / Rural repast" (9.1–4). Companionship (which means "to share bread with") between terrestrial and heavenly beings is replaced by "distance and distaste," as mortals now merit the disgust of creatures with whom they had shared "No ingrateful food" (9.9, 5.407). Where Adam had been charmingly nervous about the possibility that terrestrial food would not appeal to heavenly palates, his own act of transgressive consumption ensures that the earth is now "distasteful" to heavenly creatures.

The Fall, then, makes the consumption of food a profoundly complicated moral phenomenon. Where in Paradise eating was simply an appropriate response to God's generous plenitude (with one notable exception), after the Fall it becomes both a reward and a punishment, a celebration and a test. After Satan has succeeded in his mission to make Adam and Eve break their oath of dietary fealty to God, the fallen angels might be expected to indulge in a feast of victory. But in a bitter joke that God has at their expense (neither the first nor the last of such), instead of a lavish feast at the successful return of their leader, the fallen angels are made to feel a desire that can never be quenched. "Parcht with scalding thurst and hunger fierce," they are allowed to taste not quenching "fruit" but rather "Chewd bitter Ashes, which th'offended taste / With spattering noise rejected" (10.556–67). This distastefully unsatisfying meal, the only time we see them eat, entails an unsavory disgust appropriate to celebrating the alimentary cramming of Adam and Eve, and Death. Such unappeased desire will for Milton characterize a life of sinful aspiration. When told by Michael of the story of the Tower of Babel, Adam curiously wonders how Nimrod will eat so far from the earth: "Wretched man! What food / Will he convey up thither to sustain / Himself and his rash Armie, where thin Aire / Above the Clouds will pine his entrails gross, / And famish him of Breath, if not of Bread" (12.74–78). Nimrod's presumption is here compared to an unslaked hunger, and marked by an inherently foolish desire to be far from the earth, the immediate source of all nourishment. The most outrageous of political aspirations is here imagined to entail its own alimentary punishment.

Adam's own dietary reprisal for eating the forbidden fruit is less harsh, if related; he must labor arduously in the earth for the sustenance that was so liberally bestowed in Eden:

>   Curs'd is the ground for thy sake, thou in sorrow
>   Shalt eate, thereof all the days of thy Life;
>   . . . .
>   thou shalt eate th' Herb of th' Field,
>   In the sweat of thy Face shalt thou eat Bread,
>   Till thou return unto the ground.   (10.201–6)

Milton here paraphrases Genesis, but the contrast with paradisal ease and excess he has drawn in lavish detail is profound. Before the Fall, abundance was the source of enormous gastronomic pleasure, and entailed only a comparatively innocent anxiety – Adam and Eve offer thanks for "this delicious place / For us too large, where thy abundance wants / Partakers, and uncropt falls to the ground" (4.729–31). But after the Fall, one must labor strenuously in the anxious hope that the ground from which humans derive will produce enough to sustain a subsistence existence.

The infrequent alternative to toilsome subsistence, moreover, is an even more threatening plenitude, since as Michael warns Adam, sometimes "th'Earth shall bear / More than anough, that temperance may be tri'd" (11.804–5). After the Fall, even bounty is tainted, becoming not a blessing but a test. As Milton argues in *Areopagitica*, "though [God] command us temperance, justice, continence, yet [He] powrs out before us ev'n to a profusenes all desirable things."[57] Taking a lesson from Galenic physiology, in which almost all disease was imagined to derive from a faulty diet producing a surplus of some noxious substance, Michael shows Adam the different ways that death will come to his progeny. "Some," he announces,

> by violent stroke shall die,
> By Fire, Flood, Famin, by Intemperance more
> In Meats and Drinks, which on the Earth shall bring
> Diseases dire. (11.471-74)

In Milton's account, the deaths that will ensue from violence and conflagration, drowning and starvation, pale beside the deaths that will ensue from intemperate eating. The original act of intemperance introduces the illnesses that intemperate eating was thought in contemporary physiology to produce. Milton here relies upon a distressingly familiar version of contemporaneous physiology – one that blames the victim for her or his disease – to underpin a moral lesson in self-discipline. In order to drive this lesson home, Michael offers Adam a chilling and extensive vision of

> What miserie th'inabstinence of Eve
> Shall bring on men. Immediately a place
> Before his eyes appeard, sad, noysom, dark,
> A Lazar-house it seemd, wherein were laid
> Numbers of all diseas'd, all maladies
> Of gastly Spasm, or racking torture, qualmes
> Of heart-sick Agonie, all feaverous kinds,
> Convulsions, Epilepsies, fierce Catarrhs,
> Intestin Stone and Ulcer, Colic pangs,
> Dæmoniac Phrenzie, moaping Melancholie
> And Moon-struck madness, pining Atrophie,
> Marasmus, and wide-wasting Pestilence,
> Dropsies, and Asthma's, and Joint-racking Rheums.
> Dire was the tossing, deep the groans, despair
> Tended the sick busiest from Couch to Couch;
> And over them triumphant Death his Dart
> Shook, but delaid to strike, though oft invok't
> With vows, as thir chief good, and final hope. (11.477-93)

The diseases themselves range from those which primarily afflict the body, such as the arthritic agony of "Joint-racking Rheums," through those which affect the body through the mind, such as "Convulsions, [and] Epilepsies," through those that afflict the mind through the body – "Dæmoniac Phrenzie, moaping Melancholie, / And Moon-struck madness." The "Colic pangs" may reflect in part Milton's own digestive afflictions. In the letter to Philaris, he had complained that for ten years "my spleen and all my viscera [have been] burdened and shaken with flatulence."[58] As terrifying as this catalogue already was, Milton actually adds lines 485–87 in his revisions for the edition of 1674 – lines which focus on the torments of psychological disease (frenzy, melancholy, and madness) and of the plague, which raged through London in 1665. The deliciously studious melancholy that the young Milton had portrayed in "Il Penseroso" has given way to a torturous pathological depression issuing from the spleen. As Michael later tells Adam, such depression will emerge from the very physiology of old age: "in thy blood will reigne / A melancholly damp of cold and dry / To weigh thy Spirits down, and last consume / The Balme of Life" (11.543–46). In the invocation to Book 9, Milton worries that just such a physiological condition – "an age too late, or cold / Climat, or Years damp my intended wing / Deprest" (9.44–46) – will keep him from finishing the epic. Amid the pageant of corporeal and mental agonies that Michael displays, death becomes a consummation devoutly to be wished who is coy in proportion to the degree to which he is desired.

This hellish scenario, Michael argues, demonstrates the immense suffering that awaits those who "serve ungoverned appetite" and "pervert pure nature's healthful rules / To loathsome sickness." We create, he suggests, the physiological hells we inhabit by what we ingest. But the vision also holds out the prospect of governing such appetites. Michael promises Adam that "if thou well observe / The rule of not too much, by temperance taught / In what thou eatst and drinkst, seeking from thence / Due nourishment, not gluttonous delight," one may experience not the torturous existence culminating in a painful death Adam has just witnessed but rather live a contented life until "like ripe Fruit thou drop / Into thy Mother's lap, or be with ease / Gatherd, not harshly pluckt" (11.531–37). The proper conduct of the appetite, Michael suggests, can in part ameliorate the horrible physical effects of that first dietary transgression. If intemperance re-enacts the original Fall and intensifies its deleterious effects, temperance allows one to regain something of what was lost in that Fall. By obeying what the Lady in *Comus* calls the "holy dictate of spare temperance" (line 766), one can become like the ripe fruit that was available to Adam and Eve in Paradise before the Fall; death will be not the horrible culmination of a tortured existence but rather a gentle return to the comforting embrace of a nourishing parent.

The Milton who wrote *Paradise Lost*, however, must have sensed as well as anyone the physiological limits of the medical applications of temperance. Blind and gout-ridden, Milton was probably finishing the ten-book version of the epic as the plague raged through London in 1665.[59] One of the plague-pits for mass burials of plague victims, Bunhill Fields, was close to Milton's house in Artillery Walk, leading Milton's biographer Masson to surmise that "in no neighbourhood in all London can the death-cart, the death-bell, and all the sights and sounds of the plague, have been more familiar and incessant than close to Milton's house."[60] Amid such "widewasting pestilence," against which the "rule of not too much" would have had absolutely no effect, Milton's discussion of temperance as a cure for postlapsarian suffering sounds wistful, yet another attempt to justify the ways of an omnipotent God to his suffering creatures by blaming their sinful conduct rather than divine will. Yet it is also good physiology. As Lessius remarks in his *Hygiasticon,* "a sober Diet doth arm and fortifie against the Plague."[61] Nevertheless, as the plague ravaged the city, Milton and his family ultimately left London for the country in order to avoid exposure to the "loathsome sickness" that can like all other mortal afflictions be traced back to the Fall, but which devastated innocent and guilty, temperate and intemperate alike. Milton in the last books of *Paradise Lost* seeks in the patterns of eternal providence justifications, if not cures, for the physical afflictions from which he and those around him suffered (11.412–15).

Indeed, when in Book 11 Michael treats Adam's bleared vision, we witness a moment that must have had enormous personal resonance for Milton: the application of medicine to the eyes. It is, moreover, a scenario that advertises, as William Kerrigan points out, "the founding of our medical tradition."[62] It clearly delineates the cause and cure for moral blindness in a materialist physiology:

> but to nobler sights
> Michael from Adams eyes the Filme remov'd,
> Which that false Fruit that promis'd clearer sight
> Had bred; then purg'd with Euphrasy and Rue
> The visual Nerve, for he had much to see;
> And from the Well of Life three drops instill'd.
> So deep the power of these Ingredients pierc'd,
> Ev'n to the inmost seat of mental sight,
> That Adam now enforc't to close his eyes,
> Sunk down, and all his Spirits became intranst.   (11.411–20)

As a result of this purgation, at once moral and material, Adam is able to view the panorama of biblical history Michael proffers. "In the materialistic narrative coincident with the moral narrative," remarks Kerrigan, "Adam was developing cataractic blindness from the unpurged vapors of the fruit."[63] Lemnius suggests that rue is an appropriate medicine "when the eyes are dark and misty from superfluity of humours" because it can "dissolve the congealed and collected humours that by their thicknesse hinder the spirits to be brought thither."[64] Michael's medical intervention is only temporary, since at the beginning of Book 12, Michael declares to Adam: "I perceave / Thy mortal sight to faile" (12.8–9). At this moment, he switches from vision to pure narration. But his application of euphrasy and rue does reach to the "inmost seat of mental sight," presaging thereby a kind of inwardness which will survive the ultimate failure of the potion.

When told by Michael of the "New Heav'ns, new Earth" that will at the end of time "bring forth fruits Joy and eternal Bliss," Adam replies, in aptly alimentary terms, that "Greatly instructed I shall hence depart, / Greatly in peace of thought, and have my fil / Of knowledge, what this Vessel can contain" (12.558–60). Whereas the angels in heaven are secure of surfeit, postlapsarian humanity is a fragile receptacle whose appetites – for knowledge and for food – habitually exceed its capacity. Adam's declared awareness of the limitations of "what this vessel can contain" marks the beginning of the self-knowledge that temperance demands. Indeed, when Michael reminds Adam of the ethical need to put into practice the knowledge he has received, he follows Simon Peter (2 Peter 1.5–7) in placing temperance, the classical virtue that imposes limits on appetite, in a prominent place:

>   onely add
> Deeds to thy knowledge answerable, add Faith,
> Add vertue, Patience, Temperance, add Love,
> By name to come call'd Charitie, the soul
> Of all the rest: then wilt thou not be loath
> To leave this Paradise, but shalt possess
> A paradise within thee, happier farr.   (12.581–87)[65]

This paradise will ultimately be not a geographical place but rather a series of social and dietary practices that cultivate the inner spaces of the postlapsarian subject. It will be nurtured not through agrarian labor but rather by virtuous action. Michael had prefaced his vision of "what shall come in future days / To thee and to thy Ofspring" by telling Adam that he would need "to learn / True patience, and to *temper* joy with fear / And pious sorrow, equally inur'd / By moderation either state to beare, / Prosperous or adverse" (11.357–64; my italics). Temperance, finally, involves not only regulating appetite but also attaining a well-balanced admixture of emotions. If one brings hellish suffering on oneself by serving ungoverned appetite, Milton indicates, one can by governing appetite and emotion achieve a physiological and psychological version of Paradise within the body of the individual. Although Milton will not articulate the full importance of temperance to Christian salvation until *Paradise Regained*, where the "temperance invincible" of Jesus's refusal of a sumptuous banquet, as well as other temptations, regains for humanity what was lost in that first act of intemperate eating, in *Paradise Lost* he nevertheless makes temperance a central site of individual ethical activity.[66] Inwardness becomes for Milton the locus of both the highest reward, and the greatest agony.

Milton's Samson complains that "torment should not be confin'd / To the bodies wounds and sores . . . But must secret passage find / To th' inmost mind" (*Samson Agonistes*, 606–11). Yet the closet drama concludes with a moment of remarkable quiet – "calm of mind all passion spent" – that is achieved through the violent expenditure of passion. In the preface to *Samson Agonistes*, "Of that sort of Dramatic Poem which is call'd Tragedy," Milton explains the emotional homeopathy that tragedy performs, giving a particularly physiological emphasis to Aristotle's celebrated definition of tragedy as

of power by raising pity and fear, or terror, to purge the mind of those and such-like passions, that is to temper and reduce them to just measure with a kind of delight, stirr'd up by reading or seeing those passions well imitated.

Tragedy aspires to a tempering of the passions, but works by heightening them in order to expel them, rather than the Galenic balancing of opposites that Michael prescribes; just as in "Nature . . . so in Physic things of melancholic hue and quality are used against melancholy, sowr against sowr, salt to remove salt humours."[67] Both *Samson Agonistes* and *Paradise Lost*, then, propose recipes for a temperate inner life, but the recipes themselves arise from different medical regimes. If in *Paradise Lost* Satan's greatest torment lies in the fact that Hell is an inescapable interior state – "within him Hell / He brings, and round about him, nor from Hell / One step no more than from himself can fly / By change of place" (4.20–23) – then humanity's greatest hope lies in the corollary discovery that Paradise is ultimately a moral and physiological state rather than a geographical location.

By emphasizing such inwardness as the locus of a paradise available to all who are willing to submit to the poem's lessons, Milton allows temperance to assume the full political importance that it had only begun to intimate for Spenser. It is for Milton the essential virtue of a free individual. Indeed, the individual who cannot govern the self is for Milton unfit for other forms of citizenship. In *The Second Defence*, Milton had warned his countrymen that if they do not begin regulating their personal conduct, then it will not matter whether they have a king or not:

Unless you will subjugate the propensity to avarice, to ambition, and sensuality, and expel all luxury from yourselves and your families, you will find that you have cherished a more stubborn and intractable despot at home, than you ever encountered in the field; and even your very bowels will be continually teeming with an intolerable progeny of tyrants. Let these be the first enemies whom you subdue. . . . For who would vindicate your right of unrestrained suffrage, or of choosing what representatives you like best, merely that you might elect the creatures of your own faction, whoever they might be, or him however small might be his worth, who would give you the most lavish feasts, and enable you to drink to the greatest excess?

Thus not wisdom and authority, but turbulence and gluttony, would soon exalt the vilest miscreants from our taverns and our brothels, from our towns and villages, to the rank and dignity of senators. . . . You, therefore, who wish to remain free, either instantly be wise, or, as soon as possible, cease to be fools; if you think slavery an intolerable evil, learn obedience to reason and the government of yourselves.[68]

The privileges of citizenship emerge from the parameters of temptation successfully resisted. As in Spenser, there is no servitude more demeaning than a subjection to one's own appetites. What Milton and Spenser both urge upon the reader is "the government of yourselves," an active subordination of the passions and appetites to the rigors of reason. But where Spenser has not yet fully developed this internal government in explicit opposition to the rule of political tyrants, Milton directly connects enslavement to appetite and to monarchy.

The greatest threat to the self-government that temperance enjoins is passion, that complex of emotion and physiology that continually challenges the constitutive rule of reason. Milton's entire career, literary as well as political, could be seen as a meditation on that crucial issue of the Renaissance – the respective claims of reason and passion in the formation of the moral individual – although the answers are different at different times, and sometimes conflicted within the same text. "Wherefore did [God] creat passions within us, pleasures round about us," Milton asks in *Areopagitica*, "but that these rightly temper'd are the very ingredients of vertu?" (p. 1010). Milton here comes down aggressively against a Stoic emphasis on the eradication of the passions as the highest moral state. For Milton, in many ways, the moral effort required to temper strong passions is superior to the state of having tempered them perfectly. Yet in both *Comus* and *Paradise Regained*, Milton's protagonist is a figure whose unmoved status has led to accusations, both within the works and by subsequent critics, of Stoic indifference. In *Samson Agonistes*, by contrast, the violent expenditure of passion that is that work's main action has precipitated a critical conundrum about Milton's attitude to his protagonist. At the center of these various works and attitudes is *Paradise Lost*, an epic that stages a series of debates on the proper role of the passions before and after the Fall, and in heaven and on earth.

Milton was far from unique in allowing passion into his prelapsarian Paradise. Even Aquinas had allowed that "man was passible [i.e., capable of feeling passion] in the state of innocence," although the doctor severely restricts the meanings of passion to "understanding and sensation" in order to sustain the claim.[69] In *A Treatise of the Passions and Faculties of the Soule of Man*, Edward Reynolds suggests that passions existed before the Fall, but only turned malicious after it:

as long as Man continued intire and incorrupt, there was a sweet harmonie between all his Faculties, and such an happie subordination of them each to other, as that every Motion of the Inferiour Power was directed and governed.... But, when once Man had tasted of that murthering Fruit, and poyson'd him and all his Posteritie; then began those Swellings, and inward Rebellions, which made him as lame in his Naturall, as dead in his Spirituall Condition. Whence Passions are become, now in the state of Corruption, Beastly and Sensual, which were before, by Creation, Reasonable and Humane.[70]

Milton certainly feels that the Fall transforms the passions from obedient citizens to unruly rebels in the state of the self.

Milton, though, complicates the picture radically, by locating at the center of his Paradise a passion whose depth and force make it resemble unruly postlapsarian emotion. Adam himself describes to Raphael his primal experience of passion, at the moment when he first saw Eve: "here passion first I felt, / Commotion strange" (8.530–31). This commotion is a kind of internal disturbance that one would not expect before the Fall. Milton is at once making passion a surprising part of prelapsarian existence, and using the suspicion of it to explain in part the Fall. Raphael responds by generating a conventional distinction between love and passion:

> In loving thou dost well, in passion not,
> Wherein true Love consists not; love refines
> The thoughts, and heart enlarges, hath his seat
> In Reason, and is judicious, is the scale
> By which to heav'nly Love thou maist ascend.   (8.588–92)

Raphael, then, does not deny the role of passion, but does suggest that it should be clearly separated from the elevating experience of love, and properly subordinated to reason. Yet the very vehemence of the love Adam feels – a vehemence that derives from the way that Eve fulfills absolutely Adam's hunger for a partner – renders the distinction moot. The extremity and the intensity of Adam's love for Eve, that is, seem an appropriate response to God's wish to grant him "Thy likeness, thy fit help, thy other self, / Thy wish exactly to thy hearts desire" (8.449–50). But the extremity of even well-placed emotion runs head-on into an ethic of moderation in the stern words of Raphael. That tension we have traced in the works of Spenser, Shakespeare, and Herbert between the moderation of passion and the proper direction of extreme passion is located by Milton in the relationship between the first man and the first woman before the Fall. The epic does not so much decide the issue as suspend it.[71]

Raphael's final warning to Adam before departing delineates the connection between the discipline of self-government and the achievement of internal freedom that fascinated Milton – "take heed least Passion sway / Thy Judgement to do aught, which else free Will / Would not admit" (8.635–37). The overarching effect of the Fall, according to Michael, is that humans lose "true Libertie," and surrender the control of their passions. Thus the story of Nimrod, the first tyrant, who "affect[s] to subdue / Rational Libertie," issues in the following lesson in postlapsarian psychology:

> Since thy original lapse, true Libertie
> Is lost, which alwayes with right Reason dwells
> Twinn'd, and from her hath no dividual being:
> Reason in man obscur'd, or not obeyd,
> Immediately inordinate desires
> And upstart Passions catch the Government
> From Reason, and to servitude reduce
> Man till then free. (12.82–90)

God, Michael relates, allows tyrants to rule over those humans who have abdicated the rule of their own emotions, a rule on which any notion of individual liberty must be based:

> since hee permits
> Within himself unworthie Powers to reign
> Over free Reason, God in Judgement just
> Subjects him from without to violent Lords;
> Who oft as undeservedly enthrall
> His outward freedom. (12.90–95)

For Milton, the experience of political defeat produced a radically inward notion of freedom. In *Comus*, the Lady had defended herself by arguing that "Thou canst not touch the freedom of my minde / With all thy charms, although this corporal rinde / Thou haste immanacl'd" (lines 663–65).[72] As Milton was to learn the hard way, the only space over which political power cannot exert its ravenous claims is the inward space of the self. Where Herbert struggles to make these spaces available to his God, Milton struggles to hide them from his king. The only revolution over which one finally has control is a revolution within, cultivating the individual liberty that emerges from the disciplined application of reason to one's desires. On the physiological plane, this discipline produces health, while on the political plane it produces true liberty.

It is Milton's signal achievement in *Paradise Lost* to compose an epic that assimilates the lessons of individual liberty to a genre normally dedicated to the founding of nations. In *Elegia Sexta*, written to Charles Diodati when Milton was twenty-one and at work on his Nativity Ode, the ambitious young writer imagined that the successful composition of epic poetry depends upon the poet's stringent exercise of temperance. His opening address suggests that health and a full stomach do not go together: "With a stomach anything but full, I send you a prayer for sound health, which you, perhaps, with your stomach stuffed, may need badly." The young Milton suggests that "For elegiac poets, feasts are their privilege, and again and again to soak themselves in aged wine." But "if a poet sings of wars" in epic poetry, Milton continues, if he sings on the one hand about the holy counsels of the gods above, then of the depths where the savage hound howls, he should live a simple, frugal life, after the fashion of the teacher who came from Samos [Pythagoras]; let herbs offer him food that doesn't upset his system, let the purest of water stand near him, in a beech bowl, and let him drink soberly from a pure spring. Such a poet should be required to have a youth chaste and free of crime. (pp. 196–98)

The young Milton, then, envisaged temperance in dietary and sexual conduct as part of the process by which a poet keeps himself pure in preparation to write epic poetry. When Milton finally came to write his epic, though, he turned decidedly from the traditional material of epic – "Warrs, hitherto the onely Argument / Heroic deem'd" and "marshal'd Feast / Serv'd up in Hall with Sewers and Seneschals" (9.28–29, 37–38) – in order to install temperance as a crucial aspect of the "higher argument" of that epic. Milton, then, ultimately composes not a heroic epic enhanced by the author's personal temperance but an epic devoted to making heroic the self-discipline epic composition demands.[73] In doing so, he deliberately displaces the violent excess that traditionally defines epic emotion – "the wrath / Of stern Achilles... or rage of Turnus,... Or Neptune's ire or Juno's" (9.14–18) – with an ethic of patience and moderation. This ethic, at once Christian and Stoic, is "Not less but more Heroic" Milton argues, than the "long and tedious havoc" of conventional epic material (9.14, 30).

Milton's emphasis on the virtue of temperance in the conclusion of his epic depicting the Fall as a moment of dietary transgression thus provides a moment where the spiritual demands of Christianity seem to merge effortlessly with the moral exigencies of classical philosophy. But it also highlights a central and unresolved ambivalence in Milton's oeuvre and his culture, between the classical ideal of self-administration and the Christian ideal of self-abnegation; between, that is, a sense that the human subject could purify itself through a regimen of discipline and a recognition that the human subject can only confess its impurity before an absolute God. Adam is told by Michael that he must "add / Deeds to thy knowledge answerable," yet he also inhabits a theological universe in which the saved must "renounce / Thir own both righteous and unrighteous deeds" (3.291–92). He is told, that is, to act virtuously and yet inhabits a theological world in which mortals are asked to disavow all action. This tension between ethics and theology, between the self-sufficiency that temperance enables and the total dependency that Milton's God demands, is paralleled by a tension between the Pauline notion that "to the pure all things are pure" – a notion Milton endorses enthusiastically in *Areopagitica* – and the equally Pauline proclamation, also endorsed in *Areopagitica*, that "Assuredly we bring not innocence into the world, we bring impurity much rather."[74] In both cases, Milton is divided between valuing the human subject and demeaning it, between viewing it as the source of contamination and praising it as the site of moral agency. In the *Apology for Smectymnuus*, Milton quotes Paul to the effect that "the body is for the Lord and the Lord is for the body."[75] The primacy of the body in Milton's religious imagination imposes a confused urgency on all acts of consumption. Like the idea of temptation itself, something one experiences within but in response to something from without, the contingencies of consumption produce a continual negotiation of the tension between imagining the human subject as pure but in need of protection and advertising the impure subject's contamination of those around it.

Milton, Aubrey records, was "Temperate, [and] rarely dranke between meales."[76] *Paradise Lost* testifies to his wish to link *salus* and salvation, imagining that the temperance he idealized and practiced could ameliorate the physical afflictions from which he and others suffered. By tracing the origins of humanity to his culture's myth of the primal breach of table manners, Milton assimilates the classical and Renaissance regime of dietary control to the patterns of Judeo-Christian myth. This places immense pressure on the processes of consumption, but it also gives the self the crucial power to control what it consumes. If the human subject's originary act of transgressive consumption precipitates an impurity which invades both self and world, that subject can nevertheless cultivate its interior garden, if not its external environment, by rigorous control of what it ingests and excretes. The necessary fiction that by regulating such corporeal flow one could in fact mitigate the inexorable processes of decay, disease, and death – a fantasy shared by each of the authors we have studied, and still very much with us in the flurry of frequently contradictory health recommendations that flood our newspapers – is the other side of the nightmare of unmitigated corporeal suffering that Michael portrays. An act of triage on the distempered body of postlapsarian existence, temperance is imagined to ameliorate the incurable diseases that ensue from that first act of intemperate eating, and that are nourished by the gluttony that re-enacts that originary transgression. Bringing together the medical theory of his day, which imagined that physiology and morality were intimately related, and his own intense ethical imagination, in which all acts have material consequences, Milton's epic exhibits a profound dedication to the liberating aspects of the exercise of self-discipline. The rule of temperance represents an exertion of discipline over desire, of reasoned choice over sensual appetite, that constitutes for Milton the moral and physiological essence of postlapsarian ethical life.

Afterword

By focusing on the advances achieved at the cutting-edge of new knowledge, historians of science frequently exaggerate the pace at which ideas and practices actually change.[1] What seems in hindsight like an earthquake, shattering the structures of old explanations, is more frequently experienced as a glacier, imperceptibly altering the landscape and climate. This glacial pace of change seems particularly pronounced when confronting ideas and practices surrounding the body. Ancient remedies and regimes dedicated to extending life have themselves demonstrated remarkable longevity. Milton's contemporary Sir Isaac Newton, theorist of the mechanistic universe, employed in his diet "a well-known classical regimen designed to support intellectual endeavor," even though that endeavor was largely dedicated to dismantling the theoretical underpinnings of that classical regimen.[2] Similarly George Cheyne, the eighteenth-century physician after whom Cheyne Walk in Chelsea is named, proclaims in *An Essay of Health and Long Life* that "The *great Secret* of *Health* and *Long Life*, lies in keeping the Blood (and consequently the other Juices of the Body) in a due Degree of *Fluidity*."[3] His regimen for long life, in other words, remains dedicated to the patterns of salutary solubility elaborated by the writers we have been exploring. "Most chronical Diseases proceed from Repletion," relates Cheyne, "as appears from their being cured by Evacuation" (p. 74).

The idea of remedy by purgation of humoral excess, then, lingers long after its conceptual framework had been demolished. Herbert's seventeenth-century translation of Cornaro's sixteenth-century *Treatise of Temperance and Sobrietie* (itself composed of various ideas from classical Greece and Rome) was reprinted in 1938 under the title *How to Live to be 100*.[4] What is now called alternative or folk medicine, moreover, remains a sanctuary for the allopathic remedies of Galenic medicine.[5] The scientific demolition of the theoretical system of humoral physiology – a demolition triggered by Harvey's discovery of the circulation of the blood – did not destroy its enormously useful vocabulary of corporeal and psychological experience. We still catch colds, and burn with anger. We offer hearty welcomes, and wonder if we have the stomach for a particular activity. We continue to feel melancholic, or choleric, or phlegmatic, or sanguine, although we no longer locate the emotion in an excess of the concomitant humoral fluid. Our language of emotion repeatedly testifies to the fact that we imagine our organs as more than just machines for various corporal processes unrelated to who we are.[6]

A major reason for Western medicine's rejection of this material grounding of emotion is its basis in subjective corporeal experience rather than scientifically verifiable phenomena. Nevertheless, this experiential grounding may in part account for the durability of this vocabulary. It may also offer a partial explanation for the striking similarity between this medical regime and those of other cultures, far removed from the influence of the West. As I have scratched the surface of the medical learning of different cultures – primarily those of China and India – I have been struck by unexpected similarities between their accounts of the body and those available in early modern England.[7] Like Galenic medicine, these systems treat the body as a whole, and explain physiological processes in terms of sensory experience. The essential qualities of a body are frequently expressed in terms of contrasting pairs – hot and cold, dry and wet, earth and air, fire and water. These elemental oppositions serve to link the inner body to the world around it, and make it subject to environmental factors. An intimate and meaningful relationship between the matter of bodies and the matter of the world around is asserted. Health is imagined as a balance of these elemental opposites, a balance achieved through the manipulation of the body's necessary osmosis with the world in the activities of eating, drinking, defecating, and urinating. Disease is not so much a foreign invader as a breakdown in the body's balance; this breakdown, moreover, has an ethical as well as a medical dimension, since the patient is responsible for the conduct that would sustain the proper balance of the body's opposing forces. Therapeutic interventions are designed to restore this balance through diet and evacuation. The details certainly vary widely among Eastern and Western medicines, as they do even among various Western interpreters of Galen, but the structural resemblances are striking. Although attention to descriptions of corporeal experience spread across time or geography frequently inculcates a sense of estrangement, solipsism, and relativism, as if registering the vast gulfs that can separate individuals and cultures, a focus on the experience of the body in texts from other cultures sometimes appears to yield intimations of something fundamentally and wondrously human. We are in these moments like the doubting Thomas who probes the body of the resurrected Jesus with his finger and discovers that the deepest spiritual mystery imaginable is also material and tangible. Searching the wondrous transubstantiation of spirit into matter that constitutes another's inner being, we confront the quotidian mystery of our own incarnation.

It would be easy to convert our admiration for the structures of embodied feeling that this earlier regime produced into nostalgia for a world in which a common language was available to both health practitioners and patients, in which patients were clearly linked to their environment, and in which a holistic account of the patient was assumed. This is a nostalgia that I wish to acknowledge, but not to indulge. Today's medical regime can seem a study in alienation where the patient and doctor speak different languages, where the patient is dealt with by a series of specialists who have little feeling for the whole organism, and where some major health markers – e.g., blood counts, blood pressure, cholesterol – are ineffable, registered only through tests, numbers, and gauges. But it has also produced enormous gains in longevity, and in ease of suffering. The interventions advised by this earlier medicine, by contrast, probably caused more suffering than they assuaged, and shortened more lives than they extended. By making people responsible for their health, moreover, this earlier medical regime abetted the pernicious (and continuing) practice of condemning patients for the afflictions they arbitrarily suffer.[8]

We nevertheless long for the holistic explanatory power that this earlier regime possessed. "The current success of alternative medicine," suggests Antonio Damasio, "is a symptom of public dissatisfaction with traditional medicine's inability to consider humans as a whole." Tellingly, though, contemporary medical science has recently become much more willing to entertain a notion of the mind–body nexus that resembles the model available in early modern England. Much current scientific work in neurobiology, for example, is explicitly devoted to remedying what Damasio terms the "Cartesian-based neglect of the mind in Western biology and medicine."[9] By postulating that ingestion of a material substance – now an antidepressant pharmaceutical rather than an allopathic remedy – can alleviate illnesses whose arena is primarily mental, the burgeoning field of psychopharmacology restores a biological basis to emotional and mental states.[10]

Perhaps this archaic vocabulary of corporeal experience has proven durable, over the centuries and over geography, because it makes sense, very literally, of the inevitably messy and ineluctably decaying matter of bodies. Providing images and metaphors that convey the internal workings and meanings of the body with remarkable power and grace, it produced a poetics of corporeal experience. Each of the works I have explored in this book testifies to a lingering desire to make visible and ethically meaningful the mysterious organization of the body, a desire which is still very much with us, even if the model of organization has changed immeasurably. The lyrical yet clinical descriptions recently offered by Dr. Sherwin Nuland of the intricate processes by which we live and die – I am thinking here of *How We Die* and *The Wisdom of the Body* – could have been read by any of these authors with sympathy and joy.[11] The title of an extremely popular alternative health manual for women – *Our Bodies, Our Selves*[12] – inherits the tradition of self-medication of body and soul that this book has investigated.

We continue to fret about the relationship between bodies and selves. Anxieties about the tense relationship between bodies and selves emerge frequently in the public mythology and policy issues surrounding organ transplants. Resistance to the idea of moving organs from a dead body to a living one, even when such a procedure is necessary to sustain life, and reports of organ-transplant patients taking on the personality traits of those whose organs they have received, indicate that we still believe these organs to be more than just identically replaceable parts, cogs in a machine we inhabit. We continue to believe that the unique bundle of desires, traumas, hopes, and anxieties that we term personality is tied to the corporal stuff in which we dwell.[13]

What, then, do we imagine the body–self nexus to be? We know that in the end, however carefully we maintain them, bodies always fail us. The inscrutable and absurd vagaries of mortal flesh demand that we impose meaning upon their delicious pleasures and random afflictions. Mortality urges a confrontation with arbitrariness to which many of us remain unwilling to surrender – whether out of courage or cowardice, I am not sure. This book has tracked the processes by which an earlier regime attempted to wring meaning from the matter of existence. By recognizing the accomplishments and limitations of four writers working within this regime, we can perhaps begin to reconceive the terms in which we frame our own conversations about the relationships between the bodies we all inhabit and the selves these bodies encourage us to imagine.

Notes

1 BODIES OF RULE: EMBODIMENT AND INTERIORITY IN EARLY MODERN ENGLAND

1. I cite the translation of Joseph Leo Koerner, *The Moment of Self-Portraiture in German Renaissance Art* (University of Chicago Press, 1993), p. 177. Koerner calls melancholy "Dürer's characteristic, character-determining ailment" (p. 181).
2. Jonathan Sawday, *The Body Emblazoned: Dissection and the Human Body in Renaissance Culture* (Routledge, 1995). Koerner, *Self-Portraiture*, p. 179. See, though, Sawday's discussion of this drawing in "Self and Selfhood in the Seventeenth Century," in *Rewriting the Self: Histories from the Renaissance to the Present*, ed. Roy Porter (Routledge, 1997), pp. 41–43.
3. Katharine Maus, *Ben Jonson and the Roman Frame of Mind* (Princeton University Press, 1985), pp. 26–27.
4. On Galenism, see Oswei Temkin, *Galenism: Rise and Decline of a Medical Philosophy* (Cornell University Press, 1973); and Nancy Siraisi, *Medieval and Early Renaissance Medicine* (University of Chicago Press, 1990).
5. Andrew Wear, "Medicine in Early Modern Europe, 1500–1700," in *The Western Medical Tradition 800 BC to AD 1800*, ed. Lawrence I. Conrad *et al.* (Cambridge University Press, 1995), p. 253.
6. Thomas Walkington, *The Optick Glasse of Humors (1631)*, ed. John A. Popplestone and Marion White McPherson (Scholars' Facsimiles & Reprints, 1981), p. xvii.
7. Peter Brown, *The Body and Society: Men, Women, and Sexual Renunciation in Early Christianity* (Columbia University Press, 1988), p. 17.
8. Lodowick Bryskett, *A Discourse of Civill Life*, ed. Thomas E. Wright (San Fernando Valley State College, 1970), pp. 176–77.
9. Sir Thomas Elyot, *The Castel of Helthe (1541)*, ed. Samuel A. Tannenbaum (Scholars' Facsimiles & Reprints, 1937), p. 2. Tannenbaum estimates that *The Castel of Helthe* went through "not less than fifteen editions between the years 1539 and 1610" (p. iii).
10. Siraisi, *Medieval and Early Renaissance Medicine*, p. 106.
11. Katharine Maus, *Inwardness and Theater in the English Renaissance* (University of Chicago Press, 1995), p. 195.
12. In *The Language of the Heart, 1600–1750* (University of Pennsylvania Press, 1997), Robert A. Erickson offers a learned account of the multiple meanings of the heart available to the early modern period.

13 David Hillman, "Visceral Knowledge," in *The Body in Parts: Fantasies of Corporeality in Early Modern Europe*, ed. David Hillman and Carla Mazzio (Routledge, 1997), p. 83. See also Gail Kern Paster, "Nervous Tension," in *The Body in Parts*, p. 111: "That which is bodily or emotional figuration for us, preserved metaphors of somatic consciousness, was the literal stuff of physiological theory for early modern scriptors of the body."

14 For a cogent discussion of the ways that contemporary neurology encourages a rethinking of Cartesian presuppositions about the relationships of selves and bodies, see Antonio Damasio, *Descartes' Error: Emotion, Reason, and the Human Brain* (Putnam's, 1994). On "how recent and parochial the Cartesian distinction [between mind and body] is," see also Richard Rorty, *Philosophy and the Mirror of Nature* (Princeton University Press, 1979), pp. 43–59, and Wallace I. Matson, "Why Isn't the Mind–Body Problem Ancient?" in *Mind, Matter, and Method*, ed. Paul Feyerabend and Grover Maxwell (University of Minnesota Press, 1966), pp. 92–102.

15 See the discussion of Plato's *Timaeus* in Anthony Levi, *French Moralists: The Theory of the Passions 1585 to 1649* (Clarendon Press, 1964), pp. 8–11.

16 *Galen: Selected Works*, tr. P. N. Singer (Oxford University Press, 1997), pp. 175–76.

17 Juan Huarte, *The Examination of Men's Wits (1594)*, ed. Carmen Rogers (Scholars' Facsimiles & Reprints, 1959), pp. 21–23.

18 *The Optick Glasse of Humors*, pp. 9, 12–13.

19 Edward Reynolds, *A Treatise of the Passions and Faculties of the Soule of Man (1640)*, ed. Margaret Lee Wiley (Scholars' Facsimiles & Reprints, 1971), pp. 4–11.

20 Slavoj Zizek, *The Sublime Object of Ideology* (Verso, 1989), pp. 207–09.

21 Anthony Fletcher, *Gender, Sex and Subordination in England 1500-1800* (Yale University Press, 1996), p. 290.

22 Quoted in Sawday, *Body Emblazoned*, p. 145, from Descartes, *Philosophical Letters*, ed. and tr. Anthony Kenny (Basil Blackwell, 1970), p. 142.

23 Damasio, *Descartes' Error*, pp. 249–50.

24 See Plato, *Timaeus*, 86b, discussing "disorders of the soul, which depend upon the body." He argues that "sexual intemperance is a disease of the soul due chiefly to the moisture and fluidity which is produced in one of the elements by the loose consistency of the bones. And in general, all that which is termed the incontinence of pleasure and is deemed a reproach under the idea that the wicked voluntarily do wrong is not justly a matter for reproach. For no man is voluntarily bad, but the bad become bad by reason of an ill disposition of the body and bad education – things which are hateful to every man and happen to him against his will. And in the case of pain, too, in like manner the soul suffers much evil from the body" (*The Collected Dialogues of Plato*, ed. Edith Hamilton and Huntington Cairns [Princeton University Press, 1961], p. 1206). So even Plato, articulator of the central dualism of Western civilization, offers a physiological explanation for a moral transgression.

25 See Sawday, *Body Emblazoned*, pp. 156-57.

26 John Purcell, *A Treatise on Vapours or, Hysterick Fits* (London, 1702), preface. I refer here not only to the already discussed Damasio, *Descartes' Error*, and Danah Zohar, *The Quantum Self* (Bloomsbury, 1990), which views Cartesian

ontology and Newtonian science as co-collaborators in our current world-view, but also to the fascinating work in psychology by Jerome Kagan, *Galen's Prophecy: Temperament in Human Nature* (Basic Books, 1994), which argues that every human inherits a physiology that determines emotional temperament and shapes the larger psychological profile.

27 Charles Taylor, *Sources of the Self: The Making of the Modern Identity* (Harvard University Press, 1989), p. 159.
28 Henry Peacham, *The Complete Gentleman, The Truth of Our Times, and The Art of Living in London*, ed. Virgil B. Heltzel (Cornell University Press, 1962), p. 144.
29 Phineas Fletcher, *The Purple Island or The Isle of Man* (Cambridge University Press, 1633), "To the Readers."
30 Michel Foucault, *The Archaeology of Knowledge*, tr. A. M. Sheridan Smith (Pantheon, 1972); *Discipline and Punish: The Birth of the Prison*, tr. Alan Sheridan (Pantheon, 1977); *The Order of Things: An Archaeology of the Human Sciences* (Pantheon, 1971).
31 Michel Foucault, *The Use of Pleasure*, and *The Care of the Self*, vols. II and III of *The History of Sexuality*, tr. Robert Hurley (Random House, 1986).
32 Mikhail Bakhtin, *Rabelais and his World*, tr. Helene Iswolsky (M. I. T. Press, 1968).
33 Important work that has been influenced by Bakhtin includes Peter Stallybrass and Allon White, *The Politics and Poetics of Transgression* (Cornell University Press, 1986); Stallybrass, "Patriarchal Territories: The Body Enclosed," in *Rewriting the Renaissance: The Discourses of Sexual Difference in Early Modern Europe*, ed. Margaret Ferguson *et al.* (University of Chicago Press, 1986), pp. 123–42; *idem*, "Reading the Body: *The Revenger's Tragedy* and the Jacobean Theater of Consumption," *Renaissance Drama* 18 (1987): 121–48; Gail Kern Paster, *The Body Embarrassed: Drama and the Disciplines of Shame in Early Modern Europe* (Cornell University Press, 1993); and Bruce Thomas Boehrer, *The Fury of Men's Gullets: Ben Jonson and the Digestive Canal* (University of Pennsylvania Press, 1997).
34 Levinus Lemnius, *The Secret Miracles of Nature* (London, 1658), p. 343.
35 Linda Pollock, *With Faith and Physic: The Life of a Tudor Gentlewoman Lady Grace Mildmay 1552–1620* (Collins & Brown, 1993), p. 110. On female healers, see Lucinda Beier, *Sufferers and Healers: The Experience of Illness in Seventeenth-Century England* (Routledge, 1987), pp. 166–72; and Doreen Nagy, *Popular Medicine in Seventeenth-Century England* (Bowling Green State University Press, 1988), ch. 5.
36 Elyot, *Castel*, pp. 61v–62. See also Levinus Lemnius, *The Touchstone of Complexions*, tr. T. Newton (London, 1581), p. 143v, "Of a Cold and Dry Complexion," who notes that many have been made ill "by the stayinge of their Hemorrhoides, and stopping of their naturall Purgations or Flowers, or by the restraynt of some ordinary and accustomed issue." This entails a fascinating situation where what we imagine as illness is construed as salubrious if inconvenient.
37 Thomas Venner, *Via Recta ad Vitam Longam. Or, A Treatise wherein the right way and best manner of living for attaining a long and healthfull life, is clearly demonstrated* (London, 1650), pp. 321–22.

38 Michel Jeanneret, *A Feast of Words: Banquets and Table Talk in the Renaissance*, tr. Jeremy Whiteley and Emma Hughes (University of Chicago Press, 1991), p. 73. Jeanneret also notes that "As a medical student in Montpellier, and then a practitioner, Rabelais was well aware of the theories of Hippocrates and Galen. In 1532, he published *Hippocratis et Galeni libri aliquot* and edited the *Epistolae medicinales* by the Italian doctor, Manardi" (p. 73, n. 18).
39 See, too, Paster's essay in *The Body in Parts*, "Nervous Tension: Networks of Blood and Spirit in the Early Modern Body," pp. 106–25.
40 *Body Embarrassed*, pp. 16–19. Norbert Elias, *The Civilizing Process*, vol. I, *The History of Manners*, tr. Edmund Jephcott (Urizen, 1978).
41 Thomas Wright, *The Passions of the Minde in Generall (1604)*, ed. Thomas O. Sloane (University of Illinois Press, 1971), pp. 4, 63. Thomas Venner, *Via Recta ad Vitam Longam*, p. 330. J. B. Bamborough, *Little World of Man* (Longman, 1952), p. 119, citing *The copie of a letter written by E. D. Doctour of Physicke to a gentleman by whom it was publisht* (1606), pp. 14–15.
42 Maus, *Ben Jonson*, p. 92.
43 *Ibid.*, p. 93.
44 Jean Calvin, *The Institution of Christian Religion*, tr. Thomas Norton (London, 1562), II. ii. 3.
45 Stephen Greenblatt, "Psychoanalysis and Renaissance Culture," in *Literary Theory / Renaissance Texts*, ed. Patricia Parker and David Quint (Johns Hopkins University Press, 1986), p. 215. The essay is discussed by Meredith Skura in "Understanding the Living and Talking to the Dead: The Historicity of Psychoanalysis," in *The Uses of Literary History*, ed. Marshall Brown (Duke University Press, 1995), pp. 93–105. See also the essays collected in *Desire in the Renaissance: Psychoanalysis and Literature*, ed. Valeria Finucci and Regina Schwartz (Princeton University Press, 1994).
46 Levi, *French Moralists*, p. 68.
47 Augustine, *The City of God*, 9.5, quoted in Maus, *Ben Jonson and the Roman Frame of Mind*, p. 79; see, though, *City of God*, 14.9, where, according to Levi, *French Moralists*, p. 15, "In the sense of an absence of all affections, apathy is to be rejected. In the sense of an absence of those affections only which are contrary to reason, '*mentemque perturbant,*' it is an ideal which cannot be realized in this life."
48 William Bouwsma, "The Two Faces of Humanism: Stoicism and Augustinianism in Renaissance Thought," in *A Usable Past: Essays in European Cultural History* (University of California Press, 1990), pp. 19–73. "Renaissance psychologies," remarks Debora Shuger, "vacillate alarmingly between what Bouwsma terms the Stoic and the Augustinian poles of interpretation" (*Sacred Rhetoric: The Christian Grand Style in the English Renaissance* [Princeton University Press, 1988], p. 79, n. 86). She cites Thomas Wright's *Passions of the Minde* as exemplary of this vacillation: "Stoic, Thomist, and Augustinian categories mingle throughout the work without any acknowledgment of their fundamental incommensurability." See also Richard Strier, *Resistant Structures: Particularity, Radicalism, and Renaissance Texts* (University of California Press, 1995), p. 34: "The psychological and social thinking and feeling of many figures in the Renaissance was deeply and incoherently divided between Stoic ideals of self-sufficiency on the one hand, and Christian and other ideals of mutuality and community on the other."

49 J. H. Salmon, "Seneca and Tacitus in Jacobean England," in *The Mental World of the Jacobean Court*, ed. Linda Levy Peck (Cambridge University Press, 1991), pp. 187–88. On continental Neostoicism, see Gerhard Oestrich, *Neostoicism and the Early Modern State* (Cambridge University Press, 1982), p. 14.
50 Claude Levi-Strauss, *The Origin of Table Manners*, tr. John and Doreen Weightman (Harper and Row, 1978); and Mary Douglas, *Purity and Danger: An Analysis of the Concepts of Pollution and Taboo* (Routledge, 1966).
51 Julia Kristeva, *Powers of Horror: An Essay on Abjection*, tr. Leon S. Roudiez (Columbia University Press, 1982), p. 113.
52 Maud Ellmann, *The Hunger Artists: Starving, Writing, and Imprisonment* (Harvard University Press, 1993).
53 Anne Ferry, *The "Inward" Language: Sonnets of Wyatt, Sidney, Shakespeare, Donne* (University of Chicago Press, 1983), p. 7.
54 Some representative works include Ruth L. Anderson, *Elizabethan Psychology and Shakespeare's Plays* (University of Iowa Press, 1927); Bamborough, *Little World of Man*; Herschel Baker, *The Image of Man* (Harvard University Press, 1947); John W. Draper, *The Humors and Shakespeare's Characters* (Duke University Press, 1945); Lily B. Campbell, *Shakespeare's Tragic Heroes: Slaves of Passion* (Cambridge University Press, 1930); Lawrence Babb, *The Elizabethan Malady* (Michigan State University Press, 1951); and Bridget Gellert Lyons, *Voices of Melancholy: Studies in Literary Treatments of Melancholy in Renaissance England* (Routledge, 1971).
55 Juan Luis Vives, *On Education [1531]: A translation of the "de tradendis Disciplinis" of Juan Luis Vives*, ed. Foster Watson (1913; repr. Rowman and Littlefield, 1971), p. 216.
56 Elyot, *Castel of Helthe*, pp. 15v–16. William Harrison explains the predilections of English diet by reference to the English climate: "The situation of our region, lying near unto the north, doth cause the heat of our stomachs to be of somewhat greater force; therefore our bodies do crave a little more ample nourishment than the inhabitants of the hotter regions are accustomed withal, whose digestive force is not altogether so vehement, because their internal heat is not so strong as ours, which is kept in by the coldness of the air that from time to time (especially in winter) doth environ our bodies" (*Description of England [1587]*, ed. Georges Edelen [Cornell University Press, 1968], pp. 123–24).
57 Robert Burton, *Anatomy of Melancholy [1632]*, ed. Thomas C. Faulkner, Nicholas Kiessling, and Rhonda Blair, 2 vols. (Clarendon Press, 1989), II: 27. *Paracelsus: Selected Writings*, ed. Jolande Jacobi, tr. Norbert Guterman (Bollingen, 1951), p. 87.
58 Huarte, *Examination of Men's Wits*, p. 175.
59 Sir Francis Bacon, "Of Regiment of Health," in *Works*, ed. James Spedding *et al.*, 15 vols. (Hurd and Houghton, 1869), V: 188–90.
60 Burton, *The Anatomy of Melancholy*, II: 18. Sawday, "The Uncanny Body," *The Body Emblazoned*, pp. 141–82, discusses the curious blend of familiarity and estrangement in Renaissance accounts of the interior body.
61 Michael MacDonald, *Mystical Bedlam: Madness, Anxiety, and Healing in Seventeenth-Century England* (Cambridge University Press, 1981), p. 187; Mildmay quoted in Pollock, *With Faith and Physic*, p. 119.

178   Notes to pages 24–30

62 Lemnius, *Touchstone of Complexions*, pp. 138v, 141v.
63 Oswei Temkin, *Hippocrates in a World of Pagans and Christians* (Johns Hopkins University Press, 1981), p. 47.
64 William Vaughan, *Directions for Health, Naturall and Artificiall* (London, 1626), p. 62.
65 *Certaine Sermons or Homilies Appointed to be Read in Churches in the Time of Queen Elizabeth (1547–1571): A Facsimile Reproduction of the Edition of 1623*, ed. Mary Ellen Rickey and Thomas B. Stroup, 2 vols. in 1 (Scholars' Facsimiles & Reprints, 1968), II: 98.
66 Burton, *Anatomy of Melancholy* I: 144–46.
67 Bacon, *Historia Vitae et Mortis*, in *Works*, V: 294.
68 Elyot, *Castel of Helthe*, p. 74v. The locus classicus for discussions of the stomach is Cicero, *De Natura Deorum*, 2.54–55, tr. H. Rackham (Loeb, 1933), pp. 253–57. The relationship between Hell and digestion in the Middle Ages has been explored by Robert Durling, "Deceit and Digestion in the Belly of Hell," in *Allegory and Representation: Selected Papers from the English Institute, 1979–80*, ed. Stephen Greenblatt (Johns Hopkins University Press, 1981), pp. 61–93; and Caroline Walker Bynum, "Why all the Fuss about the Body?" *Critical Inquiry* 22, vol. 1 (Autumn 1995): 1–33.
69 John Veslingus, *The Anatomy of the Body of Man*, tr. Nicholas Culpepper (London, 1677), pp. 11–12. Thomas Vicary, *A Profitable Treatise of the Anatomie of Mans Body* (London, 1577), pp. 67, 69. Sir Thomas Elyot likewise explains how the liver, a hot organ, "is to the stomake, as fyre under the pot" (*Castel of Helthe*, p. 46v).
70 Vaughan, *Directions for Health*, p. 168. *Du Bartas His Divine Weekes and Workes*, tr. Joshua Sylvester (London, 1605), Sixth Day, First Week, lines 712–36, in *The Complete Works of Joshuah Sylvester*, ed. A. B. Grosart, 2 vols. (AMS Press, 1967), I: 78. For a further discussion of the blood and veins, see Paster, "Nervous Tension: Networks of Blood and Spirit in the Early Modern Body," in *The Body in Parts*.
71 See Kenneth Muir, "Menenius's Fable," *Notes and Queries* 198 (June 1953): 240–42, and Leonard Barkan, *Nature's Work of Art: The Human Body as Image of the World* (Yale University Press, 1975), pp. 95–109, on the various deployments of the fable from Plutarch through Shakespeare. Fletcher, *The Purple Island*, p. 20, marginalia, note to canto 2, stanza 14.
72 The larger patterns of eating in *Coriolanus* have been analyzed well from a psychoanalytic perspective by Janet Adelman, "'Anger's My Meat': Feeding, Dependency, and Aggression in *Coriolanus*," in *Representing Shakespeare: New Psychoanalytic Essays*, ed. Murray Schwartz and Coppelia Kahn (Johns Hopkins University Press, 1980), pp. 129–49. *Coriolanus* 1.1.98–146, from *The Riverside Shakespeare*, ed. G. Blakemore Evans *et al*. (Houghton Mifflin, 1974), pp. 1397–98.
73 Carole Rawcliffe, *Medicine and Society in Later Medieval England* (A. Sutton, 1995), p. 45, quotes Russell from S. B. Chrimes, *English Constitutional Ideas in the Fifteenth Century* (Cambridge University Press, 1936), p. 175. Rawcliffe, though, does not cite the classical precedent.
74 Reynolds, *A Treatise of the Passions*, p. 80.

75 Peter Lowe, *The Whole Course of chirurgerie* (London, 1597), p. C3v. Vicary, *A Profitable Treatise*, p. 66.
76 Lemnius, *Touchstone of Complexions*, "Of a Compound Complexion," pp. 84–84v.
77 Vaughan, *Directions for Health*, p. 137.
78 Huarte, *Examination of Men's Wits*, pp. 289–90.
79 Vicary, *A Profitable Treatise*, p. 65; Elyot, *Castel of Helthe*, p. 53.
80 On the penchant for diaries in the period, see Stuart Sherman, *Telling Time: Clocks, Diaries, and English Diurnal Form, 1660–1785* (University of Chicago Press, 1996).
81 Richard Baxter, *Reliquiae Baxterianae* (London, 1696), Part 1, p. 9; Part 3, p. 173.
82 Baxter, *Reliquiae*, Part 1, p. 10; Part 1, p. 11. This is a less festive regime than it might first appear to modern palates, since beer was at once a far more common drink and a far less alcoholic drink than it is today.
83 Venner, *Via Recta ad Vitam Longam*, p. 314.
84 *Diary of Ralph Josselin 1616-1683*, ed. Alan Macfarlane (The British Academy, 1976), pp. 112, 122. On Josselin, see Lucinda Beier, "In Sickness and in Health: A Seventeenth-Century Family's Experience," and Andrew Wear, "Puritan Perceptions of Illness," in *Patients and Practitioners: Lay Perceptions of Medicine in Pre-Industrial Society*, ed. Roy Porter (Cambridge University Press, 1985). Sir John Harington, *A New Discourse of a Stale Subject, Called the Metamorphosis of Ajax*, ed. Elizabeth Story Donno (Columbia University Press, 1962), p. 92.
85 *The Riverside Milton*, ed. Roy Flanagan (Houghton Mifflin, 1998), p. 1006.
86 I have elsewhere explored the use of the discourse of gender by male and female writers; see my "Gender and Conduct in *Paradise Lost*," in *Sexuality and Gender in Early Modern Europe: Institutions, Texts, Images*, ed. James G. Turner (Cambridge University Press, 1993), pp. 310-38, and "The Gender of Religious Devotion: Amelia Lanyer and John Donne," in *Religion and Culture in the English Renaissance*, ed. Debora Shuger and Claire McEachern (Cambridge University Press, 1997), pp. 209–33.
87 See, for example, Thomas Laqueur, *Making Sex: Body and Gender from the Greeks to Freud* (Harvard University Press, 1990); Paster, *Body Embarrassed*; Fletcher, *Gender, Sex and Subordination*.
88 Lemnius, *Secret Miracles of Nature*, pp. 273–74.
89 Anthony Gibson, *A woman's woorth, defended against all the men in the world*, tr. John Wolfe (London, 1599), p. 19.
90 See, for example, Mark Breitenberg's description of the humoral body as "a body characteristically 'feminine' in its unruly fluidity and orificial vulnerability" ("Fearful Fluidity: Burton's Anatomy of Melancholy," in *Anxious Masculinity in Early Modern England* [Cambridge University Press, 1996], pp. 36–7, 42, 43).
91 Walkington, *Optick Glasse of Humors*, p. 58.
92 Sawday, *Body Emblazoned*, p. 160; my italics.
93 Robert Burton, *Anatomy of Melancholy*, I: 145.
94 On the Tilbury speech, see Carole Levin, *The Heart and Stomach of a King:*

Elizabeth I and the Politics of Sex and Power (University of Pennsylvania Press, 1994), pp. 143–45.
95 Quoted in Sawday, *Body Emblazoned*, p. 230; see Lisa T. Sarahsohn, "A Science Turned Upside Down: Feminism and the Natural Philosophy of Margaret Cavendish," *Huntington Library Quarterly* 47 (1984): 289–307.
96 See Caroline Walker Bynum, *Holy Feast and Holy Fast: The Religious Significance of Food to Medieval Women* (University of California Press, 1987).
97 See, though, Sawday's essay, "Self and Selfhood in the Seventeenth Century," in *Rewriting the Self*, pp. 29–48.
98 Katharine Maus, *Inwardness and Theater*.

2 FORTIFYING INWARDNESS: SPENSER'S CASTLE OF MORAL HEALTH

1 Norman Maclean, *Young Men and Fire* (University of Chicago Press, 1992), p. 294.
2 Lodowick Bryskett, *A Discourse of Civill Life*, ed. Thomas E. Wright (San Fernando Valley State College, 1970), pp. 202–3.
3 *Spenser: The Faerie Queene*, ed. A. C. Hamilton (Longman, 1977). All citations of *The Faerie Queene* are to this edition.
4 William Bouwsma, "The Two Faces of Humanism: Stoicism and Augustinianism in Renaissance Thought," in *A Usable Past: Essays in European Cultural History* (University of California Press, 1990), pp. 19–73.
5 William Ames, *The Marrow of Theology*, tr. John D. Eusden (Labyrinth Press, 1983), p. 231.
6 On continence as feeling temptations but resisting them, see Aristotle, *Nicomachean Ethics*, tr. Martin Ostwald (Bobbs-Merrill, 1962), 7. 1–10 (pp. 174–202); on temperance, see *Nicomachean Ethics*, 3.10–12, (pp. 77–82).
7 Cited from Ben Jonson, *The Complete Poems*, ed. George Parfitt (Yale University Press, 1982).
8 Baldassare Castiglione, *The Book of the Courtier*, tr. Thomas Hoby (J. M. Dent, 1928), p. 270.
9 For an account of this notion of temperance in literature, see David Reynolds, *The Serpent in the Cup: Temperance in American Literature* (University of Massachusetts Press, 1998).
10 *The Sermons of John Donne*, ed. George R. Potter and Evelyn M. Simpson, 10 vols. (University of California Press, 1953–62), v:171–72.
11 Where C. S. Lewis argues that the Bower of Bliss is a place of inactive looking, Graham Hough wryly remarks: "I do not suppose the toil referred to is watering the garden" (C. S. Lewis, *The Allegory of Love: A Study in Medieval Tradition* [Oxford University Press, 1958], pp. 331–32; Graham Hough, *A Preface to The Faerie Queene* [Duckworth, 1962], p. 164).
12 Bryskett, *Discourse of Civill Life*, p. 162.
13 Levinus Lemnius, *The Secret Miracles of Nature* (London, 1658), p. 153.
14 On the Aristotelian mean, see Joshua Scodel, "'Mediocrities' and 'Extremities': Francis Bacon and the Aristotelian Mean," in *Creative Imitation: New Essays on Renaissance Literature in Honor of Thomas M. Greene* (Medieval & Renaissance Texts & Studies, 1996), pp. 89–127; and "John Donne and the Religious

Politics of the Mean," in *John Donne's Religious Imagination: Essays in Honor of John T. Shawcross*, ed. Raymond-Jean Frontain and Frances M. Malpezzi (University of Central Arkansas Press, 1995), pp. 45–80.
15 Kathleen Williams, *Spenser's World of Glass* (University of California Press, 1966), p. 44.
16 Stephen Orgel, ed., *Ben Jonson: Selected Masques* (Yale University Press, 1970), p. 341.
17 Thomas Wright, *The Passions of the Minde in Generall (1604)*, ed. Thomas O. Sloane (University of Illinois Press, 1971), pp. 68–70.
18 *Montaigne: Complete Works*, tr. Donald Frame (Stanford University Press, 1967), pp. 853, 855 (Essay 3.13, "Of Experience").
19 Wright, *Passions of the Minde*, p. 150.
20 On the brothers' alignment with the humors, see Harry Berger, *The Allegorical Temper: Vision and Reality in Book II of Spenser's "Faerie Queene"* (Yale University Press, 1957), pp. 59–61, and James Carscallen, "The Goodly Frame of Temperance: The Metaphor of Cosmos in *The Faerie Queene*, Book II," in *Essential Articles: Edmund Spenser*, ed. A. C. Hamilton (Archon Books, 1972), pp. 347–65.
21 Liquid, suggests A. Kent Hieatt, supplies "the general image of the intemperance of appetite in Book 2 at large, as in Cymochles' name, in the Idle Lake and boat of Phaedria, and in the Odyssean sea journey to the floating isle of Acrasia herself" (*Chaucer, Spenser, Milton: Mythopoeic Continuities and Transformations* [McGill-Queen's University Press, 1975], p. 194). See also *The Faerie Queene* 1.7.7, in which Redcrosse is "Pourd out in loosnesse on the grassy grownd, / Both carelesse of his health, and of his fame."
22 See, for example, Thomas Laqueur, *Making Sex: Body and Gender from the Greeks to Freud* (Harvard University Press, 1990), and Gail Kern Paster, *The Body Embarrassed: Drama and the Disciplines of Shame in Early Modern Europe* (Cornell University Press, 1993). In the next chapter, we will see how heat in fact can become identified with disease, and coolness with a kind of health.
23 In *Paradise Regained*, Milton compares Christ's defeat of Satan with Hercules' victory over Antaeus. Arthur, though, must not only hold Maleger up but also throw his corpse into water.
24 John Hughes, *An Essay on Allegorical Poetry (1715)*, in *Spenser: The Critical Heritage*, ed. R. M. Cummings (Barnes and Noble, 1971), pp. 267–68.
25 This notion still underpins Bakhtin's separation of grotesque from classical bodies. Bakhtin, that is, inverts the hierarchy, but does not undo it. But Alma is a perfect example of just how anachronistic this is. Though grotesque to us, Alma is deeply "classical" to the regime Spenser articulates. See Mikhail Bakhtin, *Rabelais and his World*, tr. Helene Iswolsky (M. I. T. Press, 1968).
26 Robert Burton, *The Anatomy of Melancholy*, ed. Thomas C. Faulkner, Nicholas Kiessling, and Rhonda Blair, 2 vols. (Clarendon Press, 1989) II: 139–40.
27 Stephen Greenblatt, "To Fashion a Gentleman: Spenser and the Destruction of the Bower of Bliss," in *Renaissance Self-Fashioning: From More to Shakespeare* (University of Chicago Press, 1980), pp. 157–92; David Lee Miller, *The Poem's Two Bodies: The Poetics of the 1590 "Faerie Queene"* (Princeton University Press, 1988).

28 James A. Riddell and Stanley Stewart, *Jonson's Spenser: Evidence and Historical Criticism* (Duquesne University Press, 1995), p. 183.
29 *The Works of Edmund Spenser: A Variorum Edition, The Faerie Queene Book Two*, ed. Edwin Greenlaw et al. (Johns Hopkins University Press, 1933), II: 472. See also Riddell and Stewart, *Jonson's Spenser*, which argues throughout that Jonson's marginalia is the source of Digby's observations.
30 See, though, Jonathan Sawday's assertion that the House of Alma "is undoubtedly feminine," a claim which is less convincing than his brief but cogent observation on "the sexually undifferentiated body-interior" (*The Body Emblazoned: Dissection and the Human Body in Renaissance Culture* [Routledge, 1995], pp. 162–63, 160).
31 See Hamilton's note to stanza 29, p. 252.
32 William Vaughan, *Directions for Health, Naturall and Artificiall* (London, 1626), p. 168.
33 For a cogent critique of Descartes from the viewpoint of modern neurophysiology, see Antonio Damasio, *Descartes' Error: Emotion, Reason, and the Human Brain* (Putnam's, 1994).
34 *A View of the Present State of Ireland*, ed. W. L. Renwick (Clarendon Press, 1970), p. 68. Spenser's authorship of the *View* has been disputed by Jean R. Brink, "Constructing the *View of the Present State of Ireland*," *Spenser Studies* 11 (1994): 203–28. Spenser's authorship has been reasserted vigorously by Willy Maley, *Salvaging Spenser: Colonialism, Culture and Identity* (St. Martin's, 1997), pp. 163–94.
35 Bryskett, *A Discourse of Civill Life*, p. 40.
36 Lemnius, *Secret Miracles*, p. 257.
37 Burton, *Anatomy of Melancholy*, II: 18.
38 Vaughan, *Directions for Health*, p. 168.
39 Carol Rawcliffe, *Medicine and Society in Later Medieval England* (A. Sutton, 1995), p. 44.
40 Miller, *The Poem's Two Bodies*, p. 190.
41 See Debora Shuger, *The Renaissance Bible: Scholarship, Sacrifice, Subjectivity* (University of California Press, 1995), pp. 176–81.
42 Michel Foucault, *The History of Sexuality*, vol. III, *The Care of the Self*, tr. Robert Hurley (Pantheon, 1986), p. 141.
43 Juan Huarte, *The Examination of Men's Wits (1594)*, tr. Richard Carew, ed. Carmen Rogers (Scholars' Facsimiles & Reprints, 1959), p. 26. In *The Book of Memory: A Study of Memory in Medieval Culture* (Cambridge University Press, 1990), pp. 165–66, Mary Carruthers observes that "Metaphors which use digestive activities are so powerful and tenacious that 'digestion' should be considered another basic functional model for the complementary activities of reading and composition, collection and recollection."
44 Augustine, *Confessions*, 10.14, tr. R. S. Pine-Coffin (Penguin, 1961), pp. 220–21.
45 Riddell and Stewart, *Jonson's Spenser*, p. 125.
46 Thomas Wright's *Passions of the Minde*, p. 17. Hamilton's note cites Sir Thomas Elyot, *Governor*, 1. 10, where the two passions are described as important qualities in a youth: "By Shamfastnes, as it were with a bridell, they rule as well theyr dedes as their appetites. And desire of prayse addeth to a sharpe spurre to their disposition toward lernyng and vertue." Hamilton suggests a source in

Aristotle, *Nicomachean Ethics*, III.vii.1116a, on the balance between fear of shame and desire for honour in the brave. Riddell and Stewart, *Jonson's Spenser*, p. 128, also cites the passage from Wright.
47 Miller, *The Poem's Two Bodies*, pp. 179–80.
48 Wright, *Passions of the Minde*, pp. 16–17.
49 *Ibid.*, p. 62.
50 *Ibid.*, p. 60.
51 Thomas Healy, *New Latitudes: Theory and English Renaissance Culture* (Edward Arnold, 1992), pp. 99–100. See also the *Variorum*, p. 282.
52 Richard A. McCabe, "Edmund Spenser, Poet of Exile," *Proceedings of the British Academy* 80 (1993): 85.
53 Greenblatt, *Renaissance Self-Fashioning*, p. 173, citing Freud's *Civilization and Its Discontents*.
54 Wright, *Passions of the Minde*, p. 73.
55 Healy, *New Latitudes*, pp. 100–1. For an elaboration of the ways that bodily process and foreign policy can be metaphors for each other, see also Healy, "Sound Physic: Phineas Fletcher's *The Purple Island* and the Poetry of Purgation," *Renaissance Studies* 5 (1991): 341–52.
56 "To the right worshipfull, my singular good friend, M. Gabriell Harvey," cited from *The Shorter Poems of Edmund Spenser*, ed. William Oram *et al.* (Yale University Press, 1989), p. 773.
57 Foucault, *The History of Sexuality*, vol. II, *The Use of Pleasure*, tr. Robert Hurley (Pantheon, 1988), p. 77
58 Sawday, *Body Emblazoned*, p. 219.
59 Riddell and Stewart, *Jonson's Spenser*, p. 169.
60 M. Andreas Laurentius, *A Discourse of the Preservation of the Sight: of Melancholike Diseases; of Rheumes, and of Old Age*, tr. Richard Surphlet (1599), ed. Sanford Larkey (Shakespeare Association Facsimiles no. 15, 1938), Book 2, Chapter 2, pp. 80–81.
61 McCabe, "Poet of Exile," p. 86.
62 Bryskett, *A Discourse of Civill Life*, p. 128.
63 D. M. Vieth, ed., *The Complete Poems of John Wilmot, Earl of Rochester* (Yale University Press, 1968).

3 THE MATTER OF INWARDNESS: SHAKESPEARE'S SONNETS

1 Friedrich Nietzsche, "On the Despisers of the Body," in *Thus Spake Zarathustra*, tr. Thomas Common (Modern Library, 1951).
2 Sir Thomas Elyot, *The Book Named The Governor*, ed. S. E. Lehmberg (Everyman, 1962), pp. 205–6.
3 On the Sonnets as a particularly literary form of subjectivity, see Joel Fineman, *Shakespeare's Perjured Eye: The Invention of Poetic Subjectivity in the Sonnets* (University of California Press, 1986), and Margreta de Grazia, "The Motive for Interiority: Shakespeare's *Sonnets* and *Hamlet*," *Style* 23 (1989): 430–44. For the debate about *Hamlet* and modern subjectivity, see Catherine Belsey, *The Subject of Tragedy: Identity and Difference in Renaissance Drama* (Methuen, 1985), pp. 33–52; Jonathan Dollimore, *Radical Tragedy: Religion, Ideology, and Power in the Drama of Shakespeare and His Contemporaries* (University of Chicago

Press, 1984), pp. 173–81; and Francis Barker, *The Tremulous Private Body: Essays on Subjection* (Methuen, 1984), Recent attempts to reclaim for Hamlet the prospect of an authentic proto-modern interiority include Katharine Eisaman Maus, *Inwardness and Theater in the English Renaissance* (University of Chicago Press, 1995); Peter Iver Kaufman, *Prayer, Despair, and Drama: Elizabethan Introspection* (University of Illinois Press, 1996), pp. 103–49; and, most recently, Harold Bloom, *Shakespeare: The Invention of the Human* (Riverhead Books, 1998).

4 See, for example, Lawrence Babb, *The Elizabethan Malady: A Study of Melancholia in English Literature from 1580 to 1642* (Michigan State University Press, 1951); Bridget Gellert Lyons, *Voices of Melancholy: Studies in Literary Treatments of Melancholy in Renaissance England* (Norton, 1975), and Winfred Schleiner, *Melancholy, Genius, and Utopia in the Renaissance* (In Kommission bei Otto Harrassowitz, 1991).

5 Helen Vendler, *The Art of Shakespeare's Sonnets* (Harvard University Press, 1997), p. 17.

6 Throughout the essay I will quote the Sonnets from Stephen Booth's admirable edition, *Shakespeare's Sonnets* (Yale University Press, 1977), drawing on the 1609 Quarto facsimile contained therein, and occasionally referring to the accompanying modernized text.

7 J. B. Leishman, *Themes and Variations in Shakespeare's Sonnets* (Harper and Row, 1966), p. 120, remarks of the poem: "If it were possible to use the word 'conventional' in an unpejorative sense, I think it might be said that this is Shakespeare's nearest approach to an expression both of conventional Platonism and of conventional Christianity." In his annotations, Booth offers a provocative discussion of the use and abuse of convention to interpret this poem (*Shakespeare's Sonnets*, pp. 507–17).

8 Helen Vendler makes a strong case for "Feeding" in *The Art of Shakespeare's Sonnets*, pp. 611–14.

9 A similar sentiment is expressed in *Love's Labour's Lost* 1.1.25–27: "The mind shall banquet, though the body pine." In a poem entitled "Lent," George Herbert notes that by fasting, one "banquet[s]" the soul (*The Works of George Herbert*, ed. F. E. Hutchinson [Clarendon Press, 1941], lines 47–48). I discuss this poem, and Herbert's larger meditation on eating and devotion, in the next chapter.

10 Nicholas Culpepper, *Health for the Rich and Poor, by Diet, without Physick* (London, 1670), p. 124. Thomas Wright, *The Passions of the Minde in Generall (1604)*, ed. Thomas O. Sloane (University of Illinois Press, 1971), pp. 86–87. The medieval heritage of such conceptions is explored by Caroline Walker Bynum, *Holy Feast and Holy Fast: The Religious Significance of Food to Medieval Women* (University of California Press, 1987).

11 Lily B. Campbell, *Shakespeare's Tragic Heroes: Slaves of Passion* (Cambridge University Press, 1930), p. 81. Wright, *Passions of the Minde*, pp. 89–90.

12 Fineman, *Shakespeare's Perjured Eye*, argues that the maddeningly divided subjectivity articulated here is the source of the modern poetic subject. In *Love's Labour's Lost*, 4.3.93–96, Dumaine identifies his love as an illness – "I would forget her, but a fever she / Reigns in my blood, and will rememb'red be" – to which Berowne responds with a witty suggestion of an appropriate medical

therapy, bleeding the patient to decrease the troublesome heat: "A fever in your blood! why then incision / Would let her out in saucers."

13 If the arguments of John Kerrigan and Katherine Duncan-Jones about *A Lover's Complaint* as the end of the sequence are accepted, then we get a portrait there, as Duncan-Jones argues, of a woman who "proves to be just as powerfully driven by negative and self-destructive desire as the lust-mad 'men' of sonnet 129" (*Shakespeare's Sonnets*, ed. Katherine Duncan-Jones [Arden Shakespeare, 1998],p. 95); see also *Shakespeare: The Sonnets and A Lover's Complaint*, ed. John Kerrigan (Penguin, 1986), pp. 7–64.

14 According to F. David Hoeniger, *Medicine and Shakespeare in the English Renaissance* (University of Delaware Press, 1992), p. 169, the "stuff," is "melancholy or burned humors produced by her passionate condition."

15 Juan Huarte, *The Examination of Men's Wits*, tr. Richard Carew (London, 1594), p. 322.

16 See Booth's note on these lines in *Shakespeare's Sonnets*, pp. 395–96.

17 Stephen Booth, *An Essay on Shakespeare's Sonnets* (Yale University Press, 1969), pp. 150–51.

18 *Ibid.*, p. 167.

19 John Crowe Ransom, "Shakespeare at Sonnets," in *The World's Body* (Scribner's, 1938), p. 297.

20 This tension is not peculiar to this poem, but is in fact a critical issue in Western Christianity, particularly as it dealt with its Roman inheritance. See the wonderful essay by William J. Bouwsma, "The Two Faces of Humanism: Stoicism and Augustinianism in Renaissance Thought," in *A Usable Past: Essays in European Cultural History* (University of California Press, 1990), pp. 19–73. On the Christian assimilation of Roman ideas, see also Peter Brown, *The Body and Society: Men, Women, and Sexual Renunciation in Early Christianity* (Columbia University Press, 1988), and Michel Foucault, *The History of Sexuality*, vol. II, *The Use of Pleasure*, and vol. III, *The Care of the Self*, tr. Robert Hurley (Pantheon, 1985, 1986).

21 Edward Hubler, *The Sense of Shakespeare's Sonnets* (Princeton University Press, 1952), p. 103; William Empson, "They That Have Power: Twist of Heroic-Pastoral Ideas into an Ironical Acceptance of Aristocracy," in *Some Versions of Pastoral* (1935; New Directions, 1974), pp. 89–115.

22 Booth, *Essay*, p. 162.

23 See Bouwsma, "The Two Faces of Humanism," pp. 19–73. See also Geoffrey Miles, *Shakespeare and the Constant Romans* (Clarendon Press, 1996), on Shakespeare's dramatic emphasis on Stoic constancy in the Roman plays. On the philosophical debate over whether a wise man should destroy or manage affect, see also Charles Schmitt, Quentin Skinner, and Eckhard Kessler, eds., *The Cambridge History of Renaissance Philosophy* (Cambridge University Press, 1988), pp. 360–65.

24 Katharine Maus, *Ben Jonson and the Roman Frame of Mind* (Princeton University Press, 1985), p. 92.

25 J. H. Salmon, "Seneca and Tacitus in Jacobean England," in *The Mental World of the Jacobean Court*, ed. Linda Levy Peck (Cambridge University Press, 1991), p. 170.

26 Campbell, *Shakespeare's Tragic Heroes*, p. 70.

186   Notes to pages 85–88

27 Edward Reynolds, *A Treatise of the Passions and Faculties of the Soule of Man* (London, 1640), pp. 47–48.
28 Sir John Davies, *Nosce Teipsum*, lines 381–82, quoted from *The Renaissance in England: Non-dramatic Prose and Verse of the Sixteenth Century*, ed. Hyder E. Rollins and Herschel Baker (D. C. Heath and Company, 1954), p. 480.
29 Quoted in Gilles Monsarrat, *Light from the Porch: Stoicism and English Renaissance Literature* (Didier-Erudition, 1984), pp. 106–7. This passage was dropped in the 1603 edition of the *Basilikon*, perhaps for political reasons. On attitudes to Seneca in Jacobean England, see also Salmon, "Seneca and Tacitus in Jacobean England," p. 186.
30 Richard Wilson, "Shakespeare and the Jesuits," *Times Literary Supplement* 4942 (19 Dec., 1997): 11–13.
31 On the link between heat and masculinity, see Thomas Laqueur, *Making Sex: Body and Gender from the Greeks to Freud* (Harvard University Press, 1990), pp. 27–40, 141–42, and Gail Kern Paster, *The Body Embarrassed: Drama and the Disciplines of Shame in Early Modern Europe* (Cornell University Press, 1993).
32 For a Pyrochles-like anger in a Shakespearean play, see *King John*, 3.1.340–45. The King declares to Philip: "France, I am burned up with inflaming wrath – / A rage whose heat hath this condition, / That nothing can allay, nothing but blood," to which Philip replies: "Thy rage shall burn thee up, and thou shalt turn / To ashes, ere our blood shall quench that fire."
33 Huarte, *Examination of Men's Wits*, pp. 56–58.
34 Wright, *Passions of the Minde*, pp. 38–40. Perhaps this is why Ferdinand chooses a similar discourse of internal coolness to reassure Prospero of his conduct with Miranda: "I warrant you, sir / The white cold virgin snow upon my heart / Abates the ardour of my liver" (4.1.54–56). See also *Passions of the Minde*, p. 40, where Wright explains how women's comparative dearth of physiological heat – frequently a sign of innate inferiority – could bestow upon them the material basis of superior conduct: "Women, by nature, are enclined more to mercie and pietie than men, because the tendernesse of their complexion moveth them more to compassion. They surpasse men also in pitie and devotion.... Neither are they so prone to incontinency as men, for lacke of heate."
35 In M. Andreas Laurentius, *A Discourse of the Preservation of the Sight*, tr. Richard Surphlet (1599), ed. Sanford Larkey (Oxford University Press, 1938), pp. 141–42. Laurentius sees himself here as siding with Galen over Aristotle, since Aristotle says that the brain is cold "onely to coole the heart." Leontes describes his onset of irrational jealousy – whose first verbal manifestation is the phrase "Too hot" – as "the infection of my brains" (*Winter's Tale*, 1.2.145).
36 Huarte, *Examination of Men's Wits*, pp. 56–57.
37 Huarte, *Ibid.*, pp. 88–89. One could perhaps usefully invoke the line from *The Tempest*, on how the physical and mental tribulations to which Prospero has subjected Gonzalo, Alonso, Sebastian, and Antonio, have made their "brains, / Now useless, boil'd within [their] skull[s]" (5.1.60). They have literally been over-heated by the ordeals they have suffered. This issue of the material underpinnings of behavior, central to Renaissance moral philosophy, has returned in contemporary psychopharmacology, particularly surrounding antidepressants such as Prozac.

38 Robert Burton, *The Anatomy of Melancholy*, ed. Thomas C. Faulkner, Nicholas Kiessling, and Rhonda Blair (2 vols. Clarendon Press, 1989) I: 255–56.
39 *Ibid.*, I: 256.
40 As Maus argues, "Sexual desire is, in erotic comedy, the linchpin of the human psyche and the primary motive for community life. The forces of repression need to be overcome; the rule of the game is not to deny one's emotional nature but to employ it in some acceptable manner" (*Ben Jonson and the Roman Frame of Mind*, pp. 79–80).
41 Richard Ford, *Women with Men* (Knopf, 1997) p. 91, at the end of "The Womanizer."
42 Hubler, *Sense*, p. 104.
43 Sir Thomas Elyot, *The Castel of Helthe (1541)*, ed. Samuel A. Tannenbaum (Scholars' Facsimiles & Reprints, 1937), p. 64.
44 Henry Peacham, *The Complete Gentleman (1622)*, ed. Virgil B. Heltzel (Cornell University Press, 1962), p. 144.
45 Empson, *Some Versions*, p. 90. L. C. Knights likewise views the poem as filled with "irony" that is "serious and destructive" ("Shakespeare's Sonnets," *Scrutiny* 3 [1934]: 146).
46 Wright, *Passions of the Minde*, pp. 90–103.
47 Hubler, *Sense*, p. 103. Ransom, *The World's Body*, p. 297, notes that the advice here is "exactly opposite to the argument of the sonnets which open the sequence."
48 See the reading by Joseph Pequigney, *Such is My Love: A Study of Shakespeare's Sonnets* (University of Chicago Press, 1985), pp. 104–7, which aptly juxtaposes this passage with Prince Hal's soliloquy in *1 Henry IV*, Act I, scene 2.
49 In this context, it is important to remember Leontes' description of his mental infirmity in *The Winter's Tale*, 1.2.145, as "the infection of my brains." The word was closely linked to *fester* which means "To putrefy, to rot; to become pestiferous or loathsome by corruption" (*OED*, citing Sonnet 94 and *Henry V* 4.3.28).
50 John Abernathy, *A Christian and Heavenly Treatise: Containing Physicke for the Soule* (London, 1630), p. 442.
51 The final line of Sonnet 94 is quoted in or from the play *The Reign of King Edward the Third* (1596), an anonymous play that may or may not be by Shakespeare, in a scene where a monarch's abuse of power for sexual purposes is being resisted. The quotation is from Thomas Cogan, *The Haven of Health* (London, 1584), p. 51. Such accounts of the intrinsic heat or cold of a given plant, though, are frequently disputed; the anonymous *Treasurie of Hidden Secrets* (London, 1637), Chapter 113, entitled "The sundry vertues of Lillies," notes that "Lillies are cold and dry in the third degree ... it is good for all manner of burnings and scaldings."
52 Kerrigan, ed., *The Sonnets and A Lover's Complaint*, p. 290.
53 Wordsworth, "Scorn Not the Sonnet." In "The Motive for Interiority," *Style* 23 (1989): 430-44, Margreta de Grazia astutely analyzes the processes by which the character and biography of Shakespeare began to be read into the Sonnets after 1780.
54 See Foucault, *Care of the Self*, vol. III of *The History of Sexuality*.

55 Indeed, when confronting not erotic passion but the emotion of grief Shakespeare repeatedly suggests that suppression is dangerous and ventilation therapeutic. In *Venus and Adonis*, lines 331–36, for example, he notes that "An oven that is stopp'd ... Burneth more hotly ... so of concealed sorrow may be said: / Free vent of words love's fire doth assuage." A similar point is urged in *Titus Andronicus* (2.4.36–37): "Sorrow concealed, like an oven stopped, / Doth burn the heart to cinders where it is."

4 DEVOTION AND DIGESTION: GEORGE HERBERT'S CONSUMING SUBJECT

1 "On Food and Happiness," *Antaeus* 68 (Spring 1992): 24.
2 *The Works of George Herbert*, ed. F. E. Hutchinson (Clarendon Press, 1941). All subsequent references to Herbert's English works are to this edition.
3 "Outworks" may also contain a pun on an archaic term for *hors d'œuvres*, although the *OED's* first recorded usage is from Evelyn in 1693.
4 On the relationship between architecture and the configurations of power, see Murray Baillie, "Etiquette and the Planning of the State Apartments in Baroque Palaces," *Archaeologia* 101 (1967): 169–99; David Starkey, "Intimacy and Innovation: The Rise of the Privy Chamber, 1485–1547," and Neil Cuddy, "The Revival of the Entourage: The Bedchamber of James I, 1603–1625," both in *The English Court from the Wars of the Roses to the Civil War*, ed. David Starkey et al. (Longman, 1987), pp. 71–118, 173–225. On the use of images from architecture and cabinetry to represent the interior self, see Anne Ferry, *The "Inward" Language: Sonnets of Wyatt, Sidney, Shakespeare, Donne* (University of Chicago Press, 1984), pp. 46–49, and Patricia Fumerton, *Cultural Aesthetics: Renaissance Literature and the Practice of Social Ornament* (University of Chicago Press, 1991), pp. 67–70, 137.
5 Robert Burton, *The Anatomy of Melancholy*, ed. Thomas C. Faulkner, Nicholas Kiessling, and Rhonda Blair, 2 vols. (Clarendon Press, 1989) I: 141.
6 Levinus Lemnius, *The Touchstone of Complexions*, tr. T. Newton (London, 1581), pp. 7–7v.
7 *Certaine Sermons or Homilies Appointed to be Read in Churches in the Time of Queen Elizabeth (1547–1571): A Facsimile Reproduction of the Edition of 1623*, ed. Mary Ellen Rickey and Thomas B. Stroup, 2 vols. in 1 (Scholars' Facsimiles & Reprints, 1968), II: 98.
8 *The Paradoxical Discourses of F. M. Van Helmont; Concerning the Macrocosm and Microcosm of the Greater and Lesser World, and their Union* (London, 1685), p. 97. I owe this reference to David Hillman.
9 I cite the translation from *The Latin Poetry of George Herbert*, tr. Mark McCloskey and Paul R. Murphy (Ohio University Press, 1965), p. 107.
10 Levinus Lemnius, *The Secret Miracles of Nature* (London, 1658), p. 296.
11 The most intense version of this dilemma is the poem "The Altar," which I discuss in Chapter 4 of *Prayer and Power: George Herbert and Renaissance Courtship* (University of Chicago Press, 1991), pp. 161–67.
12 On suffering in Herbert, see "'Storms are the Triumph of His Art': The Politics of Affliction," Chapter 3 of *Prayer and Power*, pp. 117–53.
13 Lemnius, *Touchstone of Complexions*, p. 22v.

14 See Keith Thomas, "Cleanliness and Godliness in Early Modern Europe," in *Religion, Culture and Society in Early Modern Britain: Essays in Honour of Patrick Collinson*, ed. Anthony Fletcher and Peter Roberts (Cambridge University Press, 1994).

15 Carol Rawcliffe, *Medicine and Society in Later Medieval England* (Alan Sutton, 1995), p. 42.

16 *The Autobiography of Edward, Lord Herbert of Cherbury*, ed. Sidney Lee (Dutton, 1906), p. 113. On the relationship between smell and status, see Georges Vigarello, *Concepts of Cleanliness: Changing Attitudes in France since the Middle Ages*, tr. Jean Birrell (Cambridge University Press, 1988). I explore the correlation between cleanliness and rank in the work of one of Herbert's contemporaries in "The Art of Disgust: Civility and the Social Body in *Hesperides*," in *Robert Herrick*, a special issue of the *George Herbert Journal* (1990/91): 127–54.

17 On the "indissoluble link between gentility and household generosity" in the period, see Felicity Heal, *Hospitality in Early Modern England* (Clarendon Press, 1990).

18 The Paracelsian view of nature here is discussed by Gillian Beer, *Darwin's Plots: Evolutionary Narrative in Darwin, George Eliot, and Nineteenth-Century Fiction* (Routledge & Kegan Paul, 1983). *Paracelsus: Selected Writings*, ed. Jolande Jacobi, tr. Norbert Guterman (Bollingen, 1951), p. 91.

19 Richard Todd, *The Opacity of Signs: Acts of Interpretation in George Herbert's "Temple"* (University of Missouri Press, 1986), p. 105.

20 For a rich discussion of the ambivalent status of pigs in Renaissance culture – they functioned at once as ambulatory garbage disposals and as sources of food – see Peter Stallybrass and Allon White, *The Politics and Poetics of Transgression* (Cornell University Press, 1986), pp. 44–59.

21 I have learned much about the dynamics of this process from Norbert Elias, *The Civilizing Process*, vol. I, *The History of Manners*, tr. Edmund Jephcott (Urizen, 1978); Mary Douglas, *Purity and Danger: An Analysis of the Concepts of Pollutions and Taboo* (Routledge, 1966); and Julia Kristeva, *Powers of Horror: An Essay on Abjection*, tr. Leon S. Roudiez (Columbia University Press, 1982).

22 Stanley Fish, *The Living Temple: George Herbert and Catechizing* (University of California Press, 1978), p. 131.

23 On the psychological weirdness of these lines, see Richard Strier, "Sanctifying the Aristocracy: 'Devout Humanism' in François de Sales, John Donne, and George Herbert," *Journal of Religion* 69 (1989): 46, n. 41, and my *Prayer and Power*, pp. 251–52, and p. 324, n. 70. The *Homilie Against Gluttonie and Drunkennesse* finds a biblical precedent for drunken incest in the story of Lot, who "being overcome with wine, committed abominable incest with his owne daughters. So will almighty GOD give over drunkards, to the shamefull lusts of their own hearts" (*Certaine Sermons or Homilies*, II: 96).

24 Thomas Hobbes, *Leviathan*, ed. C. B. Macpherson (Penguin, 1978), pp. 141–42.

25 Lines 25, 41, 47. The *Homilie Against Gluttony and Drunkennesse* warns that "drunkards and gluttons [are] altogether without power of themselves" (*Certaine Sermons or Homilies*, II: 98).

26 *Autobiography of Edward, Lord Herbert*, ed. Lee, p. 11.
27 Richard Allestree's *Almanac* (London, 1623), sig. B6r, quoted in Gail Kern Paster, *The Body Embarrassed: Drama and the Disciplines of Shame in Early Modern England* (Cornell University Press, 1993), p. 97.
28 James Boyd White, *"This Book of Starres": Learning to Read George Herbert* (University of Michigan Press, 1994), p. 180.
29 Richard Strier, *Love Known: Theology and Experience in George Herbert's Poetry* (University of Chicago Press, 1983), p. 187; see Chapter 7, "The Heart's Privileges," pp. 174–217, *passim*, and pp. 144–45. Peter Sacks, "George Herbert and Our Contemporaries," in *George Herbert in the Nineties: Reflections and Reassessments*, ed. Jonathan F. S. Post and Sidney Gottlieb (George Herbert Journal Special Studies and Monographs, 1995), p. 44.
30 I explore the political meanings of this poem in *Prayer and Power*, pp. 62–63.
31 Izaak Walton, *The Lives*, ed. George Saintsbury (Oxford University Press, 1927), p. 284. Frank Huntley discusses Herbert's illness and its date in "The Williams Manuscript, Edmund Duncon, and Herbert's Quotidian Fever," *George Herbert Journal* 10, 1–2 (1986/87): 23–32.
32 Cornaro's contribution to medicine is discussed in Nancy G. Siraisi, *The Clock and the Mirror: Girolamo Cardano and Renaissance Medicine* (Princeton University Press, 1997), pp. 79–81. Elizabeth Bishop once mentioned Herbert's translation of Cornaro's treatise in a letter of 11 August 1957 to Robert Lowell in which she admonished him to "please please take care of yourself"; cited in Brett Candlish Miller, "Modesty and Morality: George Herbert, Gerard Manley Hopkins, and Elizabeth Bishop," *Kenyon Review* ns. 9, no. 22 (Spring 1989): 50.
33 Edward Herbert recommends the works of Fernel in his *Autobiography*, p. 23: "Among writers of Physick, I do expecially commend after Hipocrates a[nd] gallen, Fernelius, Lud: Mercatus, and Dan: Sennertus, and Heurnius." According to Hutchinson, *Works*, p. 561, Edward Herbert left three of Fernel's works to Jesus College, Oxford. See Charles Sherrington, *The Endeavour of Jean Fernel, with a List of the Editions of his Writings* (Cambridge University Press, 1946), especially pp. 66–73.
34 Sherrington, *Endeavour of Jean Fernel*, p. 68. Later in *The Country Parson*, amid yet another discussion of food and health, Herbert endorses the alimentary lessons of "*Gerson*, a spirituall man, [who] wisheth all to incline rather to too much, then to too little; his reason is, because diseases of exinanition are more dangerous then diseases of repletion" (p. 267). Here Jean Charlier de Gerson (1363–1429), the "probable author of the *Imitatio*," is invoked as a guide to commensal conduct rather than to religious devotion. I cite the annotation of Hutchinson, *Works*, p. 561, quoting Evelyn Underhill on Gerson from the *Cambridge Medieval History*, 8 vols. (Cambridge University Press, 1911–36), VIII: 810.
35 In the last two volumes of *The History of Sexuality* – vol. II, *The Use of Pleasure*, and vol. III, *The Care of the Self*, tr. Robert Hurley (Pantheon, 1985, 1986) – Michel Foucault explored the emergence of subjectivity from the parameters of Stoic discipline.
36 Lemnius, *Secret Miracles*, pp. 343–44.
37 Leonard Lessius, *Hygiasticon, or The Right Course of Preserving Health* (Cam-

bridge, 1634), p. 98.
38 I am thinking here of Mikhail Bakhtin, *Rabelais and His World*, tr. Helene Iswolsky (M.I.T. Press, 1968), and Caroline Walker Bynum, *Holy Feast and Holy Fast: The Religious Significance of Food to Medieval Women* (University of California Press, 1987).
39 Terry Sherwood, *Herbert's Prayerful Art* (University of Toronto Press, 1989), p. 76. Sherwood explains well the power of Herbert's sensory experience of God, but pays little attention to the "physiological reality" he invokes here.
40 Sidney Gottlieb, "Herbert's Case of 'Conscience': Public or Private Poem?" *Studies in English Literature* 25 (1985): 109–26.
41 See David Cressy, *Bonfires and Bells: National Memory and the Protestant Calendar in Elizabethan and Stuart England* (University of California Press, 1989), p. 35. The poem has been largely ignored until recently, when it has received detailed theological treatment in Christopher Hodgkins, *Authority, Church, and Society in George Herbert: Return to the Middle Way* (University of Missouri Press, 1993), pp. 64–86, and Stanley Stewart, "Investigating Herbert Criticism," *Renascence* 45 (1993): 131–58.
42 *Latin Poetry of George Herbert*, pp. 97–99.
43 C. Anne Wilson, *Food and Drink in Britain* (Penguin, 1984; Constable, 1992); W. Nelson, ed., *A Fifteenth Century School Book* (Oxford University Press, 1956), p. 8.
44 Keith Thomas, *Religion and the Decline of Magic* (Scribner's, 1971), p. 6, notes that "The well-to-do" in Renaissance England "ate too much meat and were frequently constipated." Their chronic constipation was also precipitated by their preference for refined white bread, leaving the roughage-rich brown bread to the poor.
45 Timothy Bright, *A Treatise of Melancholy* (London, 1586), p. 154.
46 Don Cameron Allen, *Image and Meaning: Metaphoric Traditions in Renaissance Poetry* (Johns Hopkins University Press, 1960), Chapter 4, "George Herbert: 'The Rose,'" pp. 102–14, elucidates with great erudition the sensual and Christian meanings of the rose available to Herbert. The remarkable thing, however, is how little Herbert does with the Christian meanings in this poem (meanings that are important to "Church-rents and schisms"), preferring instead to focus on the link between sensual pleasure and medicinal purgative. On the larger significance of flowers in Western culture, see Jack Goody, *The Culture of Flowers* (Cambridge University Press, 1993).
47 Levinus Lemnius, *An Herbal for the Bible*, tr. Thomas Newton (London, 1587), p. 220.
48 In an interesting psychoanalytic reading of the poem, Robert Rogers hears in this line "a pain-giving sphincteral contraction caused by the purgative" (*Metaphor: A Psychoanalytic View* [University of California Press, 1978], p. 127).
49 At the conclusion of Shakespeare's *1 Henry IV*, Falstaff offers a similar moralization of physical purgation: "If I do grow great, I'll grow less, for I'll purge and leave sack, and live cleanly as a nobleman should do" (5.4.163–65, in *The Riverside Shakespeare*, ed. G. Blakemore Evans *et al.* [Houghton Mifflin, 1974]).
50 *The Diary of Ralph Josselin 1616–1683* (The British Academy, 1976), p. 112. By employing "the use of pleasure" I am deliberately invoking Michel Foucault's

The History of Sexuality, vol. II, *The Use of Pleasure*, and vol. III, *The Care of the Self*, parts of a provocative but incomplete inquiry into the classical origins of the process of self-cultivation – a process that I am arguing Herbert's entire corpus participates in.
51 Stephen Greenblatt, "Filthy Rites," in *Learning to Curse: Essays in Early Modern Culture* (Routledge, 1990), p. 72. See Erik Erikson, *Young Man Luther* (Norton, 1962), pp. 61–62, on Luther's adherence to the "homeopathic" notion "That the devil can be completely undone if you manage to fart into his nostrils." Erikson suggests that for Luther "the devil and his home, and feces and the recesses of their origin, are all associated in a common underground of magic danger." The devil has very little presence in Herbert's spiritual imagination (in contrast to Donne or Milton), but in "Sinne (II)," Herbert suggests that "devils are our sinnes in perspective" (line 10). Dante's use of digestive punishments in his *Inferno* are explored by Robert Durling, "Deceit and Digestion in the Belly of Hell," in *Allegory and Representation: Selected Papers from the English Institute, 1979–80*, ed. Stephen Greenblatt (Johns Hopkins University Press, 1981), pp. 61–93.
52 Elias, *History of Manners*, pp. 82–83, 130–35, traces the changes in the Renaissance attitude to farting, from prescribing it as a necessary purgative of malignant fumes to proscribing it as conduct offensive to society. One can already see signs of its stigmatization in the Middle Ages, though; in *European Literature and the Latin Middle Ages*, tr. Willard R. Trask (Princeton University Press, 1953), Ernst R. Curtius includes in his Excursus on "Jest and Earnest in Medieval Literature" the story of a woman who on a Friday expresses doubts that the body of St. Gangolf works the miracles it is reputed to accomplish; "During all the rest of her life the woman could not speak a word on a Friday but that it was followed by a detonation," that is, a fart (p. 435).
53 "Ritual Man: On the Outside of Herbert's Poetry," *Psychiatry* 48 (1985): 69–70.
54 *Antony and Cleopatra* 2.2.236–37; quoted from *The Riverside Shakespeare*.
55 Richard Strier, "Changing the Object: Herbert and Excess," *George Herbert Journal* 2 (1978): 24.
56 I discuss this remarkable poem in far more detail in *Prayer and Power*, Chapter 5, "Standing on Ceremony: The Comedy of Manners in 'Love (III),'" and Chapter 6, "'That Ancient Heat': Sexuality and Spirituality in *The Temple*."
57 William Butler Yeats, "A General Introduction For My Work," *Essays and Introductions* (Macmillan, 1961), p. 509.

5 TEMPERANCE AND TEMPTATION: THE ALIMENAL VISION IN *PARADISE LOST*

1 Percy Bysshe Shelley, *Queen Mab* (J. P. Mendum, 1853), p.107.
2 *The Complete Essays of Montaigne*, ed. Donald M. Frame (Stanford Universty Press, 1967), p. 844.
3 Claude Levi-Strauss, *The Origin of Table Manners*, tr. John and Doreen Weightman (Harper and Row, 1978), pp. 503–4, 508. Tracking the historical development of commensal discipline, Norbert Elias has taught us much about

the ways that table manners reflect the larger civilizing processes of western Europe; see *The Civilizing Process*, vol. I, *The History of Manners*, tr. Edmund Jephcott (Urizen, 1978). "Nothing in table manners is self-evident or the product, as it were, of a 'natural' feeling of delicacy," Elias reminds us (p. 107). Among the most profound lessons to emerge from Elias's work is an understanding of just how thoroughly constructed the threshold of physical disgust is for any given culture, and how thoroughly enmeshed it is in the language of social hierarchy.
4 *The Riverside Milton*, ed. Roy Flanagan (Houghton Mifflin, 1998), pp. 870–71. All citations of Milton are to this edition, unless otherwise specified.
5 W. B. C. Watkins, *An Anatomy of Milton's Verse* (Louisiana State University Press, 1955), p. 117.
6 As Regina Schwartz argues, "The poem centers on the distinction between forbidden and permitted food. An ur-dietary law governs Paradise" (*Remembering and Repeating: Biblical Creation in Paradise Lost* [Cambridge University Press, 1988], p. 15).
7 Flanagan, ed., *Riverside Milton*, p. 1194. I am assuming that *On Christian Doctrine* is by Milton, but acknowledge the heated controversy surrounding this issue.
8 William Kerrigan, *The Sacred Complex: On the Psychogenesis of Paradise Lost* (Harvard University Press, 1983), p. 31.
9 Watkins, *Anatomy*, pp. 16–17. On the importance of food and digestion in the poem, see also Kerrigan, *Sacred Complex*, pp. 193–245; Michael Lieb, *The Dialectics of Creation: Patterns of Birth and Regeneration in Paradise Lost* (University of Massachusetts Press, 1970), pp. 16–34, and "Further Thoughts on Satan's Journey through Chaos," *Milton Quarterly* 12 (1978): 126–33; and Stephen M. Fallon, *Milton Among the Philosophers: Poetry and Materialism in Seventeenth-Century England* (Cornell University Press, 1991), pp. 102–6, 209–10.
10 Quoted in Caroline Walker Bynum, *Holy Feast and Holy Fast: The Religious Significance of Food to Medieval Women* (University of California Press, 1982), p. 36. In his Commonplace Book, Milton records Tertullian's statement that gluttony "deserves to be punished by the penalty of hunger ... because our first parents yielded to it" (*The Works of John Milton*, ed. Frank Allen Patterson *et al.*, 18 vols. [Columbia University Press, 1931–38], XVIII: 132). Hereafter cited as Columbia Milton.
11 *Homilie Against Gluttony and Drunkennesse*, in *Certaine Sermons or Homilies Appointed to be Read in Churches in the Time of Queen Elizabeth (1547–1571): A Facsimile Reproduction of the Edition of 1623*, ed. Mary Ellen Rickey and Thomas B. Stroup, 2 vols. in 1 (Scholars' Facsimiles & Reprints, 1968), II. 96.
12 Steven N. Zwicker, *Lines of Authority: Politics and English Literary Culture 1649–1689* (Cornell University Press, 1992), shows how Milton in the Eden books of *Paradise Lost* struggles to "reclaim" from the Restoration court "the aesthetics and the politics of chaste union" (p. 120).
13 As William Kerrigan and Gordon Braden argue, Satan is the enemy of pleasure in Milton's Paradise (*The Idea of the Renaissance* [Johns Hopkins University Press, 1989]).

Notes to pages 136–143

14 On the Eucharist and its connections to the practices of eating and food preparation, see Bynum, *Holy Feast and Holy Fast*. In the 1640s, Puritans instituted days of national fasting, in which Milton must have participated.
15 Columbia Milton, XVI: 197, 199.
16 It is important to note that line 636 is inserted in the edition of 1674, giving the angels a flowery sensuousness appropriate to the feast. Lines 5.637–39, moreover, are revised in the edition of 1674, when Milton changes "refection" to "communion" and adds the lines on "secure / Of surfeit where full measure only bounds / Excess." It is telling that Milton keeps revising the lines about physiology, and eating, to extend their pleasurable connotations before the Fall, and to distend their agonies afterwards.
17 See Claude Levi-Strauss, *The Raw and the Cooked*, tr. John and Doreen Weightman (Harper and Row, 1969).
18 *Paradise Lost*, 7.119–20, 126–30. On this topos see Michel Jeanneret, *A Feast of Words: Banquets and Table Talk in the Renaissance*, tr. Jeremy Whiteley and Emma Hughes (University of Chicago Press, 1991), pp. 113–39. The comparison between intellectual assimilation and digestion derives ultimately from Quintilian, *Institutio oratoria*, 10.1.19; it is manifested in Milton's frequent pun on "sapience," from *sapere*, meaning both to have flavor and to have knowledge.
19 Juan Huarte, *The Examination of Men's Wits (1594)*, ed. Carmen Rogers (Scholars' Facsimiles & Reprints, 1959), p. 11.
20 Milton's materialism has been explored recently, and with great cogency, by Fallon, *Milton Among the Philosophers*; Harinder Singh Marjara, *Contemplation of Created Things: Science in Paradise Lost* (University of Toronto Press, 1992); and John Rogers, *The Matter of Revolution: Science, Poetry, and Politics in the Age of Milton* (Cornell University Press, 1996). See also Kerrigan, *The Sacred Complex*.
21 See Robert H. West, *Milton and the Angels* (University of Georgia Press, 1955).
22 Kerrigan, *Sacred Complex*, pp. 222–23.
23 Jonathan Richardson, *Explanatory Notes and Remarks on Milton's Paradise Lost* (London, 1734), p. 227.
24 Kerrigan, *Sacred Complex*, p. 210
25 *The Complete Prose Works of John Milton*, ed. Don M. Wolfe *et al.*, 8 vols. (Yale University Press, 1953–82),VI: 554, 560. Hereafter cited as *Complete Prose Works*.
26 *Basic Writings of Saint Thomas Aquinas*, ed. Anton C. Pegis, 2 vols. (Random House, 1945), I: 927; *Summa Theologica* 97.3.
27 Thomas Venner, *Via Recta ad Vitam Longam. Or, A Treatise wherein the right way and best manner of living for attaining a long and healthfull life, is clearly demonstrated* (London, 1650), p. 314.
28 On "Balmy sweat" as an oxymoron that "brings language close to a limit of expression," see Geoffrey Hartman, "Adam on the Grass with Balsamum," *English Literary History* 36 (1969): 168–92. Hartman develops the connection between "balmy" and "balsamum," but overreads the negative connotations of "reeking."
29 Juan Huarte, *Examination of Men's Wits*, p. 243.

30 Flanagan's note to the passage is apt: "The Spirit seems to excrete the regions of Hell" (p. 545, n. 82).
31 Alan Debus, *The English Paracelsians* (Oldbourne, 1965), pp. 30–31.
32 Rogers, *The Matter of Revolution*, p. 133.
33 *Ibid.*, p. 111.
34 Levinus Lemnius, *The Touchstone of Complexions*, tr. T. Newton (London, 1581), pp. 20–22. On the Thomistic theological background of such dreams, see William B. Hunter, "Eve's Demonic Dream," in *The Descent of Urania: Studies in Milton, 1946–1988* (Bucknell University Press, 1989), pp. 46–55.
35 Donald M. Friedman, "Divisions on a Ground: 'Sex' in *Paradise Lost*," in *Of Poetry and Politics: New Essays on Milton and His World*, ed. Paul G. Stanwood (Medieval & Renaissance Texts & Studies, 1995) p. 204, n.4.
36 This ideal is described in detail by Jeanneret, *A Feast of Words*.
37 I discuss the sexual politics of this episode more fully in "Gender and Conduct in *Paradise Lost*," in *Sexuality and Gender in Early Modern Europe*, ed. James Turner (Cambridge University Press, 1993), pp. 310–38.
38 The quotation is from Diane Kelsey McColley, *A Gust for Paradise: Milton's Eden and the Visual Arts* (University of Illinois Press, 1993), p. 86, who explains well the positive medicinal features of paradisal plants, but does not explore how strange it is to include cures before they are needed.
39 Tobias Whitaker, *The Tree of Humane Life or the Bloud of the Grape* (London, 1638); quoted in Andrew Wear, "Health and the Environment in Early Modern England," in *Medicine in Society: Historical Essays*, ed. Andrew Wear (Cambridge University Press, 1992), p. 140.
40 Debora Shuger, "'Gums of Glutinous Heat' and the Stream of Consciousness: The Theology of Milton's *Maske*," in *Representations* 60 (Fall 1997): 1–48. Shuger offers an erudite reading of the phrase in the context of discussion about volition and wet dreams.
41 Flanagan, ed., *Riverside Milton*, p. 940.
42 *Homilie Against Gluttony and Drunkennesse*, p. 99.
43 Lemnius, *Touchstone of Complexions*, p. 84v.
44 Venner, *Via Recta ad Vitam Longam*, p. 150.
45 Flanagan, ed., *Riverside Milton*, pp. 983, 985.
46 Kerrigan, *Sacred Complex*, p. 202.
47 Flanagan, ed., *Riverside Milton*, p. 1055.
48 Venner, *Via Recta ad Vitam Longam*, p. 322. See also the numerous medical writings cited by Kerrigan, *Sacred Complex*, pp. 202–3.
49 Flanagan, ed., *Riverside Milton*, p. 3.
50 See Zera Fink, "Milton and the Theory of Climatic Influence," *Modern Language Quarterly* 2 (1941): 73–74.
51 Kerrigan, *Sacred Complex*, p. 249.
52 Michael Lieb, *Poetics of the Holy: A Reading of Paradise Lost* (University of North Carolina Press, 1981), p. 114.
53 Perhaps significantly, Milton in *An Apology for Smectymnuus* denies the accusation that he had been "vomited [that is, expelled] out of Cambridge," and argues that Cambridge "vomits now out of sicknesse, but ere it be well with her, she must vomit by strong physick" (Columbia Milton, III: 297–98). In *The*

Matter of Revolution, p. 149, Rogers argues that "the figuration of the expulsion points, I believe, to a physiological process other than emesis," and cites Fallon's suggestion (in *Milton Among the Philosophers*, p. 241) that "The physiological paradigm shaping Milton's image for this organismic expulsion of polluted matter could very well be the recently formulated principle of tissue irritability." It seems to me far more likely that Milton is here simply referring to the standard medical treatment of purging noxious matter that he refers to in the preface to *Samson Agonistes*, the passage quoted above from the *Apology*, and elsewhere.

54 McColley, *A Gust for Paradise*, pp. 152–53. In *Il Penseroso*, Milton similarly refers to "eating Cares" (line 135).
55 Schwartz, *Remembering and Repeating*, p. 16.
56 Lieb, *Dialectics of Creation*, pp. 28–30, and "Further Thoughts on Satan's Journey Through Chaos."
57 Flanagan, ed., *Riverside Milton*, p. 1010.
58 *Ibid.*, p. 1055.
59 In a letter to Hermann Mylius written in the early 1650s, Milton describes "what is now almost a perpetual enemy of mine, bad health" (Columbia Milton, XII: 53). Milton may have finished the epic as early as 1663.
60 David Masson, *The Life of John Milton*, 7 vols. (London, 1859–94), VI: 489–90.
61 Leonard Lessius, *Hygiasticon or the Right Course of Preserving Health* (London, 1634), pp. 117–18. Herbert's translation of Cornaro's *Treatise of Temperance and Sobrietie*, discussed at length in the previous chapter, first appeared in this volume. See also Stephen Bradwell, *A Watch-Man for the Pest* (London, 1625), p. 2, on how "The Plague, is a popular Disease: sent immediately from God; wrought by the Constellations of the Heavens, the Corruption of the Aire, and *the Disorder of Mans Diet*" (my italics).
62 Kerrigan, *Sacred Complex*, p. 253.
63 *Ibid.*
64 Levinus Lemnius, *The Secret Miracles of Nature* (London, 1658), p. 251. I have not found any references to euphrasy used for blindness.
65 Perhaps relevantly for the blind Milton, 2 Peter 1.9 continues: "But was hee that lacketh these things, is blind, and cannot see farre off, and hath forgotten that hee was purged from his old sinnes."
66 *Paradise Regained*, 2.408–9. On the centrality of temperance to *Paradise Regained*, see Arnold Stein, *Heroic Knowledge: An Interpretation of Paradise Regained and Samson Agonistes* (University of Minnesota Press, 1957).
67 See Sherman Hawkins, "Samson's Catharsis," *Milton Studies* 2 (1970): 211–30.
68 *Complete Prose Works* I: 295, 299.
69 *Summa Theologica*, 97.2, in *Basic Writings*, ed. Pegis, I: 925.
70 Edward Reynolds, *A Treatise of the Passions and Faculties of the Soule of Man* (London, 1640), pp. 62–63.
71 I discuss Adam's argument with Raphael more fully in "Gender and Conduct in *Paradise Lost*" in *Sexuality and Gender in Early Modern Europe*, pp. 310–38.
72 On the potential political radicalism of the Lady's separation of bodies and minds, see John Thelwall, a late eighteenth-century radical, whose *Poems written in close confinement in the Tower and Newgate, under a charge of High*

Treason, has the motto, "Fool, do not boast: Thou can'st not touch the freedom of my mind" (*The Politics of English Jacobinism: Writings of John Thelwall*, ed. Gregory Claeys [Pennsylvania State University Press, 1995]).
73 See Edwin Greenlaw, "A Better Teacher than Aquinas," *Studies in Philology* 14 (1917): 196–217, which argues that temperance, learned from Spenser, is the true theme of *Paradise Lost*.
74 Flanagan, ed., *Riverside Milton*, pp. 1005, 1006. See Titus 1.15
75 *Apology for Smectymnuus*, (Columbia Milton, III: 306). See 1 Cor. 6.13.
76 Flanagan, ed., *Riverside Milton*, p. 3. Bishop Newton records in his 1749 edition of *Paradise Lost* that Milton "was very temperate in his eating and drinking, but what he had he always loved to have of the best" (Columbia Milton, XVIII: 391–92). Kerrigan, *Sacred Complex*, p. 205, points out that in Milton's third marriage contract, "should Elizabeth Minshull, cousin to a trusted physician, prepare food to his instructions, she would inherit his estate" (see J. Milton French, ed., *Life Records of John Milton*, 5 vols. [Rutgers University Press, 1949–58], v. 220).

AFTERWORD

1 This is the argument in part of Steven Shapin, *The Scientific Revolution* (University of Chicago Press, 1996).
2 Rob Iliffe, "Isaac Newton: Lucatello Professor Mathematics," in *Science Incarnate*, ed. Christopher Lawrence and Steven Shapin (University of Chicago Press, 1998), p. 123.
3 George Cheyne, *An Essay of Health and Long Life* (London, 1724), p. 230.
4 Luigi Cornaro, *How to Live to be 100* (Rodale Publications, 1938).
5 See the fascinating account of alternative medicine in Robert and Michele Root-Bernstein, *Honey, Mud, Maggots, and Other Medical Marvels: The Science Behind Folk Remedies and Old Wives' Tales* (Houghton-Mifflin, 1997). The authors focus on ancient treatments that seem ludicrous to us, but that are "making a comeback at the cutting edge of modern clinical practice" (p. 3).
6 See Mark Seltzer, *Bodies and Machines* (Routledge, 1992).
7 See, for example, the essays collected in *The Buddha's Art of Healing: Tibetan Paintings Rediscovered*, ed. John F. Avedon et al. (Rizzoli, 1998).
8 On how this condemnation of the patient has continued in contemporary attitudes to cancer, tuberculosis, and AIDS, see Susan Sontag, *Illness as Metaphor; And AIDS and its Metaphors*, 2nd edition (Doubleday, 1990).
9 Antonio Damasio, *Descartes' Error: Emotion, Reason, and the Human Brain* (Putnam's, 1994), pp. 257, 256.
10 See Peter Kramer, *Listening to Prozac* (Viking, 1993), and David Healy, *The Antidepressant Era* (Harvard University Press, 1998).
11 See Sherwin Nuland, *How We Die: Reflections on Life's Final Chapter* (Knopf, 1994), and *The Wisdom of the Body* (Knopf, 1997).
12 *Our Bodies, Our Selves: A Course By and For Women* (Boston Women's Health Course Collective, 1971).
13 See Stuart J. Youngner, "Some Must Die," in *Organ Transplantation: Meanings and Realities*, ed. Stuart J. Youngner et al. (University of Wisconsin Press, 1996), pp. 51–52.

Index

Abernathy, John, 187 n. 50
Adelman, Janet, 178 n. 72
Allen, Don Cameron, 191 n. 46
Allestree, Richard, 110, 190 n. 27
Ames, William, 42, 180 n. 5
Anatomy, 1, 37–38
Anderson, Ruth L., 177 n. 54
Aquinas, Thomas, 141, 164, 194 n. 26, 196 n. 69
Aristotle, 3, 87, 180 n. 6, 180 n. 14, 182–83 n. 46, 186 n. 35
Aubrey, John, 152, 168
Augustine, 16, 18, 63, 176 n. 47, 182 n. 44
Avedon, John F. 197 n. 7

Babb, Lawrence 177 n. 54, 184 n. 4
Bacon, Francis, 22, 25, 177 n. 59, 178 n. 67
Baillie, Murray, 188 n. 3
Baker, Herschel, 177 n. 54, 186 n. 28
Bakhtin, Mikhail, 13–15, 60, 119, 175 n. 32, 175 n. 33, 181 n. 25, 191 n. 38
Bamborough, J. B., 176 n. 41, 177 n. 54
Barkan, Leonard, 178 n. 71
Barker, Francis, 184 n. 3
Baxter, Richard, 32–33, 179 n. 81, 179 n. 82
Beer, Gillian, 189 n. 18
Beier, Lucinda, 175 n. 35, 179 n. 84
Belly, The Fable of the, 28–30
Belsey, Catherine, 183 n. 3
Berger, Harry, 181 n. 20
Bible, books of,
 Genesis, 135, 158
 Leviticus, 133
 Leviticus 28.25, 154
 Jeremiah 9.15, 124
 Matthew 6.28, 43, 94
 Matthew 16.18, 86
 John 6.56, 94
 Romans 7.15, 89
 1 Corinthians 3.16, 130

2 Peter 1.5–7, 162
2 Peter 1.9, 196 n. 65
Bishop, Elizabeth, 190 n. 32
Blindness, and indigestion, 152–53
Bloom, Harold, 184 n. 3
Body–soul relationship, 6–11, 40–41, 56–57, 60, 77–79, 98–102
Boehrer, Bruce Thomas, 175 n. 33
Book of Common Prayer, 120
Booth, Stephen, 76–77, 83, 85, 184 n. 6, 184 n. 7, 185 n. 16, 185 n. 17, 185 n. 18, 185 n. 22
Bouwsma, William, 18–19, 176 n. 48, 180 n. 4, 185 n. 20, 185 n. 23
Braden, Gordon, 193 n. 13
Bradwell, Stephen, 196 n. 61
Breitenberg, Mark, 179 n. 90
Bright, Timothy, 124–25, 191 n. 45
Brink, Jean R., 182 n. 34
Brown, Peter, 4, 173 n. 7, 185 n. 20
Browning, Robert, 95
Bryskett, Lodowick, 6–7, 40, 46, 60, 72, 173 n. 8, 180 n. 2, 180 n. 12, 182 n. 35, 183 n. 62
Burton, Robert, 21–23, 25, 37, 52, 61, 88–89, 100, 177 n. 57, 177 n. 59, 178 n. 66, 179 n. 93, 181 n. 26, 182 n. 37, 187 n. 38, 187 n. 39, 188 n. 5
Bynum, Caroline Walker, 38, 119, 178 n. 68, 180 n. 96, 184 n. 10, 191 n. 38, 193 n. 10, 194 n. 14

Calvin, John, 176 n. 44
Calvinism, 41, 46
Campbell, Lily B., 78, 85, 177 n. 54, 184 n. 11, 185 n. 26
Carruthers, Mary, 182 n. 43
Carscallen, James, 181 n. 20
Castiglione, Baldassare, 42–43, 180 n. 8
Cavendish, Margaret, 37

Index

Certaine Sermons or Homilies, 24, 100, 135–36, 150, 178 n. 65, 188 n. 7, 189 n. 23, 189 n. 25, 193 n. 11, 195 n. 42
Cheyne, George, 169, 197 n. 3
China, medical traditions of, 170
Chrimes, S. B., 178 n. 73
Christianity, 19–20
Cicero, 16, 178 n. 68
Climate, and temperament, 177 n. 56
Cogan, Thomas, 94, 187 n. 51
Collinson, Patrick, 189 n. 14
Constancy, 74–75, 85–86, 89–102, 111–12
Cornaro, Alvise (Luigi), 115–16, 169, 190 n. 32, 196 n. 61, 197 n. 4
Cressy, David, 191 n. 41
Cuddy, Neil, 188 n. 3
Culpepper, Nicholas
   Anatomy of the Body of Man, 26–27, 178 n. 69
   Health for the Rich and Poor, 77, 184 n. 10
Curtius, Ernst R., 192 n. 52

Damasio, Antonio, 10, 171, 174 n. 14, 174 n. 23, 182 n. 33, 197 n. 9
Danvers, Sir John, 123
Davies, Sir John, 86, 186 n. 28
Debus, Alan, 144, 195 n. 31
Decorum, 52, 141, 181 n. 25
De Grazia, Margreta, 183 n. 3, 187 n. 53
Descartes, Rene, 8, 10–11, 174 n. 22, 182 n. 33
Desire, 41–42; see also Emotion
   as disease, 78–83
   of food vs. love, 81–82
Diet, 19–33, 115–19, 133–34, 145–51, 191 n. 44, 197 n. 76
Digby, Kenelm, 55–57
Digestion
   technology of, 25–28
   as moral discrimination, 132–34, 139–46
Discipline, linked to freedom, 69–70, 162–68
Disease
   and intemperance, 158–60
   as infection, 93
   as obstruction, 61, 118–19, 156, 175 n. 36, 191 n. 44
   venereal, 94
Dollimore, Jonathan, 183–84, n. 3
Donne, John, 45, 180 n. 10
Douglas, Mary, 19, 177 n. 50, 189 n. 21
Downame, John, 24, 111
Draper, John W., 177 n. 54
DuBartas, Guillaume, 28, 178 n. 70
Duncan-Jones, Katherine, 185 n. 13

Dürer, Albrecht, 1, 24, 115, 152, 173 n. 1
Durling, Robert, 178 n. 68, 192 n. 51

Elias, Norbert, 15, 176 n. 40, 189 n. 21, 192 n. 52, 192–93 n. 3
Elizabeth I, 37
Ellmann, Maud, 20, 177 n. 52
Elyot, Thomas
   The Castel of Helthe, 7, 14, 21, 26, 31, 66, 91, 152, 173 n. 9, 175 n. 36, 177 n. 56, 178 n. 68, 178 n. 69, 179 n. 79, 187 n. 43
   The Governor, 74–75, 182–83 n. 46, 183 n. 2
Emotion, 16–17, 49–50, 164–65, 176 n. 47
   vs. reason, 47–49, 78–80, 111–13, 164–67
   as spur to virtue, 64–66
Empson, William, 84–85, 91, 185 n. 21, 187 n. 45
Erickson, Robert A., 173 n. 12
Erikson, Erik, 192 n. 51
Eucharist, 97–101, 120–21, 129–30, 136–37, 140, 141, 194 n. 14
Excrement (see Waste), 32–33, 127, 132–33, 140–43, 154, 156, 194 n. 28, 196 n. 53

Fallon, Stephen, 193 n. 9, 194 n. 20, 196 n. 53
Fasting, 46–47, 77–79, 121–24, 136, 194 n. 14
Featley, Daniel, 12
Fernel, Jean, 116–17, 190 n. 33
Ferry, Anne, 20, 177 n. 53, 188 n. 4
Fineman, Joel, 183 n. 3, 184 n. 12
Finucci, Valeria, 176 n. 45
Fink, Zera, 195 n. 50
Fish, Stanley, 108, 189 n. 22
Flanagan, Roy, 193 n. 7, 195 n. 30, 195 n. 41, 195 n. 45, 195 n. 47, 195 n. 49, 196 n. 57, 196 n. 57, 196 n. 58, 197 n. 74, 197 n. 76
Fletcher, Anthony, 10, 174 n. 21, 189 n. 14
Fletcher, Phineas, 12, 29, 175 n. 29, 178 n. 71, 183 n. 55
Fludd, Robert, 3–5
Ford, Richard, 90, 187 n. 41
Foucault, Michel, 12–13, 62, 70, 95, 175 n. 31, 182 n. 42, 183 n. 57, 185 n. 20, 187 n. 54, 190 n. 35, 191–92 n. 50
French, J. Milton, 197 n. 76
Friedman, Donald M., 147, 195 n. 35
Freud, Sigmund, 15–18, 62, 67, 89, 183 n. 53
Fumerton, Patricia, 188 n. 3

Galen, 2–4, 9, 87, 119, 150, 149–50, 169–70, 174 n. 16, 186 n. 35
Gender, 35–37, 148, 178 n. 86, 182 n. 30

Index

and humoral temperature, 51, 57, 87–88, 186 n. 34
Gerson, Jean, 190 n. 34
Gibson, Anthony, 36, 179 n. 89
Goody, Jack, 191 n. 46
Gottlieb, Sidney, 120, 190 n. 29, 191 n. 40
Greenblatt, Stephen, 17–18, 52–71, 176 n. 45, 178 n. 68, 181 n. 27, 183 n. 53, 192 n. 52
Greenlaw, Edwin, 182 n. 29, 197 n. 73

Hamilton, A. C., 57, 180 n. 3, 181 n. 20, 182 n. 31, 182–83 n. 46
Harington, Sir John, 33, 179 n. 84
Harrison, William, 177 n. 56
Hartman, Geoffrey, 194 n. 28
Harvey, Gabriel, 69, 183 n. 56
Harvey, William, 169
Hawkins, Sherman, 196 n. 67
Heal, Felicity, 189 n. 17
Healy, David, 197 n. 10
Healy, Thomas, 67–69, 183 n. 51, 183 n. 55
Hegel, G. W. F., 10
Herbert, Edward, 106, 110, 189 n. 16, 190 n. 26, 190 n. 33
Herbert, George, 25, 34, 45, 92, 96–130, 132, 133
  The Country Parson, 105, 107, 116–19, 122–23, 127, 129, 130
  Lucus: 'In Thomam Didymum,' 101; 'In Gulosum,' 121–22
  The Temple: 'Affliction (I),' 102, 124; 'Affliction (V),' 105, 127; 'The Agonie,' 128–29; 'The Altar,' 112; 'The Bag,' 102; 'The Banquet,' 128–29; 'The Church-porch,' 105, 107–12, 114–15, 117, 120, 123, 124; 'Church-musick,' 102; 'The Collar,' 109–10, 117, 130; 'Confession,' 102–4, 119; 'Conscience,' 120–21; 'Constancie,' 111–12; 'The Crosse, 102; 'L'Envoy,' 127, 156; 'Faith,' 129; 'The Familie,' 113; 'The Flower,' 111; 'Frailtie,' 112; 'Giddinesse,' 103–4, 109–110; 'The Glimpse,' 128; 'H. Communion,' 97–102, 104–5, 127; 'Home,' 120; 'Humilitie,' 112; 'Invitation,' 128; 'Lent,' 121–23, 184 n. 9; 'Longing,' 127–28; 'Love (III),' 129; 'Love Unknown,' 112; 'Man,' 106–7; 'Mans Medley,' 119; 'Miserie,' 109, 111; 'Nature,' 125; 'The Odour,' 128; 'An Offering,' 103; 'The Pearl,' 96; 'Prayer (I),' 127; 'Providence,' 106–7, 127; 'Praise (I),' 99; 'The Priesthood,' 120–21; 'Repentance,' 124; 'The Rose,' 126–27; 'Sighs and Grones,' 124; 'The Size,' 119; 'Superliminare,' 108; 'The Temper (I),' 110, 113–14, 117; 'The Temper (II),' 110, 114; 'The 23d Psalme,' 129; 'Ungratefulnesse,' 119;
  Outlandish Proverbs, 106, 112
  Poems from the Williams Manuscript: 'H. Communion,' 97; 'The Knell,' 125
  Treatise of Temperance and Sobrietie, 96, 115, 125, 169, 196 n. 61
Herrick, Robert, 189 n. 16
Hieatt, A. Kent, 181 n. 21
Hillman, David, 8, 174 n. 13, 188 n. 8
Hippocrates, 2
Hobbes, Thomas, 108–9, 189 n. 24
Hodgkins, Christopher, 191 n. 41
Hoeniger, F. David, 185 n. 14
Hough, Graham, 180 n. 11
Huarte, Juan, 9, 22, 31, 63, 80–81, 87–88, 139, 142–43, 174 n. 17, 177 n. 58, 179 n. 78, 182 n. 43, 185 n. 15, 186 n. 33, 186 n. 36, 185 n. 37, 194 n. 19, 194 n. 29
Hubler, Edward, 84, 90–91, 93, 185 n. 21, 187 n. 42, 187 n. 47
Hughes, John, 52, 181 n. 24
Humors, 2–39, 49, 56, 76–77, 109–11, 115–17
Hunter, William B., 195 n. 34
Huntley, Frank L., 190 n. 31
Hutchinson, F. E., 188 n. 2, 190 n. 34

Iliffe, Rob, 197 n. 2
India, medical traditions of, 170
Indigestion (see Stomach) 121–27, 138–39, 150–53, 156–57
Inwardness, 1–2, 20–23, 132–35, 162–68, 183–84 n. 3

James I, 86, 186 n. 29
Jeanneret, Michel, 14, 176 n. 38, 194 n. 18, 198 n. 36
Jesus, suffering body of, 1, 101, 128–29
Jonson, Ben, 2, 110, 180 n. 7, 181 n. 16
  Masques: *Hymenaei*, 49, *Pleasure Reconciled to Virtue*, 25
  Poems: 'Epo–de,' 42; 'To Penshurst,' 148
  Notes on Spenser, 54, 71, 182 n. 28
Josselin, Ralph, 33, 127, 179 n. 84, 191 n. 50

Kagan, Jerome, 175 n. 26
Kaufman, Peter Iver, 184 n. 3
Kerrigan, John, 95, 185 n. 13, 187 n. 52
Kerrigan, William, 127, 135, 140, 141, 152, 153, 161, 192 n. 53, 193 n. 8, 193 n. 9,

Index

193 n. 13, 194 n. 20, 195 n. 46, 195 n. 48, 195 n. 51, 197 n. 76
Kessler, Eckhard, 185 n. 23
Knights, L. C., 187 n. 45
Koerner, Joseph Leo, 1–2, 173 n. 1, 173 n. 2
Kramer, Peter, 197 n. 10
Kristeva, Julia, 19–20, 177 n. 50, 189 n. 21

Laqueur, Thomas, 35–36, 179 n. 87, 181 n. 22, 186 n. 31
Laurentius, M. Andreas, 72, 87–88, 183 n. 60, 186 n. 35
Leishman, J. B., 184 n. 7
Lemnius, Levinus
  An Herbal for the Bible, 191 n. 47
  The Secret Miracles of Nature, 13, 36–37, 60, 175 n. 34, 179 n. 88, 180 n. 13, 182 n. 36, 188 n. 10, 190 n. 36, 196 n. 64
  The Touchstone of Complexions, 23–24, 31, 47, 100, 102, 104–5, 118, 126, 147, 151, 161, 175 n. 35, 178 n. 62, 179 n. 76, 188 n. 6, 188 n. 13, 195 n. 34, 195 n. 43
Lessius, Leonard, 119, 161, 190–91 n. 37, 196 n. 61
Levi, Anthony, 18, 174 n. 15, 176 n. 46
Levin, Carol, 179–80 n. 94
Levi-Strauss, Claude, 19, 131, 177 n. 50, 192 n. 3, 194 n. 17
Lewis, C. S., 180 n. 11
Lieb, Michael, 154, 156, 193 n. 9, 195 n. 52, 196 n. 56
Lipsius, Justus, 18, 85
Lowe, Peter, 30–31, 179 n. 95
Lowell, Robert, 190 n. 32
Luther, Martin, 127, 192 n. 51
Lyons, Bridget Gellert, 177 n. 54, 184 n. 4

MacDonald, Michael, 23, 177 n. 61
Maclean, Norman, 40, 180 n. 1
McCabe, Richard, 67, 72, 183 n. 52, 183 n. 61
McCloskey, Mark, 188 n. 9
McColley, Diane, 155, 195 n. 38, 196 n. 54
McEachern, Claire, 179 n. 86
Maley, Willy, 182 n. 34
Manners, 149, 192–93 n. 3
Marjara, Harinder Singh, 194 n. 20
Masson, David, 160, 196 n. 60
Matson, Wallace I., 174 n. 14
Maus, Katharine, 2, 8, 16–17, 38, 85, 173 n. 3, 173 n. 11, 176 n. 42, 176 n. 43, 176 n. 47, 180 n. 98, 184 n. 3, 185 n. 24, 187 n. 40
Mazzio, Carla, 174 n. 13
Memory, and digestion, 63, 138–39, 161–62, 182 n. 43, 194 n. 18
Mildmay, Lady Grace, 13, 23
Miles, Geoffrey, 185 n. 23
Miller, Brett Candlish, 190 n. 32
Miller, David Lee, 52–65, 181 n. 27, 182 n. 40, 183 n. 47
Milton, John, 34–35, 59, 97, 121, 124, 130, 131–68
  Comus, 25, 122, 132, 134–35, 143, 149, 150, 160, 164, 166
  Elegies, 132, 166–67
  Paradise Lost, 19, 100, 131–68
  Paradise Regained, 19, 132, 134, 135, 147, 162, 164, 181 n. 23, 195 n. 66
  Samson Agonistes, 135, 143, 162–63, 164, 196 n. 53
  Poems: 'Il Penseroso,' 159–60, 196 n. 54
  Prose: *Apology for Smectymnuus*, 168, 195 n. 53, 197 n. 75; *Areopagitica*, 132–33, 134–35, 147, 158, 164, 167; *On Christian Doctrine*, 134, 136, 141; Commonplace Book, 193 n. 10; *The Doctrine and Discipline of Divorce*, 149; *Of Education*, 151; Prolusions, 132; *Second Defense of the English People*, 163
Monsarrat, Gilles, 196 n. 29
Montaigne, Michel de, 50, 131, 181 n. 18, 192 n. 2
Muir, Kenneth, 178 n. 71
Murphy, Paul R., 188 n. 9
Mylius, Hermann, 196 n. 59

Nagy, Doreen, 175 n. 35
Nelson, William, 191 n. 43
New Historicism, 11–12
Newton, Bishop, 197 n. 76
Newton, Isaac, 169
Nietzsche, Friedrich, 74, 183 n. 1
Nilus, Abbot, 135
Nuland, Dr. Sherwin, 171–72, 197 n. 11

Oestrich, Gerhard, 177 n. 49
Organ transplants, 172
Orgel, Stephen, 181 n. 16
Our Bodies, Our Selves, 172, 197 n. 12

Paracelsus, 3, 21, 106–7, 144–45, 177 n. 57, 189 n. 18
Paster, Gail Kern, 15, 174 n. 13, 175 n. 33, 176 n. 39, 176 n. 40, 178 n. 70, 179 n. 87, 181 n. 22, 186 n. 31, 190 n. 27
Patterson, Frank Allen, 193 n. 10
Paul, Saint, 20, 167–68
Peacham, Henry, 12, 91, 175 n. 28, 187 n. 44
Peck, Linda Levy, 177 n. 49

Index

Pequigney, Joseph, 187 n. 48
Petrarch, 82–83
Philaris, Leonard, 152
Plato, 8–9, 150, 174 n. 24
Pleasure, 66, 119–22, 126–29, 136–38, 147, 191 n. 46, 193 n. 12, 194 n. 16
Pollock, Linda, 175 n. 35, 177 n. 61
Porter, Roy, 173 n. 2, 179 n. 84
Post, Jonathan F. S., 190 n. 29
Powel, Gabriel, 86
Purcell, John, 11, 174 n. 26
Puritan, stereotype of, 120
  attitude to fasting, 121–22

Quintilian, 194 n. 18

Rabelais, Francois, 13–14, 176 n. 38
Ransom, John Crowe, 84, 185 n. 19, 187 n. 47
Rawcliffe, Carol, 61–62, 105, 178 n. 73, 182 n. 39, 189 n. 15
Reynolds, David, 180 n. 9
Reynolds, Edward, 9–10, 30, 85, 164–65, 174 n. 19, 178 n. 74, 186 n. 27, 196 n. 70
Richardson, Jonathan, 141
Riddell, James A., 182 n. 28, 182 n. 29, 182 n. 45, 182–83 n. 46, 183 n. 59
Roberts, Peter, 189 n. 14
Rogers, John, 144–45, 194 n. 20, 195 n. 32, 195 n. 33, 196 n. 53
Rogers, Robert, 191 n. 48
Rollins, Hyder E., 186 n. 28
Root-Bernstein, Robert and Michele, 197 n. 4
Rorty, Richard, 174 n. 14
Russell, Bishop, 29–30, 178 n. 73

Sacks, Peter, 112, 190 n. 29
Salmon, J. H., 18–19, 177 n. 49, 185 n. 25, 186 n. 29
Sarasohn, Lisa T., 180 n. 95
Sawday, Jonathan, 1, 37, 38, 71, 173 n. 2, 174 n. 22, 174 n. 25, 177 n. 60, 179 n. 92, 180 n. 95, 180 n. 97, 182 n. 30, 183 n. 58
Schleiner, Winfred, 184 n. 4
Schmitt, Charles, 185 n. 23
Schoenfeldt, Michael, 188 n. 11, 188 n. 12, 189 n. 16, 189 n. 23, 190 n. 30, 192 n. 56, 195 n. 37, 196 n. 71
Schwartz, Regina, 155–56, 176 n. 45, 196 n. 55
Scodel, Joshua, 180–81 n. 14
Seltzer, Mark, 197 n. 6
Seneca, 17, 186 n. 29
Shakespeare, 2, 33–34, 36, 45, 74–95, 96, 99, 112, 132 149
Sonnets
  15: 89
  16: 83, 89
  33: 93
  45: 76–77
  56: 81
  69: 91
  75: 81
  92: 91
  93: 91
  94: 74, 83–95, 112
  95: 91, 94
  110: 93
  111: 93
  116: 89
  118: 81–82
  129: 82–83, 90
  144: 79, 83
  146: 77–79, 122
  147: 78–80, 83, 88
  151: 79, 83
  153: 79
  154: 79
Venus and Adonis, 81, 188 n. 55
Antony and Cleopatra, 81, 128, 192 n. 54
Coriolanus, 28–30, 178 n. 72
Hamlet, 2, 73, 75
Henry IV, 1 and 2, 91, 187 n. 48, 191 n. 49
Henry V, 90–91
King John, 186 n. 32
Love's Labour's Lost, 184 n. 9, 184 n. 12
Macbeth, 79–80
Measure for Measure, 84–85
Merchant of Venice, 90
The Reign of King Edward the Third (?), 187 n. 51
The Tempest, 186 n. 34, 186 n. 37
Titus Andronicus, 188 n. 55
Troilus and Cressida, 79
Twelfth Night, 1, 3, 81
The Winter's Tale, 186 n. 35, 187 n. 49
Shapin, Steven, 197 n. 1
Shelley, Percy Bysshe, 131, 192 n. 1
Sherman, Stuart, 179 n. 80
Sherrington, Charles, 116, 190 n. 33, 190 n. 34
Sherwood, Terry, 119, 191 n. 39
Shuger, Debora, 62, 176 n. 48, 179 n. 86, 182 n. 41, 195 n. 40
Simic, Charles, 96, 188 n. 1
Siraisi, Nancy, 7, 173 n. 4, 173 n. 10, 190 n. 32

Index

Skinner, Quentin, 185 n. 23
Skura, Meredith, 176 n. 45
Sloane, Thomas O., 176, n. 41
Smell, 105–6, 189 n. 16
Sontag, Susan, 197 n. 8
Soul, see Body–soul relationship
Spenser, Edmund, 12, 17, 33, 35, 74–75, 77, 86, 87, 96, 99, 132, 134, 135, 136, 140, 150, 152, 156, 157, 164
  Amoretti, 80
  The Faerie Queene, Book 2, 40–73
  View of the Present State of Ireland, 60, 67–69, 182 n. 34
  'To the Right Worshipfull . . . Gabriel Harvey,' 69, 183 n. 56
Spirit, 82–83, 99–100, 116–17, 146–47
Stallybrass, Peter, 175 n. 33, 189 n. 20
Starkey, David, 188 n. 3
Stein, Arnold, 196 n. 66
Stewart, Stanley, 182 n. 28, 182 n. 29, 182 n. 45, 182–83 n. 46, 183 n. 59, 191 n. 41
Stoicism, 12–13, 16–19, 41–43, 45, 46, 85–87, 111–14, 164–67, 176 n. 47, 176 n. 48, 177 n. 49, 185 n. 23, 186 n. 29
Stomach, 21–35, 51–64, 97–102, 138–40
Strier, Richard, 112, 128, 176 n. 48, 189 n. 23, 190 n. 29, 192 n. 55
Sylvester, Joshua, 28, 178 n 70

Taylor, Charles, 11, 175 n. 27
Temkin, Oswei, 24, 173 n. 4, 178 n. 63
Temperance, 40, 110–23, 132–33, 157–62, 166–68
  and abstinence, 43, 180 n. 9
  and pleasure, 50
  as Aristotelian mean, 48
  in food versus sex, 46–47, 134–35
  vs. continence, 42–43, 180 n. 6
Tertullian, 193 n. 10
Thomas, Doubting, 101–2, 170–71
Thelwall, John, 196–97 n. 72
Thomas, Keith, 189 n. 14, 191 n. 44
Todd, Richard, 107, 189 n. 19
Transubstantiation, 97–101, 140–41
Turner, James G., 179 n. 86, 195 n. 37

Underhill, Evelyn, 190 n. 34

Van Helmont, Franciscus, 101, 188 n. 8
Vaughan, William, 23, 24, 28, 31, 61, 178 n. 64, 178 n. 70, 179 n. 77, 182 n. 32, 182 n. 38
Vendler, Helen, 76, 184 n. 5, 184 n. 8
Venner, Thomas, 14, 16, 32, 142, 151, 152, 175 n. 37, 179 n. 83, 194 n. 27, 195 n. 44, 195 n. 48
Vicary, Thomas, 26–28, 30, 31, 178 n. 69, 179 n. 79
Vieth, D. M., 183 n. 63
Vigarello, Georges, 189 n. 16
Vives, Juan Luis, 20–21, 177 n. 55

Walkington, Thomas, 3–4, 9, 76–77, 173 n. 6, 174 n. 18, 179 n. 91
Walton, Izaak, 115, 190 n. 31
Waste, 60–62, 143–47, 155–56
Watkins, W. B. C., 132, 135, 193 n. 5, 193 n. 9
Wear, Andrew, 2, 173 n. 5, 179 n. 84, 195 n. 39
West, Robert H., 194 n. 21
Whitaker, Tobias, 148, 195 n. 39
White, Allon, 175 n. 33, 189 n. 20
White, James Boyd, 190 n. 28
Williams, Kathleen, 48, 181 n. 15
Wilmot, John, Earl of Rochester, 73, 183 n. 63
Wilson, C. Anne, 191 n. 43
Wilson, Richard, 86–87, 186 n. 30
Wolfe, Don M. 194 n. 25
Wordsworth, William, 95, 187 n. 53
Wright, Thomas, 16, 49, 50–51, 65–66, 68, 77–79, 92, 176 n. 41, 176 n. 48, 181 n. 17, 181 n. 19, 182 n. 46, 183 n. 48, 183 n. 49, 183 n. 50, 183 n 54, 184 n. 10, 184 n. 11, 186 n. 34

Yeats, William Butler, 129, 192 n. 57
Youngner, Stuart J., 197 n. 13

Zizek, Slavoj, 10, 174 n. 20
Zohar, Danah, 174–75 n. 26
Zwicker, Steven, 193 n. 12

Cambridge Studies in Renaissance Literature and Culture

General editor
STEPHEN ORGEL
Jackson Eli Reynolds Professor of Humanities, Stanford University

1. Douglas Bruster, *Drama and the market in the age of Shakespeare*
2. Virginia Cox, *The Renaissance dialogue: literary dialogue in its social and political contexts, Castiglione to Galileo*
3. Richard Rambuss, *Spenser's secret career*
4. John Gillies, *Shakespeare and the geography of difference*
5. Laura Levine, *Men in women's clothing: anti-theatricality and effeminization, 1579–1642*
6. Linda Gregerson, *The reformation of the subject: Spenser, Milton, and the English Protestant epic*
7. Mary C. Fuller, *Voyages in print: English travel to America, 1576–1624*
8. Margreta de Grazia, Maureen Quilligan, Peter Stallybrass (eds.), *Subject and object in Renaissance culture*
9. T. G. Bishop, *Shakespeare and the theatre of wonder*
10. Mark Breitenberg, *Anxious masculinity in early modern England*
11. Frank Whigham, *Seizure of the will in early modern English drama*
12. Kevin Pask, *The emergence of the English author: scripting the life of the poet in early modern England*
13. Claire McEachern, *The poetics of English nationhood, 1590–1612*
14. Jeffrey Masten, *Textual intercourse: collaboration, authorship, and sexualities in Renaissance drama*
15. Timothy J. Reiss, *Knowledge, discovery and imagination in early modern Europe: the rise of aesthetic rationalism*
16. Elizabeth Fowler and Roland Greene (eds.), *The project of prose in early modern Europe and the New World*
17. Alexandra Halasz, *The marketplace of print: pamphlets and the public sphere in early modern England*
18. Seth Lerer, *Courtly letters in the age of Henry VIII: literary culture and the arts of deceit*
19. M. Lindsay Kaplan, *The culture of slander in early modern England*
20. Howard Marchitello, *Narrative and meaning in early modern England: Browne's skull and other histories*

21. Mario DiGangi, *The homoerotics of early modern drama*
22. Heather James, *Shakespeare's Troy: drama, politics, and the translation of empire*
23. Christopher Highley, *Shakespeare, Spenser, and the crisis in Ireland*
24. Elizabeth Hanson, *Discovering the subject in Renaissance England*
25. Jonathan Gil Harris, *Foreign bodies and the body politic: discourses of social pathology in early modern England*
26. Megan Matchinske, *Writing, gender and state in early modern England: identity formation and the female subject*
27. Joan Pong Linton, *The romance of the New World: gender and the literary formations of English colonialism*
28. Eve Rachele Sanders, *Gender and literacy on stage in early modern England*
29. Dorothy Stephens, *The limits of eroticism in post-Petrarchan narrative: conditional pleasure from Spenser to Marvell*
30. Celia R. Daileader, *Eroticism on the Renaissance stage: transcendence, desire, and the limits of the visible*
31. Theodore B. Leinwand, *Theatre, finance, and society in early modern England*
32. Heather Dubrow, *Shakespeare and domestic loss: forms of deprivation, mourning, and recuperation*
33. David Posner, *The performance of nobility in early modern European literature*
34. Michael C. Schoenfeldt, *Bodies and selves in early modern England: physiology and inwardness in Spenser, Shakespeare, Herbert, and Milton*

Printed in Great Britain
by Amazon